NORTH AMERICAN
AIRLINES HANDBOOK

© Airways International Inc 1997

Design: Marvin Reguindin
Production coordinator: Gretchen Bender

Printed in Singapore

Published by Airways International Inc, PO Box 1109, Sandpoint, Idaho 83864, USA

First edition 1997

All rights reserved. No part of this publication may be reproduced or transmitted in any form or by any means, electronic or mechanical including photocopying, recording, or by any information retrieval system, without written permission from the publisher.
While every effort was made to ensure the accuracy of the information contained in this publication, and each operator was contacted for verification, the editors and publisher cannot be held responsible for any errors or omissions, or for any financial loss or damage caused by any person using these data.

ISBN 0-9653993-1-1

INTRODUCTION

In response to numerous requests from readers of *Airways* and *Airline & Commercial Aircraft Report (ACAR) International* and our many industry friends, we have compiled our first guide to the airlines of North America.

For our purposes, 'North America' is defined as all 50 states of the USA—plus the commonwealth of Puerto Rico and the territory of the Virgin Islands, Canada, Greenland (part of the Danish realm), Saint-Pierre et Miquelon (a French *département*, or territory, off the coast of eastern Canada), México, and the islands of the Caribbean. American Samoa and the Federated States of Micronesia, associated with the USA, are omitted (although Continental Micronesia is included in the US listing).

With some exceptions, all regularly scheduled and charter passenger airlines operating turbine-powered aircraft of not less than 19 seats, and scheduled and charter all-cargo operators of heavy pure-jet equipment receive a one-page entry, including a color photograph depicting current aircraft equipment.

Other airlines which operate regularly scheduled passenger and/or cargo services, plus selected charter operators, are recorded in the relevant addenda.

Inevitably, despite our best attempts, some of the information will be out of date before the book returns from the printer. All route network and detailed fleet changes plus other news items are recorded in our monthly *Airline & Commercial Aircraft Report (ACAR) International* illustrated news magazine, and major features on North American carriers appear regularly in *Airways* magazine.

Any corrections, updates, suggestions, and new slides and photographs will be welcomed by the editors for future editions.

John Wegg (Managing Editor)
Tom Norwood (USA)
Glen Etchells (Canada)
Jorge Seguí Martin (México)
Joe Wolf (Caribbean)

Airways International Inc
PO Box 1109, Sandpoint ID 83864-0872, USA
Tel: +1 208 263 2098
Fax: +1 208 263 5906
Email: airways@nidlink.com
URL: http://www.flightdata.com/airways

EXPLANATION OF ENTRIES & ABBREVIATIONS
(in order of appearance)

IATA Two-letter designator ('airline code') assigned by the International Air Transport Association and used for ticketing and other purposes.

ICAO Three-letter designator ('airline code') assigned by the International Civil Aviation Organization and used for air traffic control and other purposes.

IATA/ARC Three-digit code assigned by IATA or the Airline Reporting Corp (USA) for accounting purposes.

RADIO Radio call-sign assigned by ICAO and used in air traffic control (ATC) communications.

CONTACTS Admin = Administrative, PR = Public/Press/Media Relations/Corporate Communications, Res = Reservations

OPERATION It has been assumed that many primarily scheduled carriers also operate charters. Cities/airports served on a scheduled or regular charter basis are listed alphabetically by IATA three-letter codes (*see decode*) and, if the territory served includes areas outside of the airline's home section, then separate geographic entries are made.

FFP Frequent Flyer Program

HISTORY/STRUCTURE CEO = Chief Executive Officer, COO = Chief Operating Officer, GM = General Manager

OWNERSHIP Publicly traded companies stock market abbreviations: AMEX = American Stock Exchange, NASDAQ = National Association of Securities Dealers Automated Quotations, NYSE = New York Stock Exchange

FLEET Listed in order of size of aircraft. **Seating configurations:** C or J = Business-Class, F = First-Class, or Y = Economy-Class (Coach). **Engines** Manufacturer prefixes: CFM = CFM International (SNECMA/General Electric); CO = Continental; GA = Garrett; GE = General Electric; IAE = International Aero Engines (Rolls-Royce/Pratt & Whitney/Japanese Aero Engines/FIAT); IV = Ivchyenko; IZ = Izotov; KU = Kuznetsov; LO = Lotarev; LY = Lycoming; PW = Pratt & Whitney; PWC = Pratt & Whitney Canada; RR = Rolls-Royce; SH = Shvetsov; SO = Soloviev

Information for companies in the addenda is listed in the sequence: name, IATA/ICAO/ARC/Radio, mail address, telephone and fax number, Email address, name of CEO/president, type of operation, fleet information.

DOUGLAS DC-8-63F

ABX AIR (dba Airborne Express)

IATA: GB **ICAO:** ABX **IATA/ARC:** 382 **RADIO:** Abex

CONTACTS:

Mail
145 Hunter Drive
Wilmington, OH 45177

Telephone/FAX
Admin: +1 937 382 5591
Fax: +1 937 382 2452
Info: 1 800 247 2676

Internet: http://www.airborne-express.com

OPERATION:

Type: Scheduled cargo
Cities Served: US: ABE ABQ ALB ANC ATL ATW AUS BDL BFI BHM BIL BNA BOI BOS BTV BUF BWI CAE CHA CHO CID CLE CLT CNW COS COU CWF DAL DEN DFW DSM DTW ELP EWR FAR FAT FLL FNT FSD GEG GRR GSO GSP HRL HSV IAD IAH ICT ILN ISP JAN JAX JFK LAS LAX LBB LGB LIT MCI MCO MDT MDW MEM MHR MHT MIA MKE MSN MSP MSY MWA OAK OKC OMA ONT ORD ORF PDX PHL PHX PIA PIT PNS PVD PWM RDU RFD RIC RNO ROA ROC RST SAN SAT SBN SGF SHV SJC SLC STL SWF SYR TPA TRI TUL TUS TYS YNG **Canada:** YYZ **Caribbean:** SJU
Other markets served by contract carriers

HISTORY/STRUCTURE:

Founded: April 17, 1980 **Start Date:** 1980
President/CEO: Carl Donaway **Ownership:** Airborne Freight Corp

FLEET:

Type	No	Engines
NAMC YS-11A-205	8	RR Dart 542-10
DC-9-15	2	PW JT8D-7A/-7B
DC-9-30	43	PW JT8D-7A/-7B/-9/-9A/-11
DC-9-40	21	PW JT8D-11/-15
DC-8-61F	13	PW JT3D-3B
DC-8-62F	6	PW JT3D-7
DC-8-63F	16	PW JT3D-7
Ordered		
Boeing 767-200	12	GE CF6A-80

DOUGLAS C-118A (DC-6A) LIFTMASTER

AIR CARGO EXPRESS

IATA: 3K **ICAO:** FXG **RADIO:** Cargo Express

CONTACTS:

Mail
PO Box 61680
Fairbanks, AK 99706

Telephone/FAX
Admin: +1 907 474 3488
Fax: +1 907 474 4602

OPERATION:

Type: Scheduled cargo
Area Served: Alaska

HISTORY/STRUCTURE:

Founded: 1994
CEO: Robert Everts

Start Date: October 1994
Ownership: Tatonduk Outfitters Ltd

FLEET:

Type	No	Engines
DC-6A (C-118A)	2	PW R-2800-CB16
DC-6B	1	PW R-2800-CB16

BEECH 1900D

AIR MIDWEST

IATA: ZV   **ICAO:** AMW   **IATA/ARC:** 471   **RADIO:** Air Midwest

CONTACTS:

Mail
PO Box 7724
Wichita, KS 67277

Telephone/FAX
Admin: +1 316 942 6137
Fax: +1 316 945 0947
Res: 1 800 428 4322

Internet: http://www.mesa-air.com/amw.htm

OPERATION:

Type: Scheduled passenger
Cities Served: CID DDC DSM FOE FYV GBD GCK HYS ICT LIT LNK MCI MHK OMA SGF SLN
All service operated as US Airways Express using only US flight numbers
FFP: US Airways Dividend Miles

HISTORY/STRUCTURE:

Founded: May 1965 (as Aviation Services)
Start Date: April 1967
President: Dick Paquette
Ownership: Mesa Air Group

FLEET:

Type	No	Seats	Engines
Beech 1900D	12	Y19	PWC PT6A-67D

BOEING 737-200 (ADVANCED)

AIR SOUTH

IATA: WV   **ICAO:** KKB   **IATA/ARC:** 399   **RADIO:** Khaki Blue

CONTACTS:

Mail
PO Box 11129
Columbia, SC 29211

Internet: http://airsouth.com

Telephone/FAX
Admin: +1 803 822 3170
Fax: +1 803 822 0801
Res: 1 800 247 7688

OPERATION:

Type: Scheduled passenger
Cities Served: ATL CAE CHS GSP JAX JFK MDW MIA MYR ORF SAV

HISTORY/STRUCTURE:

Founded: 1993
President/CEO: John Tague

Start Date: August 22, 1994
Ownership: Privately held

FLEET:

Type	No	Seats	Engines
Boeing 737-200	7	Y122	PW JT8D-9A/-15

DOUGLAS DC-8-62F

AIR TRANSPORT INTERNATIONAL

IATA: 8C   **ICAO:** ATN   **IATA/ARC:** 346   **RADIO:** Air Transport

CONTACTS:

Mail
3800 Rodney Parham Road
Little Rock, AR 72212

Telephone/FAX
Admin: +1 501 224 8175
Fax: +1 501 224 3240

OPERATION:

Type: Charter cargo
Areas Served: Operates contract services for major freight carriers, with several aircraft on exclusive contract with Burlington Air Express

HISTORY/STRUCTURE:

Founded: 1978 (as US Airways)   **Start Date:** 1979
CEO: Charles Adami (YIP Group)   **Ownership:** YIP Group

FLEET:

Type	No	Engines
DC-8-61	1	PW JT3D-3B
DC-8-62	8	PW JT3D-3B/-7
DC-8-63	9	PW JT3D-7
DC-8-71	11	PW CFM56-2C1

BAe 146-300A

AIR WISCONSIN

IATA: ZW   **ICAO:** AWI   **RADIO:** Wisconsin

CONTACTS:

Mail
6390 Challenger Drive, Suite 203
Appleton, WI 54915

Telephone/FAX
Admin: +1 414 739 5123
Fax: +1 414 739 9722
Res: 1 800 241 6522

OPERATION:

Type: Scheduled passenger
Cities Served: ASE ATW COS CRW DEN ICT LEX MKE MLI MSN ORD PIA SBA SDF SGF
(Seasonal: EGE LAX)
All service operated as United Express using only UA flight numbers
FFP: United Airlines Mileage Plus

HISTORY/STRUCTURE:

Founded: 1965
President/CEO: Geoffrey Crowley
Start Date: August 23, 1965
Ownership: CJT Holdings

FLEET:

Type	No	Seats	Engines
BAe 146-100A	2	Y86	ALF502R-5
BAe 146-200A	8	Y100	ALF502R-5
BAe 146-300A	5	Y100	ALF502R-5

BOEING

TWA 175 STL-SFO

KC Ctr: 134.75
DEN Ctr: 135.606
SLC Ctr: 134.35
OAK ctr 132.26
BAY APP: 135.65

BOEING 737-200 (ADVANCED)

AIRTRAN AIRWAYS

IATA: FL   **ICAO:** MTE   **IATA/ARC:** 332   **RADIO:** Manatee

CONTACTS:

Mail
6280 Hazletine National Drive, Suite 100
Orlando, FL 32822

Telephone/FAX
Admin: +1 407 859 1579
Fax: +1 407 856 5867
Res: 1 800 247 8726

OPERATION:

Type: Scheduled passenger
Cities Served: ABE ALB BMI BUF CAE CAK CHS CVG DAY DSM GSO GSP MCI MCO MDT MLI OMA RIC SWF SYR TOL TYS

HISTORY/STRUCTURE:

Founded: 1993 (as Conquest Sun Airlines)
Start Date: October 6, 1994
President/CEO: Robert D Swenson
Ownership: Airways Corp (NASDAQ: AAIR)

FLEET:

Type	No	Seats	Engines
Boeing 737-200	11	Y128	PW JT8D-9A/-15/-17

BOEING 737-400

ALASKA AIRLINES

IATA: AS **ICAO:** ASA **IATA/ARC:** 027 **RADIO:** Alaska

CONTACTS:

Mail
PO Box 68900
Seattle, WA 98168

Telephone/FAX
Admin: +1 206 433 3200
Fax: +1 206 433 3366
Res: 1 800 426 0333
PR: +1 206 433 3170/3134

Internet: http://www.alaskaair.com

OPERATION:

Type: Scheduled passenger/cargo
Cities Served: US: ADQ AKN ANC BET BRW BUR CDV DLG FAI GEG JNU KTN LAS LAX OAK OME ONT OTZ PDX PHX PSG PSP RNO SAN SCC SEA SFO SIT SJC SMF SNA WRG YAK **Canada:** YVR **México:** MZT PVR SJD **Asia:** GDX KHV PKC UUS VVO
Code-Share: ERA Aviation, Harbor Airlines, Horizon Air, Northwest Airlines, Peninsula Airways, Reeve Aleutian, Trans States Airlines, Wings West
FFP: Alaska Airlines Mileage Plan

HISTORY/STRUCTURE:

Founded: 1932 (as McGee Airways)
Start Date: June 6, 1944
President/CEO: John F Kelly
Ownership: Alaska Air Group (NYSE: ALK)

FLEET:

Type	No	Seats	Engines
Boeing 737-200C (Advanced)	8	Y111 or combination	PW JT8D-17/-17A
Boeing 737-400	24	F8Y132	CFM56-3C1
MD-82	10	F12Y128	PW JT8D-217/-217A
MD-83	32	F12Y128	PW JT8D-219
Ordered			
Boeing 737-400	13 plus 12 options		

BOMBARDIER DHC-8-102 DASH 8

ALLEGHENY AIRLINES

IATA: none   **ICAO:** ALO   **IATA/ARC:** 395   **RADIO:** Allegheny

CONTACTS:

Mail
PO Box 601
Harrisburg International Airport
Middletown, PA 17057
Internet: http://www.usairways.com

Telephone/FAX
Admin: +1 717 944 2781
Fax: +1 717 948 5548
Res: 1 800 428 4322

OPERATION:

Type: Scheduled passenger
Cities Served: ABE ALB AVP BDL BGM BOS BTV BUF BWI CHO ELM ERI EWR HTS HVN ISP ITH LGA MHT PHL PIT ROC SCE SYR
(Seasonal: ACK MVY)
All service operated as US Airways Express using only US flight numbers
FFP: US Airways Dividend Miles

HISTORY/STRUCTURE:

Founded: 1957 (as Reading Airlines)
Start Date: August 1957
President: Doug Horn
Ownership: USAir Group

FLEET:

Type	No	Seats	Engines
DHC-8-102	37	Y37	PWC PW120A

BOEING 737-200 (ADVANCED)

ALOHA AIRLINES

IATA: AQ **ICAO:** AAH **IATA/ARC:** 327 **RADIO:** Aloha

CONTACTS:

Mail
PO Box 30028
Honolulu, HI 96820

Telephone/FAX
Admin: +1 808 836 4101
Fax: +1 808 836 0303
Res: 1 800 367 5250
PR: +1 808 836 4113

Internet: http://www.alohaair.com

OPERATION:

Type: Scheduled passenger/cargo
Cities Served: HNL ITO KOA LIH OGG
Code-Share: Island Air, United Airlines
FFP: AlohaPass

HISTORY/STRUCTURE:

Founded: June 1946 (as Trans-Pacific Airlines)
Start Date: July 26, 1946
President/CEO: Glenn Zander
Ownership: Aloha Airgroup

FLEET:

Type	No	Seats	Engines
Boeing 737-200 (Advanced)	12	F10Y111 or F6Y110	PW JT8D-9A/15
Boeing 737-200QC (Advanced)	4	F10Y103 or F6Y107	PW JT8D-9A/15
Boeing 737-200 (Advanced)	1	Freighter	PW JT8D-15

BOEING 757-200

AMERICA WEST AIRLINES

IATA: HP **ICAO:** AWE **IATA/ARC:** 401 **RADIO:** Cactus

CONTACTS:

Mail
4000 East Sky Harbor Boulevard
Phoenix, AZ 85034

Telephone/FAX
Admin: +1 602 693 0800
Fax: +1 602 693 5546
Res: 1 800 235 9292
PR: +1 602 693 5729

Internet: http://www.americawest.com

OPERATION:

Type: Scheduled passenger
Cities Served: US: ABQ ANC ATL AUS BOS BUR BWI CLE CMH COS DCA DEN DFW DTW ELP EWR IAD IAH ICT IND JFK LAS LAX LGA LGB MCI MCO MDW MIA MKE MSP OAK OMA ONT ORD PDX PHL PHX RNO RSW SAN SAT SEA SFO SJC SLC SMF SNA STL TPA TUS
Canada: YVR **México:** ACA MEX MZT PVR SJD ZLO
Code-Share: British Airways, Continental, Northwest
FFP: FlightFund

HISTORY/STRUCTURE:

Founded: February 1981
Start Date: August 1, 1983
President/CEO: Richard Goodmanson
Ownership: America West Holding Corp (NYSE: AWA)

FLEET:

Type	No	Seats	Engines
Boeing 737-100	1	F8Y87	PW JT8D-9A
Boeing 737-200 (Advanced)	19	F8Y105	PW JT8D-9A/-15
Boeing 737-300	40	F8Y124	CFM56-3B1/-3B2
Airbus A320-200	26	F12Y138	IAE V2500-A1/V2525-A5
Boeing 757-200	14	F14Y176 or F12Y175	RR RB211-535E4
Ordered			
Airbus A320	12		
Airbus A319/A321	10 plus 12 options		

AIRBUS A300B4-605R

AMERICAN AIRLINES

| IATA: AA | ICAO: AAL | IATA/ARC: 001 | RADIO: American |

CONTACTS:

Mail
PO Box 619616
Dallas/Ft Worth Airport, TX 75261

Telephone/FAX
Admin: +1 817 963 1234
Fax: +1 817 967 4318
Res: 1 800 433 7300
PR: +1 817 967 1575

Internet: http://www.americanair.com

OPERATION:

Type: Scheduled passenger
Cities Served: US: ABQ ALB AMA ATL AUS BFL BDL BHM BNA BOS BUF BUR BWI CLE CLT CMH CVG DAY DCA DEN DFW DRO DSM DTW EGE ELP FAT FLL GSO GUC HDN HNL HPN HSV IAH ICT IND ISP JAC JAX JFK LAS LAX LGA LGB LIT MCI MCO MDT MEM MIA MKE MSP MSY OAK OGG OKC OMA ONT ORD ORF PBI PDX PHL PHX PIT PSP PVD RDU RIC RNO ROC RST RSW SAN SAT SDF SEA SFO SJC SLC SMF SNA STL SWF SYR TPA TUL TUS **Canada:** YOW YUL YVR YYC YYZ **México/Central America/South America:** ACA ASU BAQ BJX BOG BZE CCS CLO CNF CUN EZE GDL GIG GRU GUA GYE LIM LPB MEX MGA MTY MVD PTY PVR SAL SAP SCL SJD TGU UIO VVI **Caribbean:** ANU AUA BDA BGI CUR KIN LRM MBJ PAP PLS POP POS SDQ SJU STT STX SXM UVF **Europe:** ARN BHX BRU FRA LGW LHR MAD MAN MXP ORY ZRH (Seasonal: GLA) **Asia:** NRT
Code-Share: American Eagle (Executive, Flagship, Simmons, Wings West), Aspen Mountain Air, British Midland, Canadian, Gulf Air, Lone Star, LOT, QANTAS, South African, Singapore
FFP: AAdvantage

HISTORY/STRUCTURE:

Founded: January 25, 1930 (as American Airways)
Start Date: May 5, 1934
CEO: Robert Crandall
President: Donald Carty
Ownership: AMR Corp (NYSE: AMR)

FLEET:

Type	No	Seats	Engines
Fokker 100	75	F8Y89	RR Tay 650-15
MD-82	227	F14Y125	PW JT8D-217A/-217C
MD-83	33	F14Y125	PW JT8D-219
Boeing 727-200 (Advanced)	81	F12Y138	PW JT8D-9/-9A/-15
Boeing 757-200	90	F22Y166	RR RB211-535E4B
Boeing 767-200	8	F14C30Y128	GE CF6-80A
Boeing 767-200ER	22	F9C30Y128	GE CF6-80A2
Boeing 767-300ER	41	F14C30Y165	GE CF6-80C2B6
A300B4-605R	35	F16Y251/Y250 or F10C34Y148	GE CF6-80C2A5
DC-10-10	12	F28C52Y157 or F34Y256	GE CF6-6K
DC-10-30	4	F30Y243	GE CF6-50C2
MD-11	16	F19C35Y203 or F16C66Y163	GE CF6-80C2D1F
Ordered			
Boeing 737-800	75 plus 425 options (any 737 series)		
Boeing 757-200	12 plus 38 options		
Boeing 767-300ER	4 plus 26 options		
Boeing 777-200	12 plus 38 options		

NOTES:

LOCKHEED L-1011 TRISTAR 200 (F)

AMERICAN INTERNATIONAL AIRWAYS

| **IATA:** CB | **ICAO:** CKS | **IATA/ARC:** 571 | **RADIO:** Connie |

CONTACTS:

Mail	Telephone/FAX
842 Willow Run Airport	Admin: +1 313 484 0088
Ypsilanti, MI 48197	Fax: +1 313 484 3630

OPERATION:

Type: Scheduled/charter cargo, charter passenger
Cities Served: US (American International Freight): ATL BOS BWI CLE CLT DEN DFW DTW ELP HNL HUF IAH JFK LAX MCI MCO MEM MFE MIA MSP OGG ORD PDX PHL SEA SFO
Bases several aircraft at Miami for contract charters to South America

HISTORY/STRUCTURE:

Founded: 1972 (as Kalitta Flying Service) **Start Date:** November 1972
President/CEO: Conrad A Kalitta **Ownership:** Conrad A Kalitta

FLEET:

Type	No	Seats	Engines
Boeing 727-100F	2	-	PW JT8D-7B
Boeing 727-200F	13	-	PW JT8D-9/9A
DC-8-50F	8	-	PW JT3D-3B
DC-8-61F	5	-	PW JT3D-3B
DC-8-62F	4	-	PW JT3D-3B/-7
DC-8-63F	2	-	PW JT3D-7
L-1011-200	2	Y354	RR RB211-524B-02
L-1011-200F	6	-	RR RB211-524B-02
Boeing 747-100	2	Y476	PW JT9D-7A
Boeing 747-100F	3	-	PW JT9D-7A
Boeing 747-200F	3	-	PW JT9D-7F

BOEING 757-200

AMERICAN TRANS AIR

IATA: TZ   **ICAO:** AMT   **IATA/ARC:** 366   **RADIO:** Amtran

CONTACTS:

Mail
PO Box 51609
Indianapolis, IN 46251

Internet: http://www.ata.com

Telephone/FAX
Admin: +1 317 247 4000
Fax: +1 317 243 4165
Res: 1 800 435 9282

OPERATION:

Type: Scheduled/charter passenger
Cities Served: US: FLL HNL IND JFK LAS LAX MCO MDW MKE OGG PHX PIE RSW SRQ **Caribbean:** NAS SJU
Code-Share: Chicago Express
FFP: none

HISTORY/STRUCTURE:

Founded: August 1973 (as Ambassadair)
Start Date: March 1981
President/CEO: Stanley Pace
Ownership: Amtran Inc (NASDAQ: AMTR)

FLEET:

Type	No	Seats	Engines
Boeing 727-200 (Advanced)	24	Y168	PW JT8D-15/-15A/-17/-17A/-17R
Boeing 757-200	7	Y216	RR RB211-535E4
L-1011-1	2	Y362	RR RB211-22B
L-1011-50	11	Y362	RR RB211-22B
L-1011-100	2	Y362	RR RB211-22B
L-1011-150	1	Y362	RR RB211-22B

BOEING 727-200 (F)

AMERIJET INTERNATIONAL

IATA: JH **ICAO:** AJT **IATA/ARC:** 810 **RADIO:** Amerijet

CONTACTS:

Mail
498 SW 34th Street
Ft Lauderdale, FL 33315

Telephone/FAX
Admin: +1 954 359 0077
Fax: +1 954 359 7871
Info: 1 800 927 6059

Internet: www.amerijet.com

OPERATION:

Type: Scheduled cargo
Cities Served: US: MIA **México:** CUN GDL MEX MID **Caribbean:** ANU BGI DOM GND PAP POP SDQ SKB SLU SVD SXM UVF

HISTORY/STRUCTURE:

Founded: 1974
President/CEO: David Bassett

Start Date: 1974
Ownership: Bassett Enterprises

FLEET:

Type	No	Engines
Boeing 727-100F	5	PW JT8D-7B
Boeing 727-200F	9	PW JT8D-9A/-15/-15A

LOCKHEED L-1011 TRISTAR 200 (F)

ARROW AIR

IATA: JW **ICAO:** APW **IATA/ARC:** 404 **RADIO:** Big A

CONTACTS:

Mail
PO Box 026062
Miami, FL 33102-6062

Telephone/FAX
Admin: +1 305 526 0900
Fax: +1 305 526 0933

OPERATION:

Type: Scheduled cargo
Cities Served: US: ATL MIA **South America:** AGT ASU CCS CLO EZE GYE IQT LAP LIM MAO MDE MVD SCL SRZ UIO **Caribbean:** SJU

HISTORY/STRUCTURE:

Founded: 1947
President/CEO: Jon Batchelor
Start Date: May 26, 1981
Ownership: International Air Leases

FLEET:

Type	No	Engines
DC-8-62F	4	PW JT3D-3B/-7
DC-8-63F	3	PW JT3D-7
L-1011-200F	3	RR RB211-524B4

DORNIER 328-110

ASPEN MOUNTAIN AIR/LONE STAR AIRLINES
(Exec Express II Inc dba)

IATA: AD   **ICAO:** LSS   **IATA/ARC:** 504   **RADIO:** Lone Star

CONTACTS:

Mail
131 East Exchange Avenue, Suite 222
Fort Worth, TX 76106-8244

Telephone/FAX
Admin: +1 817 625 7050
Fax: +1 817 626 9011
Res: 1 800 877 3932

OPERATION:

Type: Scheduled passenger
Cities Served: US: ASE BWD DEN DFW DRT ELD HOT JBR PNC ROW RUI STL TYS WDG WMH **México:** CUU TRC
Code-Share: American, Frontier
FFP: none

HISTORY/STRUCTURE:

Founded: 1984 (as Exec Express)   **Start Date:** February 1985
President/CEO: Don Martin   **Ownership:** Peak International

FLEET:

Type	No	Seats	Engines
Metro III	2	Y19	GA TPE331-11U-611G/-612G
Metro 23	4	Y19	GA TPE331-12U-701G
Dornier 328-110	4	Y30/32	PWC PW119B

AI(R) BAe JETSTREAM 41

ATLANTIC COAST AIRLINES

IATA: DH **ICAO:** BLR **IATA/ARC:** 480 **RADIO:** Blue Ridge

CONTACTS:

Mail
515A Shaw Road
Sterling, VA 20166

Telephone/FAX
Admin: +1 703 406 6500
Fax: +1 703 406 6599
Res: 1 800 241 6522

Internet: http://www.atlanticcoast.com

OPERATION:

Type: Scheduled passenger
Cities Served: ABE ALB BDL BGM BOS BTV BUF BWI CHO CLE CMH CRW DAY DTW EWR GSO HPN HVN JFK LGA LYH MDT MHT ORF PHF PHL PIT PVD PWM RDU RIC ROA ROC SCE SWF SYR TYS (Seasonal: ACK MVY)
All service operated as United Express using only UA flight numbers
FFP: United Mileage Plus

HISTORY/STRUCTURE:

Founded: 1989
Start Date: December 15, 1989
President/CEO: Kerry Skeen
Ownership: Publicly traded company (NASDAQ: ACAI)

FLEET:

Type	No	Seats	Engines
Jetstream Super 31	29	Y19	GA TPE331-12UAR-701H
Jetstream 41	27	Y29	GA TPE331-14HR-805H
Ordered			
Jetstream 41	12		
Canadair R J200ER	12 plus 36 options		

BAe 146-200A

ATLANTIC SOUTHEAST AIRLINES

IATA: EV **ICAO:** ASE **IATA/ARC:** 862 **RADIO:** Asea

CONTACTS:

Mail
100 Hartsfield Center Parkway, Suite 800
Atlanta, GA 30354-1356

Telephone/FAX
Admin: +1 404 766 1400
Fax: +1 404 209 0162
Res: 1 800 221 1212

Internet: http://www.irinfo.com/asai

OPERATION:

Type: Scheduled passenger
Cities Served: ABY AEX AGS AMA ATL AVL BPT BQK CHA CLT CRP CRW CSG DFW DHN EVV FAY FLO FSM FYV GNV GPT GSO GSP GTR HOU IAH ICT ILE ILM JAN LAW LBB LEX LFT LYH MCN MEI MGM MLU MYR OAJ OKC PFN PNS ROA SDF SHV SPS TLH TRI TUL TXK VLD VPS
All service operated as Delta Connection using only DL flight numbers
FFP: Delta SkyMiles

HISTORY/STRUCTURE:

Founded: March 1979 **Start Date:** June 27, 1979
CEO: George Pickett Jr **President:** John Beiser
Ownership: ASA Holdings (NASDAQ: ASAI)

FLEET:

Type	No	Seats	Engines
EMB-120ER Brasília	63	Y30	PWC PW118
ATR72-212	12	Y64	PWC PW127
BAe 146-200A	6	Y88	ALF502R-5
Ordered			
Canadair RJ200ER	30 plus 60 options		
ATR72-200	16 options		
BAe 146	15 options		

BOEING 747-243B (F)

ATLAS AIR

IATA: 5Y **ICAO:** GTI **IATA/ARC:** 369 **RADIO:** Giant

CONTACTS:
Mail
538 Commons Drive
Golden, CO 80401-5705

Telephone/FAX
Admin: +1 303 526 5050
Fax: +1 303 526 5051

OPERATION:
Type: Charter cargo
Areas Served: Operates freight services for major airlines on an ACMI (Aircraft, Crew, Maintenance, Insurance) basis

HISTORY/STRUCTURE:
Founded: 1992 **Start Date:** February 1992
CEO: Michael Chowdry **President:** Mickey Foret
Ownership: Atlas Holdings (NASDAQ: ATLS)

FLEET:

Type	No	Engines
Boeing 747-200F	20	PW JT9D-7A/-7J or GE CF6-50E2
Ordered		
Boeing 747-200F	4	

BOEING 727-200 (ADVANCED)

AVATLANTIC

IATA: G6 **ICAO:** KYC **IATA/ARC:** none **RADIO:** Dolphin

CONTACTS:
Mail
1000 Davidson Drive, Suite 201
Savannah, GA 31408

Telephone/FAX
Admin: +1 912 964 0020
Fax: +1 912 964 0444

OPERATION:
Type: Charter passenger

HISTORY/STRUCTURE:
Founded: 1989
President/CEO: Cheryl Grue
Start Date: September 1989
Ownership: HCL Aviation

FLEET:

Type	No	Seats	Engines
Boeing 727-100	2	Y129	PW JT8D-7B
Boeing 727-200 (Advanced)	5	Y167/170/173	PW JT8D-15/-17/-17R

FAIRCHILD SA226-TC METRO II

BIG SKY AIRLINES

IATA: GQ **ICAO:** BSY **IATA/ARC:** 387 **RADIO:** Big Sky

CONTACTS:

Mail
1601 Aviation Place
Billings, MT 59105

Telephone/FAX
Admin: +1 406 245 9449
Fax:　 +1 406 259 8750
Res:　 1 800 237 7788

Internet: http://www.bigskyair.com

OPERATION:

Type: Scheduled passenger
Cities Served: BIL GDV GGW GTF HVR LWT MLS OLF SDY

HISTORY/STRUCTURE:

Founded: 1978
President/CEO: Terry Marshall

Start Date: September 15, 1978
Ownership: Big Sky Transportation

FLEET:

Type	No	Seats	Engines
Cessna 402C	1	Y9	CO TSIO-520-VB
Metro II	3	Y16	GA TPE331-10UA-511G

SAAB 340B

BUSINESS EXPRESS AIRLINES

IATA: HQ **ICAO:** GAA **IATA/ARC:** 357 **RADIO:** Bizex

CONTACTS:

Mail
14 Aviation Avenue
Portsmouth, NH 03801

Telephone/FAX
Admin: +1 603 334 4000
Fax: +1 603 334 4058
Res: 1 800 221 1212

OPERATION:

Type: Scheduled passenger
Cities Served: US: ALB BDL BGR BOS BTV BWI DCA HPN ISP JFK LEB LGA MHT PHL PVD PWM ROC SYR **Canada:** YOW YQB YUL
FFP: Delta SkyMiles, Northwest WorldPerks

HISTORY/STRUCTURE:

Founded: 1979 (as Atlantic Air)   **Start Date:** May 22, 1981
CEO: Robert Martens   **President:** Gary Ellmer
Ownership: Dimeling, Schreiber & Park

FLEET:

Type	No	Seats	Engines
SAAB 340A	17	Y34	GE CT7-5A2
SAAB 340B	21	Y34	GE CT7-9B

BOEING 727-200 (ADVANCED) (F)

CAPITAL CARGO INTERNATIONAL AIRLINES

IATA:　　　　　ICAO:　　　　　IATA/ARC:　　　　RADIO:

CONTACTS:

Mail
PO Box 622334
Orlando, FL 32837

Telephone/FAX
Admin: +1 407 855 2004
Fax:　　+1 407 855 6620
Res:　　1 800 593 9119

OPERATION:

Type: Charter cargo, including contract with Emery Worldwide

HISTORY/STRUCTURE:

Founded: September 1995　　**Start Date:** April 1996
President/CEO: Peter Fox　　**Ownership:** Privately held

FLEET:

Type	No	Engines
Boeing 727-200F	3	PW JT8D-7B/-15

AIRBUS A300B4-203

CARNIVAL AIR LINES

IATA: KW　　**ICAO:** CAA　　**IATA/ARC:** 521　　**RADIO:** Carnival

CONTACTS:

Mail
1815 Griffin Road, Suite 205
Dania, FL 33004-2213

Telephone/FAX
Admin: +1 954 923 8672
Fax:　 +1 954 923 3350
Res:　 1 800 824 7386

Internet: http://www.carnivalair.com

OPERATION:

Type: Scheduled/charter passenger
Cities Served: US: BDL EWR FLL IAD ISP JFK LAX MCO MIA PBI RSW SWF **Caribbean:** BQN NAS PSE SJU
Code-Share: Pan American World Airways, Paradise Island Airlines
FFP: FunPass

HISTORY/STRUCTURE:

Founded: 1988 (as Majestic Air)　　**Start Date:** October 1988
CEO: Reuven Wertheim　　**President:** Daniel Ratti
Ownership: Micky Arison (chairman, Carnival Cruise Lines)

FLEET:

Type	No	Seats	Engines
Boeing 737-200	2	Y125	PW JT8D-9A
Boeing 737-400	7	Y158	CFM56-3C1
Boeing 727-200 (Advanced)	7	Y173	PW JT8D-15/-17/-17A/-217C
Airbus A300B4-203	9	F24Y222/ 228/230	GE CF6-50C2

(Two more Boeing 737-400s leased during northern winter season from Pegasus, Turkey)

NOTES:

Carnival is scheduled to be merged into Pan Am in summer 1997.

BOEING 737-200

CASINO EXPRESS

IATA: XP **ICAO:** CXP **IATA/ARC:** none **RADIO:** Casino Express

CONTACTS:

Mail
976 Mountain City Highway
Elko, NV 89801-2728

Internet: none

Telephone/FAX
Admin: +1 702 738 6040
Fax: +1 702 738 1881
Res: 1 800 258 8800

OPERATION:

Type: Charter passenger
Areas Served: Midwestern/western US and Canadian cities to Elko

HISTORY/STRUCTURE:

Founded: 1987
Start Date: 1989
General Manager: Bud Phillips
CEO: Norval Nelson
Ownership: TEM Enterprises (Todd E McClasky)

FLEET:

Type	No	Seats	Engines
Boeing 737-200	2	Y124	PW JT8D-15

BAe 3101 JETSTREAM 31

CCAIR

IATA: ED **ICAO:** CDL **IATA/ARC:** 354 **RADIO:** Carolina

CONTACTS:

Mail
PO Box 19929
Charlotte, NC 28219-9929

Telephone/FAX
Admin: +1 704 359 8990
Fax: +1 704 359 0351
Res: 1 800 428 4322

OPERATION:

Type: Scheduled passenger
Cities Served: AGS AHN CHS CLT CSG CVG GSP HKY HTS INT ISO LEX LWB LYH MGM OAJ ORF PGV RDU RWI SHD SOP
All service operated as US Airways Express using only US flight numbers
FFP: US Airways Dividend Miles

HISTORY/STRUCTURE:

Founded: 1979 (as Sunbird Airlines)
Start Date: November 15, 1979
President/CEO: Kenneth W Gann
Ownership: CCAIR Inc (NASDAQ: CCAR)

FLEET:

Type	No	Seats	Engines
Jetstream 31	14	Y19	GA TPE331-10UGR-514H
Shorts 360-300	9	Y36	PWC PT6A-67R
DHC-8-102	4	Y37	PWC PW120A

BOEING 757-200PF

CHALLENGE AIR CARGO

IATA: WE **ICAO:** CWC **RADIO:** Challenge Cargo

CONTACTS:

Mail
PO Box 523979
Miami, FL 33152-3979

Telephone/FAX
Admin: +1 305 869 8333
Fax: +1 305 869 8299

OPERATION:

Type: Scheduled cargo
Cities Served: US: LAX MIA **Central America/South America:** BOG CCS CLO GUA GYE LIM LPB MAO MGA PTY SAL SJO TGU UIO VCP

HISTORY/STRUCTURE:

Founded: 1978 (as Challenge Air Transport)
Start Date: December 1986
President: William F Spohrer
Ownership: Airline Holding Co (Bill Spohrer & Associates)

FLEET:

Type	No	Engines
Boeing 707-300C	1	PW JT3D-3B
Boeing 757-200PF	3	RR RB211-535E4

BOEING 727-200

CHAMPION AIR

IATA: MG **ICAO:** CCP **IATA/ARC:** none **RADIO:** Champion

CONTACTS:

Mail
303 North 2370 West
Salt Lake City, UT 84116
Email: champair@aol.com
Internet: none

Telephone/FAX
Admin: +1 801 359 2801
Fax: +1 801 359 2103

OPERATION:

Type: Charter passenger

HISTORY/STRUCTURE:

Founded: July 1995
Start Date: 1995
President: Richard Page
Ownership: GHI-CA (Carl Pohlad 60%, NWA 40%)

FLEET:

Type	No	Seats	Engines
Boeing 727-100	1	F45	PW JT8D-7B
Boeing 727-200	4	Y125-170	PW JT8D-9/-9A

BAe 3101 JETSTREAM 31

CHAUTAUQUA AIRLINES

IATA: none   **ICAO:** CHQ   **IATA/ARC:** 363   **RADIO:** Chautauqua

CONTACTS:

Mail
Box 160
2500 South High School Road
Indianapolis, IN 46241
Internet: none

Telephone/FAX
Admin: +1 317 484 6000
Fax: +1 317 484 6060
Res: 1 800 428 4322

OPERATION:

Type: Scheduled passenger
Cities Served: US: AOO BNA BUF CLE CMH CMI DAY DTW EVV EWR FWA GRR HGR IND JST LNS MKE PIT ROC SBN SHD SYR
Canada: YHM YXU YYZ
All service operated as US Airways Express using only US flight numbers
FFP: US Airways Dividend Miles

HISTORY/STRUCTURE:

Founded: May 3, 1973
Start Date: August 1, 1974
President/CEO: Timothy Coon
Ownership: Privately held

FLEET:

Type	No	Seats	Engines
Jetstream 31	12	Y19	GA TPE331-10UG-513H
SAAB 340A	12	Y30	GE CT7-5A2

BAe JETSTREAM 31

CHICAGO EXPRESS AIRLINES

IATA: C8   **ICAO:** WDY   **IATA/ARC:** 488   **RADIO:** Windy City

CONTACTS:

Mail
5945 South Keating Avenue
Chicago, IL 60629

Telephone/FAX
Admin: +1 773 585 0585
Fax: +1 773 585 4877
Res: 1 800 264 3929

Internet: http://www.mindspring.com/~phlerb/chicagoexpress.html

OPERATION:

Type: Scheduled passenger
Cities Served: DAY DSM GRR IND MDW MKE
Code-Share: American Trans Air
FFP: none

HISTORY/STRUCTURE:

Founded: 1993
CEO: Carol Brady
Ownership: Phoenix AirlineServices

Start Date: August 9, 1993
President: Courtney Anderson

FLEET:

Type	No	Seats	Engines
Jetstream 31	9	Y19	GA TPE-331-10UG-513H
SAAB 340A	1	Y30	GE CT7-5A2

BEECH 1900C-1

COLGAN AIR

IATA: 9L **ICAO:** CJC **IATA/ARC:** 426 **RADIO:** Colgan

CONTACTS:

Mail
PO Box 1650
Manassas, VA 22110

Internet: http://www.colganair.com

Telephone/FAX
Admin: +1 703 368 8880
Fax: +1 703 331 3116
Res: 1 800 272 5488

OPERATION:

Type: Scheduled passenger
Cities Served: US: ACK AUG BHB BKW BLF BOS CHO CLT EEN EWR HYA LGA RKD RUT
All service operated as Continental Connection using only CO flight numbers

HISTORY/STRUCTURE:

Founded: 1991 (as National Capital Airways)
Start Date: December 1, 1991
President/CEO: Charles Colgan
Ownership: Michael and Charles Colgan

FLEET:

Type	No	Seats	Engines
Beech 1900C-1	5	Y19	PWC PT6A-65B
Beech 1900D	2	Y19	PWC PT6A-67D
SAAB 340B	1	Y30	GE CT7-9B

BOMBARDIER CANADAIR REGIONAL JET SERIES 100ER

COMAIR

IATA: OH **ICAO:** COM **IATA/ARC:** 886 **RADIO:** Comair

CONTACTS:

Mail
PO Box 75021
Cincinnati, OH 45275

Telephone/FAX
Admin: +1 606 525 2550
Fax: +1 606 283 5043
Res: 1 800 221 1212

Internet: http://www.flycomair.com

OPERATION:

Type: Scheduled passenger
Cities Served: US: ABE ATW AVL AVP AZO BHM BNA BOS BUF BWI CAE CAK CHA CHO CID CLE CLT CMH CRW CVG DAY DSM DTW EVV EWR EYW FWA GRR GSO GSP HPN HSV HTS IAD ICT IND JAN JAX LAN LEX LGA LIT MCI MCO MDT MDW MEM MHT MIA MKE MSN MSP MSY MYR OMA PBI PHL PIT PNS RDU RIC ROA ROC SBN SDF SRQ STL SYR TLH TOL TRI TUL TYS **Canada:** YUL YYZ
Caribbean: FPO NAS
All service operated as Delta Connection using only DL flight numbers
FFP: Delta SkyMiles

HISTORY/STRUCTURE:

Founded: 1976 (as Wings Airways) **Start Date:** April 1977
CEO: David R Mueller **President:** David Siebenburgen
Ownership: Comair Holdings (NASDAQ: COMR)

FLEET:

Type	No	Seats	Engines
EMB-120RT Brasília	40	Y30	PWC PW118
Canadair RJ 100ER	50	Y50	GE CF34-3A1
Ordered			
Canadair RJ	25 options		

RAYTHEON BEECH 1900D

COMMUTAIR

IATA: none **ICAO:** UCA **IATA/ARC:** none **RADIO:** Commutair

CONTACTS:

Mail
518 Rugar Street
Plattsburgh, NY 12901

Internet: none

Telephone/FAX
Admin: +1 518 562 2700
Fax: +1 518 562 8030
Res: 1 800 428 4322

OPERATION:

Type: Scheduled passenger
Cities Served: ALB BGM BOS BTV BUF ELM EWR HPN IAD ISP ITH LGA ORH PHL PLB POU PVD PWM ROC SLK SYR UCA
All service operated as US Airways Express using only US flight numbers
FFP: US Airways Dividend Miles

HISTORY/STRUCTURE:

Founded: 1989
President: John A Sullivan Jr
Ownership: Champlain Enterprises

Start Date: August 1, 1989
CEO: Tony von Elbe

FLEET:

Type	No	Seats	Engines
Beech 1900D	30	Y19	PWC PT6A-67D

FAIRCHILD SA227-AC METRO III

CONQUEST AIRLINES

IATA: 5C **ICAO:** CAC **IATA/ARC:** 355 **RADIO:** Conquest Air

CONTACTS:

Mail
2215 Redwood Avenue
Austin, TX 78723

Internet: http://www.conquestair.com

Telephone/FAX
Admin: +1 512 929 6706
Fax: +1 512 929 6711
Res: 1 800 722 0860

OPERATION:

Type: Scheduled passenger
Cities Served: ABI AUS BPT CRP LRD MFE SAT SJT TYR

HISTORY/STRUCTURE:

Founded: 1986
President/CEO: William Hirsh

Start Date: April 14, 1988
Ownership: AirLA Group

FLEET:

Type	No	Seats	Engines
Metro III	8	Y19	GA TPE331-11U-611G

BOEING 757-200

CONTINENTAL AIRLINES

IATA: CO   **ICAO:** COA   **IATA/ARC:** 005   **RADIO:** Continental

CONTACTS:

Mail
2929 Allen Parkway
Houston, TX 77019

Telephone/FAX
Admin: +1 713 834 5000
Fax: +1 713 834 2087
Res: 1 800 523 3273
PR: +1 713 834 5080

Internet: http://www.flycontinental.com

OPERATION:

Type: Scheduled passenger
Cities Served: US: ABQ ANC ATL AUS BDL BHM BOS BRO BUF BWI CAE CHS CLE CLT CMH COS CRP CVG DAB DAY DCA DEN DFW DTW ELP EWR FLL GSO GSP HDN HNL IAD IAH IND JAX LAS LAX LBB LFT LGA MAF MCI MCO MDW MFE MIA MKE MSP MSY MTJ OKC OMA ONT ORD ORF PBI PDX PHL PHX PIT PNS PVD PWM RDU RIC ROC RSW SAN SAT SDF SEA SFO SJC SLC SNA SRQ STL TPA TUL TUS **Canada:** YUL YVR YYZ **México/Central America/South America:** ACA BJX BOG BZE CUN CZM GDL GUA GYE LIM MGA MTY MZT PTY PVR SAL SAP SJD SJO TGU UIO ZIH **Caribbean:** ANU BDA MBJ SDQ SJU SXM **Europe:** BHX CDG DUS FRA LGW LIS MAD MAN SVO
Code-Share: Aeroflot, Air Canada, Air Nova, ALITALIA, America West, Business Air, Continental Express, Continental Micronesia, CSA, SkyWest, Transavia, Virgin Atlantic
FFP: OnePass

HISTORY/STRUCTURE:

Founded: 1934 (as Varney Speed Lines)
Start Date: July 15, 1934 (July 1, 1937 as Continental)
CEO: Gordon M Bethune
President: Greg Brenneman
Ownership: Publicly traded company (NYSE: CAIA/CAIB)

FLEET:

Type	No	Seats	Engines
DC-9-30	31	F8Y95	PW JT8D-9A/-15
Boeing 737-100	13	F8Y87	PW JT8D-7A
Boeing 737-200	17	F10Y90	PW JT8D-9A
Boeing 737-500	37	F10Y94	CFM56-3C1
Boeing 737-300	65	F10Y118	CFM56-3B1
MD-81	5	F14Y127	PW JT8D-217
MD-82	60	F14Y127	PW JT8D-217/-217A/-219
MD-83	4	F14Y127	PW JT8D-219
Boeing 727-200 (Advanced)	30	F14Y137	PW JT8D-9A/-15
Boeing 757-200	18	C16Y156 or Y24Y159	RR RB211-535E4-B
DC-10-30	23	C38Y204 or C26Y254	GE CF6-50C2/-50C2B
Ordered			
Boeing 737-500	30		
Boeing 737-600	30		
Boeing 737-800	48 plus 15 options		
Boeing 757-200	10 plus 8 options		
Boeing 777-200	5		

NOTES:

EMBRAER EMB-145ER AMAZON

CONTINENTAL EXPRESS

IATA: none **ICAO:** BTA **IATA/ARC:** none **RADIO:** Jetlink

CONTACTS:

Mail
15333 JFK Boulevard
Gateway 2 Suite 600
Houston, TX 77032
Internet: http://www.flycontinental.com

Telephone/FAX
Admin: +1 713 985 2700
Fax: +1 713 590 3820
Res: 1 800 523 3273

OPERATION:

Type: Scheduled passenger
Cities Served: US: ABE ACK ACT ACY AEX ALB AVP AZO BDL BGM BGR BPT BRO BTR BTV BWI CAK CHO CLE CLL CMH CRP CVG DAY DCA DTW EFD ERI EWR FNT FWA GPT GRR GSO HOU HRL HVN IAD IAH ILE IND ITH JAN LAN LAR LCH LEX LFT LGA LIT MBS MDT MEM MHT MKE MLU MOB MSP MVY ORF ORH PHL PIT PNS PVD PWM RDU RIC ROC SBN SDF SHV STL SYR TOL TYR TYS VCT (Seasonal: HPN) **México** MTY
All service operated using only CO flight numbers
Code-Share: none
FFP: OnePass

HISTORY/STRUCTURE:

Founded: 1956 (as Vercoa Air Service)
Start Date: 1968 (as commuter, became Britt Airlines)
President: David Siegal   **Ownership:** Continental Airlines

FLEET:

Type	No	Seats	Engines
Beech 1900D	25	Y19	PWC PT6A-67D
EMB-120RT Brasília	32	Y30	PWC PW118
ATR42-320	32	Y46	PWC PW121
ATR42-512	8	Y48	PWC PW127E
ATR72-212	3	Y64	PWC PW127
EMB-145ER	6	Y50	Allison AE3007A
Ordered			
EMB-145ER	19 plus 175 options		

McDONNELL DOUGLAS DC-10-10

CONTINENTAL MICRONESIA

IATA: CS **ICAO:** CMI **IATA/ARC:** 596 **RADIO:** Air Mike

CONTACTS:

Mail
Box 8778-G
A B Won Pat International Airport
Tamuning GU 96931
Internet: http://www.destmic.com

Telephone/FAX
Admin: +1 671 646 5125
Fax: +1 671 646 9219
Res: 1 800 231 0856

OPERATION:

Type: Scheduled passenger/cargo
Cities Served: US: HNL JON **Asia:** DPS FUK GUM HKG KHH KIX KSA KWA MAJ MNL NGO PNI ROR SDJ SEL SPK SPN TKK TPE YAP
Freight services operated for DHL
FFP: OnePass

HISTORY/STRUCTURE:

Founded: 1966 (as Air Micronesia)
Start Date: May 16, 1968
President/CEO: Donald J Breeding
Ownership: Continental Airlines/United Micronesia Development Association

FLEET:

Type	No	Seats	Engines
Boeing 727-200 (Advanced)	13	Y164	PW JT8D-15/-17/-17R
Boeing 727-200F (Advanced)	4	Freighter	PW JT8D-17R
DC-10-10	6	C18Y269	GE CF6-6D
Boeing 747-200	4	C24 or C28/402	PW JT9D-7A/-7F
Ordered			
Boeing 737	11		.
Boeing 757	5		
DC-10	2		

BOEING 727-200 (F)

CUSTOM AIR TRANSPORT

IATA: DG **ICAO:** none **RADIO:** none

CONTACTS:

Mail
4101 Ravenswood Road, Suite 214
Dania, FL 33312

Telephone/FAX
Admin: +1 954 359 9776
Fax: +1 954 792 8988

OPERATION:

Type: Charter cargo/passenger
Passenger charters, primarily to Caribbean, operated as Tropic Aire
Areas Served: US plus Middle East contract for Lufthansa

HISTORY/STRUCTURE:

Founded: 1995
President/CEO: Richard Wellman

Start Date: December 9, 1995
Ownership: Brent Aviation

FLEET:

Type	No	Engines
Boeing 727-200F	5	PW JT8D-9A/-15

BOEING 767-300 (ER)

DELTA AIR LINES
IATA: DL **ICAO:** DAL **IATA/ARC:** 006 **RADIO:** Delta

CONTACTS:
Mail
Hartsfield Atlanta International Airport
Atlanta, GA 30320

Telephone/FAX
Admin: +1 404 715 2600
Fax: +1 404 715 2596
Res: 1 800 221 1212
PR: +1 404 715 5162

Internet: http://www.delta-air.com

OPERATION:
Type: Scheduled passenger
Cities Served: US: ABE ABQ AGS ALB ANC ATL AUS BDL BGR BHM BIL BNA BOI BOS BTR BUF BWI BZN CAE CHS CLE CLT CMH COS CVG DAB DAY DCA DEN DFW DTW EGE ELP EWR FAI FAT FCA FLL FWA GEG GNV GRR GSO GSP GTF GUC HNL HSV IAD IAH IDA IND JAC JAN JAX JFK JNU LAS LGA LIT MCI MCO MDT MEM MGM MIA MLB MLU MOB MSO MSP MSY OAK OGG OKC OMA ONT ORD ORF PBI PDX PHL PHX PIT PNS PSC PVD PWM RDU RIC RNO ROC RSW SAN SAT SAV SBN SDF SEA SFO SHV SJC SLC SMF SNA SRQ STL SWF SYR TLH TOL TPA TUL TUS TYS **Canada:** YEG YUL YVR YYZ **México:** ACA GDL MEX MZT PVR **Caribbean:** BDA NAS SJU STT STX **Europe:** AMS ATH BCN BRU BUD CDG CPH DUB DUS FCO FRA GVA IST LGW MAD MAN MUC MXP NCE PRG SNN STR SVO TXL VIE WAW ZRH **Asia:** BOM NGO NRT SEL
Code-Share: Aer Lingus, AEROMEXICO, Air France, ASA, Austrian, Business Express, Comair, Finnair, Korean Air, MALÉV, SABENA, Scenic, SkyWest, Singapore, Swissair, TAP-Air Portugal
FFP: SkyMiles

HISTORY/STRUCTURE:
Founded: 1924 (as Huff-Daland Dusters)
Start Date: June 17, 1929
President/CEO: Ronald W Allen
Ownership: Publicly traded company (NYSE: DAL)

Fleet:

Type	No	Seats	Engines
Boeing 737-200 (Advanced)	54	F12Y95 or Y119	PW JT8D-15/-15A
Boeing 737-300	13	F8Y120	CFM56-3B1
MD-88	120	F14Y128	PW JT8D-219
MD-90-30	16	F12Y138	IAE V2525-D5
Boeing 727-200 (Advanced)	129	F12Y137 or F28Y91 or Y157	PW JT8D-9A/-15
Boeing 757-200	91	F24Y156	PW2037
Boeing 767-200	15	F18Y186	GE CF6-80A2
Boeing 767-300	26	F24Y228	GE CF6-80A2 or PW4060
Boeing 767-300ER	20	F10C34Y174	PW4060
L-1011-1	25	F32Y270	RR RB211-22B/-524B
L-1011-250	6	F32Y265	RR RB211-524B4
L-1011-500	17	F24Y217 or F12C35Y170 or F12C30Y183	RR RB211-524B4
MD-11	14	F18C32Y215 or F18C40Y209	PW4460
Ordered			
Boeing 737	70 plus	340 options	
Boeing 757-200	9 plus	137 options	
Boeing 767-300	12 plus	29 options	
Boeing 767-300ER	13 plus	10 options	
Boeing 767-400	21 plus	49 options	
Boeing 777-200		10 options	
MD-11	1 plus	17 options	

McDONNELL DOUGLAS MD-11

DOUGLAS DC-8-73F

DHL AIRWAYS

IATA: ER **ICAO:** DHL **IATA/ARC:** 423 **RADIO:** Dahl

CONTACTS:

Mail
PO Box 75122
Cincinnati, OH 45275

Internet: http://www.dhl.com

Telephone/FAX
Admin: +1 606 283 2232
Fax:　 +1 606 525 1998
Info:　 1 800 345 7775

OPERATION:

Type: Scheduled cargo
Cities Served: US: ATL BDL BOS BWI CVG DEN DFW DTW EWR IAH JFK LAX MCI MCO MIA MSP ORD PHL PHX SAT SEA SFO SLC STL TPA **México:** GDL MEX **Europe:** BRU EMA LHR SNN
All service operated as DHL Worldwide Express; additional cities served by contract carriers.

HISTORY/STRUCTURE:

Founded: 1969 (as DHL, by Dalsye, Hillblom & Lynn)
Start Date: 1982
President/CEO: J Patrick Foley
Ownership: DHL Corp (Japan Airlines, 25%; Lufthansa, 25%; Nisshono Iwai, 7.5%)

FLEET:

Type	No	Engines
Boeing 727-100F	11	PW JT8D-7
Boeing 727-200F	9	PW JT8D-7/15/-17/-17R
DC-8-73F	7	CFM56-2/-2C5
Ordered		
Airbus A300B4 (F)	7	

FOKKER F27 FRIENDSHIP MK 500F

EAGLE CANYON AIRLINES/ EAGLE JET CHARTER

IATA: FE　　**ICAO:** none　　**IATA/ARC:** 328　　**RADIO:** Talon

CONTACTS:

Mail
275 E. Tropicana Ave, Suite 220
Las Vegas, NV 89109

Internet: http://www.eagleair.com

Telephone/FAX
Admin: +1 702 736 3333
Fax:　 +1 702 895 7824
Res:　 31 800 446 4584

OPERATION:

Type: Scheduled/charter passenger
Cities Served: GCN LAS
Code-Share: none
FFP: none

HISTORY/STRUCTURE:

Founded: 1975 (as Lang Aire)　　**Start Date:** 1975
President: Grant Murray　　　　**Ownership:** Privately held

FLEET:

Type	No	Seats	Engines
Cessna 207	4	Y7	CO IO-520-F/TSIO-520-G/-M
Cessna 402	14	Y9	CO TSIO-520-E/-VB
F27 Mk 200/500F/600	5	Y44	RR Dart Mk 532-7

BOEING 737-200

EASTWIND AIRLINES

IATA: W9   **ICAO:** BBE   **IATA/ARC:** none   **RADIO:** Stinger Bee

CONTACTS:

Mail
6415 Airport Parkway
Terminal Building
Piedmont Triad Airport
Greensboro, NC 27049

Telephone/FAX
Admin: +1 910 393 0111
Fax: +1 910 393 0277
Res: 1 800 644 3592

OPERATION:

Type: Scheduled passenger
Cities Served: BOS GSO MCO TPA TTN

HISTORY/STRUCTURE:

Founded: 1993
Start Date: August 16, 1995
President/CEO: Gerald Albens
Ownership: United Medical Holdings of New Jersey

FLEET:

Type	No	Seats	Engines
Boeing 737-200	2	Y120	PW JT8D-9A

DOUGLAS DC-8-73F

EMERY WORLDWIDE AIRLINES

IATA: EB **ICAO:** EWW **IATA/ARC:** 591 **RADIO:** Emery

CONTACTS:

Mail
1 Emery Plaza
Vandalia, OH 45377

Telephone/FAX
Admin: +1 937 264 1212
Fax: +1 937 264 1566
Info: 1 800 227 1981

Internet: http://www.emeryworld.com

OPERATION:

Type: Scheduled cargo
Cities Served: US: ABQ ATL AUS BDL BHM BNA BOS BRO BUF BWI CAE CLE CLT DAY DEN DFW DTW EFD ELP EWR FLL FNT GRR GSO GSP HSV IAD ICT IND JAN JAX JFK LAX LRD MCI MCO MDT MHR MIA MKE MSP MSY OAK OKC ONT ORD ORF PDX PHL PHX PIA PSM RDU RIC ROA ROC SAN SAT SEA SFO SHV SJC SLC STL SWF SYR TPA TUL TUS **Canada:** YYZ **México:** GDL **Caribbean:** SJU **Europe:** BRU
Operates US Postal Service flights from Indianapolis

HISTORY/STRUCTURE:

Founded: 1987 (as Air Train)   **Start Date:** May 1987
President: David Beatson   **Ownership:** CNF Transportation

FLEET:

Type	No	Engines
DC-8F-54	2	PW JT3D-3B
DC-8-62F	8	PW JT3D-3B
DC-8-63F	9	PW JT3D-7
DC-8-71F	10	CFM56-2C/-2C1
DC-8-73F	11	CFM56-2C1

Boeing 727s operated by Express One and Ryan International (see separate entries)

CONVAIR 580

ERA AVIATION

IATA: 7H **ICAO:** ERH **IATA/ARC:** 808 **RADIO:** Erah

CONTACTS:

Mail
6160 Carl Brady Drive
Anchorage, AK 99502-9987

Telephone/FAX
Admin: +1 907 248 4422
Fax: +1 907 266 8383
Res: 1 800 866 8394

Internet: http://www.era-aviation.com

OPERATION:

Type: Scheduled/charter passenger/cargo
Cities Served: US: ADQ ANC BET CDV CYF EEK ENA GNU HOM HPB ILI KKH KPN KWK KWN MYU NME OOK PTU SCM TNK VAK VDZ WTL WWT **Canada:** YXY
Scheduled service operated as Alaska Airlines Commuter using AS flight numbers
FFP: Alaska Airlines Mileage Plan

HISTORY/STRUCTURE:

Founded: 1948
CEO: Charles Johnson

Start Date: 1948
Ownership: Rowan Companies (RDC)

FLEET:

Type	No	Seats	Engines
DHC-6-100/-200/-300	10	Y9 or Y19	PWC PT6A-20/-27
DC-3 operated by ERA Classic Airlines	2	Y21	PW R-1830-90
DHC-8-100	2	Y37	PWC PW120A/PW121
Convair 580	5	Y48	Allison 501-D13H

McDONNELL DOUGLAS DC-9-15F

EVERGREEN INTERNATIONAL AIRLINES

IATA: EZ　　**ICAO:** EIA　　**IATA/ARC:** 494　　**RADIO:** Evergreen

CONTACTS:

Mail
3850 Three Mile Lane
McMinnville, OR 97128-9496

Telephone/FAX
Admin: +1 503 472 0011
Fax:　 +1 503 434 4210

Internet: http://www.evergreenaviation.com

OPERATION:

Type: Scheduled/charter cargo
Areas Served: Operates US Postal Service flights in western US from Oakland hub and worldwide contract and charter cargo services

HISTORY/STRUCTURE:

Founded: 1975
Start Date: November 28, 1975
President: Larry Lane
Ownership: Evergreen International Aviation

FLEET:

Type	No	Engines
DC-9-15F	2	PW JT8D-7A/-7B
DC-9-32/33F	4	PW JT8D-9
Boeing 747-100/200F	8	PW JT9D-7A/-7J

AI(R) ATR72-201

EXECUTIVE AIRLINES

IATA: NA **ICAO:** EGF **RADIO:** Eagle Flight

CONTACTS:

Mail
PO Box 38082
Airport Station
San Juan, PR 00937-0082

Telephone/FAX
Admin: +1 809 791 8070
Fax: +1 809 791 5180
Res: 1 800 433 7300
PR: +1 817 967 1577

Internet: http://www.americanair.com

OPERATION:

Type: Scheduled passenger
Cities Served: Caribbean: ANU AXA BGI DOM EIS FDF LRM MAZ POP POS PSE PTP SDQ SJU SKB SLU STT STX SVD SXM TAB
All service operated as American Eagle using only AA flight numbers
FFP: AAdvantage

HISTORY/STRUCTURE:

Founded: 1979 (as Executive Air Charter)
Start Date: September 15, 1986 (as American Eagle)
President/CEO: Thomas Del Valle
Ownership: AMR Eagle

FLEET:

Type	No	Seats	Engines
Shorts 360	11	Y36	PWC PT6A-65R/-65AR
ATR42-300	10	Y46	PWC PW120
ATR72-200	4	Y64	PWC PW124B

SAAB 340B

EXPRESS AIRLINES I

IATA: 9E   **ICAO:** FLG   **IATA/ARC:** 430   **RADIO:** Flagship

CONTACTS:

Mail
1777 Phoenix Parkway, Suite 303
Atlanta, GA 30349

Telephone/FAX
Admin: +1 770 991 3333
Fax: +1 770 997 0127
Res: 1 800 225 2525

OPERATION:

Type: Scheduled passenger
Cities Served: AEX ALO ATW BHM BTR CID CSG CVG DBQ DFW DHN DLH EAU EVV FOD FSM FYV GLH GPT GRB GSP GTR HIB HSV ICT INL JAN JLN LEX LFT LIT MCI MEI MEM MGM MKL MLU MOB MSL MSP OWB PAH PFN PIA PIB PNS RFD RHI SDF SGF SHV SUX TUL TUP TYS
All service operated as Northwest Airlink using only NW flight numbers
FFP: Northwest WorldPerks

HISTORY/STRUCTURE:

Founded: February 1985   **Start Date:** June 1986
President/CEO: Philip Trenary   **Ownership:** Northwest Airlines

FLEET:

Type	No	Seats	Engines
Jetstream 31	22	Y19	GA TPE331-10UG-513H
SAAB 340A	32	Y33	GE CT7-5A2
SAAB 340B	11	Y33	GE CT7-9B

BOEING 727-200 ADVANCED

EXPRESS ONE INTERNATIONAL

IATA: EO **ICAO:** LHN **IATA/ARC:** none **RADIO:** Longhorn

CONTACTS:

Mail
3890 Northwest Highway, Suite 700
Dallas, TX 75220
Email: express1@onramp.net

Telephone/FAX
Admin: +1 214 902 2500
Fax: +1 214 350 1399

OPERATION:

Type: Charter passenger/cargo
Areas Served: Operates freight services in the US for Emery Worldwide and other forwarders, and for TNT in Europe, plus ad hoc passenger charters

HISTORY/STRUCTURE:

Founded: 1975 (as Jet East International Airlines) **Start Date:** 1975
CEO: James Wikert **President:** Kevin Good
Ownership: Alinda and James Wikert

FLEET:

Type	No	Seats	Engines
Boeing 727-100F	6	Freighter	PW JT8D-7B
Boeing 727-200F	15	Freighter	PW JT8D-9/-15/-17R
Boeing 727-200 (Advanced)	3	Y170	PW JT8D-17R
DC-9-32	2	Y94	
Ordered			
Boeing 727-200	4		

BOEING 727-200

FALCON AIR EXPRESS

IATA: F2   **ICAO:** none   **IATA/ARC:** none   **RADIO:**

CONTACTS:

Mail
7270 NW 12th Street, Penthouse 9
Miami, FL 33126

Telephone/FAX
Admin: +1 305 592 5672
Fax: +1 305 592 7298

OPERATION:

Type: Charter passenger

HISTORY/STRUCTURE:

Founded: 1995
President: Emilio Dirube

Start Date: March 1996
Ownership: Emilio Dirube

FLEET:

Type	No	Seats	Engines
Boeing 727-200	2	Y164	PW JT8D-7B

McDONNELL DOUGLAS MD-11F

FEDEX

IATA: FM   **ICAO:** FDX   **IATA/ARC:** 023   **RADIO:** Fedex

CONTACTS:

Mail
PO Box 727
Memphis, TN 38194

Internet: http://www.fedex.com

Telephone/FAX
Admin: +1 901 369 3600
Fax: +1 901 395 4928
Info: 1 800 463 3339

OPERATION:

Type: Scheduled cargo
Cities Served: US: ABE ABQ ALB ANC ATL ATW AUS BDL BHM BOI BOS BUF BTV BUR BWI CAE CHS CID CLE CLT COS CVG DAY DEN DFW DSM DTW ELP EWR FLL FNT FSD FWA GEG GFK GRR GSO GSP GTF HNL HRL IAD IAH ICT IND JAX JFK LAS LAX LBB LCK LGB MCI MCO MDT MEM MIA MHT MKE MOB MSN MSP MSY OAK OKC OMA ONT ORD ORF PDX PHL PHX PIA PIT PVD PWM RDU RIC ROA RNO ROC RSW SAN SAT SBN SEA SFO SHV SJC SLC SNA STL SWF SYR TLH TPA TUL TUS TYS **Canada:** YMX YVR YWG YYC YYZ **México/Central America/South America:** CCS EZE GDL MAO SCL TLC VCP **Caribbean:** SJU **Europe:** CDG CGN FRA MXP PIK STN **Asia:** BKK HKG MNL NAN NRT PEN SEL SIN SYD TPE
Other cities served by FedEx Feeder contract carriers

HISTORY/STRUCTURE:

Founded: 1971 (as Federal Express)
Start Date: April 17, 1973
President/CEO: Frederick W Smith
Ownership: Federal Express Corp (NYSE: FDX)

FLEET:

Type	No	Engines
Cessna 208A/B	268	PWC PT6A-114/-114A
Fokker F27 Mk 500/600	32	RR Dart 532-7/552-7R
Boeing 727-100F	68	PW JT8D-7B
Boeing 727-200F	96	PW JT8D-9A/-15/-17/-17A
Airbus A310F-200	37	PW JT9D-7R4D1/E1 or GE CF6-80A3
Airbus A300F-600	19	GE CF6-80C2A5
DC-10-10F	12	GE CF6-6D/-6D1A
DC-10-30F	22	GE CF6-80C2
MD-11F	21	GE CF6-80C2D1F

Cessna 208 Caravans and Fokker F27s operated as FedEx Feeder under contract by Baron Aviation, Corporate Air (US and Philippines), CSA Air, Empire Airlines, ERA Aviation, Morningstar Air Express (Canada—which also operates three 727-100Fs), Mountain Air Cargo, WestAir, and Wiggins Airlines

Ordered

Cessna 208B	13
Ayres LM200	50 plus 200 options
Boeing 727-200F	12 (secondhand)
Airbus A310F-200	6 (ex-Singapore)
Airbus A300F-600	17 plus 39 options
DC-10-10F	50 (ex-American/United, to be MD-10F)
MD-11F	14 plus 9 options

NOTES:

DOUGLAS DC-8F-54 JET TRADER

FINE AIR

IATA: FB **ICAO:** FBF **IATA/ARC:** none **RADIO:** Big F

CONTACTS:

Mail
PO Box 523726
Miami, FL 33152-3726

Telephone/FAX
Admin: +1 305 871 6606
Fax: +1 305 871 4232

OPERATION:

Type: Scheduled/charter cargo
Cities Served: Caribbean: POP SDQ SJU **Central/South America:** BOG CCS GUA GYE MAR MGA PTY SAL SAP SJO UIO

HISTORY/STRUCTURE:

Founded: 1992
President/CEO: J Frank Fine

Start Date: November 10, 1992
Ownership: Frank & Barry Fine

FLEET:

Type	No	Engines
DC-8-50F	12	PW JT3D-3B
DC-8-61F	3	PW JT3D-3B

SAAB 340B

FLAGSHIP AIRLINES
IATA: 8N **ICAO:** EGF **RADIO:** Eagle Flight

CONTACTS:

Mail
Two International Plaza, Suite 900
Nashville, TN 37217

Telephone/FAX
Admin: +1 615 399 6319
Fax: +1 615 399-6384
Res: 1 800 433 7300
PR: +1 817 967 1577

Internet: http://www.americanair.com

OPERATION:
Type: Scheduled passenger
Cities Served: US: ALB APF BDL BNA BOS BUF BWI CLE DCA EYW JAX JFK MIA MCO MTH PBI PHL PIT PVD RDU ROC RSW SRQ SYR TPA **Canada:** YUL **Caribbean:** FPO GGT GHB MHH NAS
All service operated as American Eagle using only AA flight numbers
Code-Share: Canadian Airlines International, South African Airways
FFP: AAdvantage

HISTORY/STRUCTURE:
Founded: 1987 (as Nashville Eagle) **Start Date:** January 1, 1988
President/CEO: David C Kennedy **Ownership:** AMR Eagle

FLEET:

Type	No	Seats	Engines
SAAB 340B	37	Y34	GE CT7-9B
ATR42-300	12	Y46	PWC PW120

DOUGLAS DC-8-61 (F)

FLORIDA WEST INTERNATIONAL AIRWAYS

IATA: RF **ICAO:** FWL **IATA/ARC:** 330 **RADIO:** Florida West

CONTACTS:

Mail
7500 NW 25th Street, Suite 237
Miami, FL 33122-1714

Telephone/FAX
Admin: +1 305 599 2500
Fax: +1 305 591 2385

OPERATION:

Type: Scheduled cargo
Cities Served: US: IAH MIA **South America:** IQT LIM SCL

HISTORY/STRUCTURE:

Founded: 1981 (as Florida West Airlines) **Start Date:** 1983
President/CEO: Richard Haberly **Ownership:** Haberly, Fast Air Group

FLEET:

Type	No	Engines
DC-8-61F	1	PW JT3D-3B

BOEING 737-200

FRONTIER AIRLINES

IATA: F9   **ICAO:** FFT   **IATA/ARC:** 422   **RADIO:** Frontier Flight

CONTACTS:

Mail
12015 East 46th Avenue
Denver, CO 80239

Internet: http://flyfrontier.com

Telephone/FAX
Admin: +1 303 371 7400
Fax: +1 303 371 7007
Res: 1 800 432 1359

OPERATION:

Type: Scheduled passenger
Cities Served: ABQ BMI DEN ELP LAS LAX MDW MSP OMA PHX SAN SEA SFO SLC STL
Code-Share: Aspen Mountain Air, Maverick Airways
FFP: Continental OnePass

HISTORY/STRUCTURE:

Founded: 1994
Start Date: July 5, 1994
President/CEO: Samuel Addoms
Ownership: Publicly traded company (NASDAQ: FrontrAir)

FLEET:

Type	No	Seats	Engines
Boeing 737-200	7	Y108	PW JT8D-9A
Boeing 737-300	4	Y136/Y138	CFM56-3B1
Ordered			
Boeing 737-300	3	Y136	CFM56-3C1

McDONNELL DOUGLAS DC-10-30F

GEMINI AIR CARGO

IATA: GR **ICAO:** GCO **IATA/ARC:** 358 **RADIO:** Gemini

CONTACTS:

Mail
PO Box 16254
Dulles International Airport
Washington, DC 20041-6254

Telephone/FAX
Admin: +1 703 260 8100
Fax: +1 703 260 8102

OPERATION:

Type: Charter cargo
Areas Served: Operates aircraft for dedicated freight services on behalf of other carriers

HISTORY/STRUCTURE:

Founded: 1995
Start Date: October 24, 1996
President: Bill Stockbridge
Ownership: Privately held

FLEET:

Type	No	Engines
DC-10-30F	7	GE CF6-50C2

McDONNELL DOUGLAS DC-9-87 (MD-87)

GREAT AMERICAN AIRWAYS

IATA: MV   **ICAO:** GRA   **IATA/ARC:** 414   **RADIO:** Great American

CONTACTS:

Mail
PO Box 10165
Reno, NV 89510

Telephone/FAX
Admin: +1 702 857 7373
Fax: +1 702 857 7321

OPERATION:

Type: Charter passenger
Areas Served: Operates contract charters and sub-services for other carriers

HISTORY/STRUCTURE:

Founded: 1979
President: Robert Stephan

Start Date: September 26, 1979
Ownership: Target Airways Ltd

FLEET:

Type	No	Seats	Engines
DC-9-15	3	Y90	PW JT8D-7A/7B
DC-9-87	2	Y133	PW JT8D-219
DC-9-83	2	F12Y135	PW JT8D-219

EMBRAER EMB-120ER BRASILIA

GREAT LAKES AIRLINES

IATA: ZK   **ICAO:** GLA   **IATA/ARC:** 846   **RADIO:** Lakes Air

CONTACTS:

Mail
7900 Xerxes Avenue South
Bloomington, MN 55431

Telephone/FAX
Admin: +1 612 767 7000
Fax: +1 612 767 7001
Res: 1 800 274 0662

Internet: http://www.greatlakesav.com

OPERATION:

Type: Scheduled passenger
Cities Served: US: ABQ AIA ALO BIS BNA BRL BWI CAE CDR CGX CHS CIU CMH DBQ DEC DEN DIK DLH DVL ESC FAR FRM FSD GRI GSP HHH HON HUF IMT ISN JAX JMS LAF LAN MBL MCK MCW MKG MOT MQT MSP MTO MVN MYR OFK OMA ORD ORF OSH OTM PGA PIR PLN RDU RHI RIC SAV SOW SPI SPW SQI SUX TUS TVC UIN YKN **México:** GYM HMO PPE
Some services operated as United Express (UA flight numbers) and Midway Connection (JI flight numbers)
FFP: United Mileage Plus

HISTORY/STRUCTURE:

Founded: April 15, 1977 (as Spirit Lake Airways)
Start Date: October 12, 1981
President/CEO: Douglas G Voss
Ownership: Great Lakes Aviation

FLEET:

Type	No	Seats	Engines
Beech 1900C	29	Y19	PWC PT6A-65B
Beech 1900D	16	Y19	PWC PT6A-67D
EMB-120ER/RT Brasília	14	Y30	PWC PW118/118A
Ordered			
Beech 1900D	4 plus 13 options		

SHORTS 360-300

GULFSTREAM INTERNATIONAL AIRLINES
IATA: 3M   **ICAO:** GFT   **IATA/ARC:** none   **RADIO:** Gulf Flight

CONTACTS:

Mail
PO Box 777
Miami Springs, FL 33266

Telephone/FAX
Admin: +1 305 871 0727
Fax: +1 305 871 4800
Res: 1 800 992 8532

OPERATION:
Type: Scheduled passenger
Cities Served: US: EYW FLL GNV JAX MCO MIA PBI TLH TPA
Caribbean: ELH FPO MHH NAS TCB
All service operated as Continental Express using only CO flight numbers
Code-Share: Continental, United
FFP: Continental OnePass, United Mileage Plus

HISTORY/STRUCTURE:
Founded: October 1988   **Start Date:** December 1, 1990
President/CEO: Thomas L Cooper   **Ownership:** Thomas L Cooper

FLEET:

Type	No	Seats	Engines
Beech 1900C	16	Y19	PWC PT6A-65B
Shorts 360-300	4	Y36	PWC PT6A-67R

McDONNELL DOUGLAS DC-10-10

HAWAIIAN AIRLINES

IATA: HA **ICAO:** HAL **IATA/ARC:** 173 **RADIO:** Hawaiian

CONTACTS:

Mail
PO Box 30008
Honolulu, HI 96820

Telephone/FAX
Admin: +1 808 835 3700
Fax: +1 808 835 3690
Res: 1 800 367 5320
PR: +1 808 838 6778

Internet: http://www.hawaiianair.com

OPERATION:

Type: Scheduled/charter passenger
Cities Served: ANC (charter) HNL ITO KOA LAS LAX LIH LNY MKK OGG PDX SEA SFO
Code-Share: Mahalo Air, Northwest, Reno Air, Wings West
FFP: Gold Plus, WorldPerks

HISTORY/STRUCTURE:

Founded: January 30, 1929
Start Date: November 11, 1929
President/CEO: Paul Casey
Ownership: Airline Investor Partnership (61%), private investors

FLEET:

Type	No	Seats	Engines
DC-9-51	13	Y139	PW JT8D-17/-17A
DC-10-10	9	F23Y256	GE CF6-6K

FOKKER F28 FELLOWSHIP MK 1000

HORIZON AIR

IATA: QX   **ICAO:** QXE   **IATA/ARC:** 481   **RADIO:** Horizon Air

CONTACTS:

Mail
PO Box 48309
Seattle, WA 98148

Telephone/FAX
Admin: +1 206 241 6757
Fax: +1 206 431 4696
Res: 1 800 547 9308
PR: +1 206 431 4672

Internet: http://www.horizonair.com

OPERATION:

Type: Scheduled passenger
Cities Served: US: ACV ALW BIL BLI BOI BTM BZN CLM EAT EUG FCA GEG GTF HLN IDA JAC LMT LWS MFR MSO MWH OAK OTH PDT PDX PIH PSC PUW RDD RDM SEA SJC SMF SUN YKM
Canada: YEG YVR YYC YYJ
Operates as an Alaska Airlines Commuter and on behalf of Northwest Airlines using only AS and NW flight numbers
FFP: Alaska Airlines Mileage Plan, Northwest WorldPerks

HISTORY/STRUCTURE:

Founded: May 1981
Start Date: September 1, 1981
President/CEO: George D Bagley
Ownership: Horizon Air Industries/Alaska Air Group

FLEET:

Type	No	Seats	Engines
Metro III	14	Y18	GA TPE331-11U-611G
Dornier 328-110	10	Y31	PWC PW119B
DHC-8-102	23	Y37	PWC PW120A
F28 Mk 1000	9	Y62	RR Spey 555-15N
F28 Mk 4000	7	Y69	RR Spey 555-15P
Ordered			
DHC-8-200	40 plus 30 options		

BOMBARDIER DHC-8-102 DASH 8

ISLAND AIR (Aloha Island Air dba)

IATA: WP **ICAO:** PRI **IATA/ARC:** 347 **RADIO:** Princeville

CONTACTS:

Mail
99 Kapalulu Place
Honolulu, HI 96819

Internet: none

Telephone/FAX
Admin: +1 808 833 7108
Fax: +1 808 833 5498
Res: 1 800 323 3345

OPERATION:

Type: Scheduled passenger
Cities Served: HNL HNM JHM LNY MKK OGG
All service operated for Aloha using only AQ flight numbers
Code-Share: none
FFP: AlohaPass

HISTORY/STRUCTURE:

Founded: 1980 (as Princeville Airways)
President: Neil M Takekawa
Start Date: September 9, 1980
Ownership: Aloha Airgroup

FLEET:

Type	No	Seats	Engines
DHC-6-300	3	Y18	PWC PT6A-27
DHC-8-102	3	Y37	PWC PW120A

BOEING 727-200 (F)

KITTY HAWK AIR CARGO

IATA: KR   **ICAO:** KHA   **IATA/ARC:** none   **RADIO:** Kitty Hawk

CONTACTS:

Mail
PO Box 612787
Dallas/Ft Worth Airport, TX 75261

Telephone/FAX
Admin: +1 972 456 2220
Fax: +1 972 456 2277

Internet: http://www.kha.com

OPERATION:

Type: Charter cargo
Areas Served: Operates charter contracts in US for major freight carriers, as well as additional contracts in Europe and the Pacific

HISTORY/STRUCTURE:

Founded: 1976 (as Kitty Hawk Airways)   **Start Date:** 1985
CEO: M Tom Christopher   **President:** Tilmon Reeves
Ownership: Kitty Hawk Group

FLEET:

Type	No	Engines
Convair 600/640	9	RR Dart 542-2
DC-9-15F	5	PW JT8D-7B
Boeing 727-200F	15	PW JT8D-9/-9A/-15/-15A

BOEING 727-200 (ADVANCED)

KIWI INTERNATIONAL AIR LINES

IATA: KP   **ICAO:** KIA   **IATA/ARC:** 538   **RADIO:** Kiwi Air

CONTACTS:

Mail
Hemisphere Center
US 1 & 9 South
Newark, NJ 07114

Telephone/FAX
Admin: +1 201 645 1133
Fax: +1 201 645 1161
Res: 1 800 538 5494

OPERATION:

Type: Scheduled passenger
Cities Served: ATL EWR LAS MCO MDW PBI

HISTORY/STRUCTURE:

Founded: 1992
Start Date: September 21, 1992
President: Jerry Murphy
Ownership: Edwards-Wasatch Enterprises

FLEET:

Type	No	Seats	Engines
Boeing 727-200 (Advanced)	7	Y150	PW JT8D-15

McDONNELL DOUGLAS DC-10-30

LAKER AIRWAYS
IATA: 6F **ICAO:** none **IATA/ARC:** none **RADIO:** none

CONTACTS:
Mail
1170 Lee Wagner Boulevard, Suite 200
Ft Lauderdale, FL 33315

Telephone/FAX
Admin: +1 954 359 0199
Fax: +1 954 359 7698
Res: 1 888 525 3724

Internet: none

OPERATION:
Type: Scheduled passenger
Cities Served: US: FLL MCO MIA **Europe:** LGW MAN

HISTORY/STRUCTURE:
Founded: 1995
Start Date: April 6, 1996
Ownership: Sir Freddie Laker, Oscar Wyatt

FLEET:

Type	No	Seats	Engines
DC-10-30	3	Y353	GE CF6-50C2
Ordered			
DC-10-30	1		

LOCKHEED 188A (F) ELECTRA

LYNDEN AIR CARGO

IATA: none **ICAO:** none **IATA/ARC:** 344 **RADIO:** none

CONTACTS:
Mail
4000 West 50th Street
Anchorage, AK 99502

Telephone/FAX
Admin: +1 907 243 0215
Fax: +1 907 245 0213

OPERATION:
Type: Scheduled/charter cargo
Cities Served: AKN ANC BET DLG KSM OME OTZ UNK

HISTORY/STRUCTURE:
Founded: 1995
President: Mike Hart

Start Date: August 31, 1995
Ownership: Lynden Inc

FLEET:

Type	No	Engines
Electra	3	Allison 501-D13A
Ordered		
L-100-30 Hercules	2	

AI(R) ATR42-320

MAHALO AIR

IATA: 8M **ICAO:** MLH **IATA/ARC:** 371 **RADIO:** Mahalo

CONTACTS:

Mail
90 Nakolo Place, Suite 215
Honolulu, HI 96819

Telephone/FAX
Admin: +1 808 833 7500
Fax:　 +1 808 833 9711
Res:　 1 800 462 4256

Internet: http://www.islander.magazine.com

OPERATION:

Type: Scheduled passenger
Cities Served: HNL JHM KOA LIH MKK OGG
Code-Share: Hawaiian Airlines (Hawaiian Connection, JHM MKK only), Northwest
FFP: none

HISTORY/STRUCTURE:

Founded: 1993 (as Island Express Air)　　**Start Date:** October 1993
President/CEO: Michael D Yocum　　**Ownership:** Privately held

FLEET:

Type	No	Seats	Engines
ATR42-320	7	Y46	PWC PW120

DE HAVILLAND CANADA DHC-7-102 DASH 7

MAVERICK AIRWAYS

IATA: 6M   **ICAO:** MVR   **IATA/ARC:** 350   **RADIO:** Mav Air

CONTACTS:

Mail
12015 East 46th Avenue, Suite 120
Denver, CO 80239

Telephone/FAX
Admin: +1 303 371 5094
Fax: +1 303 371 4623
Res: 1 800 435 9628

Internet: pending

OPERATION:

Type: Scheduled passenger
Cities Served: DEN GJT SBS
Code-Share: Frontier
FFP: none

HISTORY/STRUCTURE:

Founded: 1994
President: Cody Diekroeger

Start Date: January 20, 1997
Ownership: Privately held

FLEET:

Type	No	Seats	Engines
DHC-7-102	2	Y46	PWC PT6A-50
Ordered			
DHC-7-102	1	Y48/50	

BOMBARDIER CANADAIR REGIONAL JET SERIES 200ER

MESA AIRLINES

IATA: YV   **ICAO:** ASH   **IATA/ARC** 533   **RADIO:** Air Shuttle

CONTACTS:

Mail
Mesa Airlines
2325 East 30th Street
Farmington, NM 87401

Telephone/FAX
Admin: +1 505 326 4410
Fax: +1 505 326 4485
Res: 1 800 637 2247 (Mesa)
Res: 1 800 235 9292 (America West Express)
Res: 1 800 241 6522 (United Express)
Res: 1 800 428 4322 (US Airways Express)
PR: +1 505 326 4403

Internet: http://www.mesa-air.com

OPERATION:

Type: Scheduled passenger
Cities Served: US: ABQ ACK ACY ALM ALS ALW AMA APF ART AVP BDL BDR BFD BFF BGR BHM BLI BOS BPT BTR BWI CBE CEZ CKB CLT CNM COD COS CPR CVN CYS DCA DEN DRO DSM DUJ EAT ELM EUG EYW FAT FHU FKL FLG FLL FMN FNL GCC GCK GJT GNV GON GUC GUP HDN HGR HII HOB HVN HYA IFP IGM IPT ITH JAC JAN JAX JHW LAM LAR LBB LBE LBF LBL LEB LGA LIT LNS LRU LWS MAF MBS MCO MFR MGW MIA MLU MSS MSY MTH MTJ MVY OGS PBI PDX PFN PHL PHX PIT PKB PNS PQI PRC PSC PSP PUB RAP RDG RDM RIW RKS ROW RSW SAF SAT SBA SEA SHV SVC TEX TLH TPA VPS WRL YKM YNG YUM
FFP: America West FlightFund, United Mileage Plus, US Airways Dividend Miles

HISTORY/STRUCTURE:

Founded: 1980
Start Date: October 12, 1980
CEO/Chairman: Larry Risley (Mesa Air Group)
President: Clark Stevens (Mesa Airlines)
Divisional Presidents: Bob Dynan (United Express)
　　　　　　　　　　　Mike Lewis (America West Express)
　　　　　　　　　　　Peter Otradovec (Independent)
Ownership: Mesa Air Group (NASDAQ: MESA)

FLEET:

Type	No	Seats	Engines
Beech 1900D	107	Y19	PWC PT6A-67D
EMB-120ER Brasilia	14	Y30	PWC PW118A
DHC-8-202	12	Y37	PWC PW123
Canadair RJ 200ER	2	Y50	GE CF34-3B1
Ordered			
Beech 1900D	10		
DHC-8-202	25		
Canadair RJ 200ER	14		

RAYTHEON BEECH 1900D

BOMBARDIER DHC-8-102 DASH 8

MESABA AIRLINES

IATA: XJ **ICAO:** MES **IATA/ARC:** 582 **RADIO:** Mesaba

CONTACTS:

Mail
7501 26th Avenue South
Minneapolis, MN 55450
Email: wilk@skypoint.com
Internet: http://www.mesaba.com

Telephone/FAX
Admin: +1 612 726 5151
Fax: +1 612 725 4901
Res: 1 800 225 2525

OPERATION:

Type: Scheduled passenger
Cities Served: US: ABE ABR ATW ATY AZO BEH BGM BIS BJI BMI BRD BUF CAK CLE CMH CMI CMX CRW CVG CWA DAY DSM DTW ELM ERI ESC EVV FAR FNT FSD FWA GFK GPZ LAF LAN LEX LNK LSE MBS MKG MLI MQT MSP OMA PIR PIT PLN ROA ROC RFD RST SBN SCE SDF STC TOL TVC TVF TYS YNG
Canada: YOW YQK YQT YWG YXU
All service operated as Northwest Airlink and using only NW flight numbers
FFP: Northwest WorldPerks

HISTORY/STRUCTURE:

Founded: 1944 (as Mesaba Aviation)
Start Date: February 4, 1973
President/CEO: Bryan K Bedford
Ownership: Mesaba Holdings (NASDAQ: MAIR)

FLEET:

Type	No	Seats	Engines
SAAB 340A	13	Y30	GE CT7-5A2
SAAB 340B	21	Y34	GE CT7-9B
DHC-8-100	25	Y37	PWC PW120A
Ordered			
SAAB 340A	5		
SAAB 340B	18 plus 22 options		
Avro RJ85	12	F16Y53	(to be operated as Northwest JetLink)

BOEING 727-200 (ADVANCED)

MIAMI AIR INTERNATIONAL

IATA: GL **ICAO:** BSK **IATA/ARC::** none **RADIO:** Biscayne

CONTACTS:

Mail
PO Box 660880
Miami Springs, FL 33266-0880

Telephone/FAX
Admin: +1 305 871 3300
Fax: +1 305 871 4222

OPERATION:

Type: Charter passenger

HISTORY/STRUCTURE:

Founded: August 1990
Start Date: October 15, 1991
President: D Ross Fischer
Chairman: George A Lyall
Ownership: Fischer, Lyall & Kornmeyer

FLEET:

Type	No	Seats	Engines
Boeing 727-200 (Advanced)	7	Y173	PW JT8D-15/-15A

FOKKER 100

MIDWAY AIRLINES

IATA: JI **ICAO:** MDW **IATA/ARC:** 878 **RADIO:** Midway

CONTACTS:

Mail
300 West Morgan Street, Suite 1200
Durham, NC 27701

Telephone/FAX
Admin: +1 919 956 4875
Fax:　 +1 919 956 4801
Res:　 1 800 446 4392

OPERATION:

Type: Scheduled passenger
Cities Served: US: BDL BOS DCA EWR LGA MCO PBI PHL RDU SWF TPA **México:** CUN
Code-Share: Great Lakes Airlines
FFP: AAdvantage

HISTORY/STRUCTURE:

Founded: 1993
Start Date: November 15, 1993
CEO: Jerry Jacobs
President: Robert Ferguson
Ownership: SAS (James Goodnight) (67%), Zell/Chilmark (27%)

FLEET:

Type	No	Seats	Engines
Fokker 100	12	Y100	RR Tay 650-15
Airbus A320-200	1	F12Y138	IAE V2500-A1

McDONNELL DOUGLAS MD-88

MIDWEST EXPRESS

IATA: YX **ICAO:** MEP **IATA/ARC:** 453 **RADIO:** Midex

CONTACTS:

Mail
6744 South Howell Avenue
Oak Creek, WI 53154

Telephone/FAX
Admin: +1 414 570 4000
Fax: +1 414 570 0199
Res: 1 800 452 2022

OPERATION:

Type: Scheduled passenger
Cities Served: US: ATL ATW BOS CMH DCA DEN DFW EWR FLL GRR LAS LAX LGA MCI MCO MKE MSN OMA PHL PHX RSW SAN TPA
Canada: YYZ
Code-Share: Skyway Airlines
FFP: Midwest Express Frequent Flyer

HISTORY/STRUCTURE:

Founded: 1983
Start Date: April 29, 1984
President/CEO: Timothy Hoeksema
Ownership: Midwest Express Holdings (NYSE: MEH)

FLEET:

Type	No	Seats	Engines
DC-9-14/15	8	Y60	PW JT8D-7B
DC-9-30	16	Y84	PW JT8D-7B/-9/-9A
MD-88	2	Y112	PW JT8D-219

FAIRCHILD DORNIER 328-110

MOUNTAIN AIR EXPRESS

IATA: none **ICAO:** PKP **IATA/ARC:** none **RADIO:** Pikes Peak

CONTACTS:

Mail
2864 South Circle Drive, Suite 900
Colorado Springs, CO 80906

Telephone/FAX
Admin: +1 719 540 7800
Fax: +1 719 572 3723
Res: 1 800 930 3030

Internet: none

OPERATION:

Type: Scheduled passenger
Cities Served: ASE COS CPR CYS FNL GJT MCI OKC SAF TUL

HISTORY/STRUCTURE:

Founded: 1996
President: Thomas McClain
Start Date: December 15, 1996
Ownership: Western Pacific Airlines

FLEET:

Type	No	Seats	Engines
Dornier 328-110	4	Y32	PWC PW119B
Ordered			
Dornier 328	8 plus 12 options		

BOEING 737-200*

NATIONS AIR EXPRESS

IATA: N5   **ICAO:** NAE   **IATA/ARC:** none   **RADIO:** Nations Express

CONTACTS:

Mail
2400 Herodian Way, Suite 440
Smyrna, GA 30080

Telephone/FAX
Admin: +1 770 661 1440
Fax: +1 770 989 5772

OPERATION:

Type: Charter passenger
Areas Served: US and Caribbean

HISTORY/STRUCTURE:

Founded: 1994
Start Date: March 6, 1995
President: Mark W McDonald
Ownership: Privately held (Mofaz Air, Malaysia, 49%)

FLEET:

Type	No	Seats	Engines
Boeing 727-200	3	F8Y134	PW JT8D-7B
Currently operating for Pan Am			

*No longer operated, illustrates full color scheme

BOEING 757-200

NORTH AMERICAN AIRLINES

IATA: XG **ICAO:** NAO **IATA/ARC:** 455 **RADIO:** North American

CONTACTS:

Mail
Suite 250 Building 75
North Hangar Road
JFK International Airport
Jamaica, NY 11430

Telephone/FAX
Admin: +1 718 656 2650
Fax: +1 718 995 3372

OPERATION:

Type: Charter passenger
Areas Served: Worldwide charters including US sub-services for El Al

HISTORY/STRUCTURE:

Founded: 1989
Start Date: January 20, 1990
President/CEO: Dan McKinnon
Ownership: Dan McKinnon (75.1%), El Al (24.9%)

FLEET:

Type	No	Seats	Engines
MD-83	1	C16Y133	PW JT8D-219
Boeing 757-200	2	Y215	RR RB211-535E4

DOUGLAS DC-6A (C-118A) LIFTMASTER

NORTHERN AIR CARGO

IATA: HU **ICAO:** NAC **IATA/ARC:** 345 **RADIO:** Northern Air Cargo

CONTACTS:

Mail
3900 West International Airport
Anchorage, AK 99502
Email: nacargo@alaska.net

Telephone/FAX
Admin: +1 907 243 3331
Fax: +1 907 249 5190

Internet: http://www.nacargo.com

OPERATION:

Type: Scheduled cargo
Cities Served: ADQ ANC ANI BET BRW DLG FAI GAL ILI KSM MCG OME RDB SCC SNP STG UNK

HISTORY/STRUCTURE:

Founded: 1956 (as Sholton & Carlson Inc) **Start Date:** 1956
CEO: Rita Sholton **President:** Mary Sholton
Ownership: Sholton family

FLEET:

Type	No	Engines
DC-6A/B	13	PW R-2800-CB16
Boeing 727-100F	1	PW JT8D-7B

BOEING 747-400

NORTHWEST AIRLINES

IATA: NW **ICAO:** NWA **IATA/ARC:** 012 **RADIO:** Northwest

CONTACTS:

Mail
5101 Northwest Drive
St Paul, MN 55111-3034

Telephone/FAX
Admin: +1 612 726 2111
Fax: +1 612 726 6599
Res: 1 800 225 2525
PR: +1 612 726 2331
Job Hot Line: +1 612 727 7450

Internet: http://www.nwa.com

OPERATION:

Type: Scheduled passenger/cargo
Cities Served: US: ABE ABQ ALB ALO ANC AUS AZO BDL BHM BIL BIS BNA BOI BOS BTR BUF BWI BZN CID CLE CLT COS CMH CVG DAY DCA DEN DFW DLH DSM DTW EWR FAI FAR FCA FLL FSD FWA GEG GFK GRB GSO GSP GTF HDN HNL HOU HPN IAD ICT IND JAX JFK LAN LAS LAX LGA LIT LSE MBS MCI MCO MDT MDW MEM MIA MKE MOT MSN MSO MSP MSY OKC OMA ONT ORD ORF PBI PDX PHL PHX PIT PVD RAP RDU RIC RNO ROC RST RSW SAN SAT SBN SDF SEA SFO SJC SLC SMF SNA SRQ STL SUX SYR TPA TUS TVC TYS VPS **Canada:** YEG YQR YUL YVR YWG YXE YYC YYZ **México:** CUN CZM MEX PVR ZIH **Caribbean:** ANU GCM MBJ PLS SJU **Europe:** AMS CDG FRA LGW **Asia:** BKK BOM DEL FUK HKG KIX KUL MNL NGO NRT PEK SEL SHA SIN SPN TPE
Code-Share: Air UK, Alaska, Aloha, America West, Asiana, Business Express, Eurowings, Express Airlines I, Hawaiian, Horizon, KLM, Mahalo Air, Mesaba, Pacific Island Aviation, Trans States
FFP: WorldPerks

HISTORY/STRUCTURE:

Founded: September 1, 1926 (as Northwest Airways)
Start Date: October 1, 1926
President/CEO: John H Dasburg
Ownership: Northwest Airlines Corp (NASDAQ: NWAC)

FLEET:

Type	No	Seats	Engines
DC-9-14/15	22	F8Y70	PW JT8D-7B
DC-9-31/32	113	F12Y88 or F16Y84	PW JT8D-7B/-9A/-15
DC-9-41	12	F12Y100	PW JT8D-11
DC-9-51	35	F12Y110	PW JT8D-17
DC-9-82	8	F12Y131	PW JT8D-217
Boeing 727-200 (Advanced)	43	F12Y134	PW JT8D-15/-15A/17/-17R
A320-200	50	F12Y138	CFM56-5A1
Boeing 757-200	49	F14Y176/Y180	PW2037
DC-10-30	16	C30Y237 or C30Y249	GE CF6-50C/-50C2/-50C2B
DC-10-40	21	C32Y256 or C34Y247	PW JT9D-20/-20J
Boeing 747-100	3	C34Y420	PW JT9D-7A
Boeing 747-200	22	F8C66Y296/Y284 or F10C66Y284	PW JT9D-7F/-7Q/-7R4G2
Boeing 747-200F	8	Freighter	PW JT9D-7F/-7Q
Boeing 747-400	10	F18C62Y338	PW4056
Ordered			
A320-200	20		
A330-300	16		
Boeing 757-200	24		
Boeing 747-400	4		

McDONNELL DOUGLAS DC-10-40

BOEING 727-200 (F)

OMNI AIR EXPRESS
IATA: X9 **ICAO:** OAE **IATA/ARC:** none **RADIO:** Omni Express

CONTACTS:

Mail
PO Box 582527
Tulsa, OK 74158
Email: omniair@worldnet.att.net

Telephone/FAX
Admin: +1 918 836 5393
Fax: +1 918 834 4850

OPERATION:
Type: Cargo charter
Area Served: Worldwide

HISTORY/STRUCTURE:
Founded: 1984 (as Continental Air Transport) **Start Date:** 1984
CEO: Sanford P Burnstein **Ownership:** Privately held

FLEET:

Type	No	Seats	Engines
Lear 24	1		GE CJ610-6
Boeing 727-100C	1		PW JT8D-7B
Boeing 727-200F	2		PW JT8D-7B

BOEING 737-200

PACE AIRLINES

IATA: none **ICAO:** none **IATA/ARC:** none **RADIO:** none

CONTACTS:

Mail
3817 North Liberty Street
Winston-Salem, NC 27105

Telephone/FAX
Admin: +1 910 661 5374
Fax: +1 910 661 5702

OPERATION:

Type: Charter passenger
Areas Served: US, Canada, Caribbean, South America; contract carrier for Charlotte Hornets basketball team

HISTORY/STRUCTURE:

Founded: 1940 (as Piedmont Aviation)
Start Date: January 2, 1996
President/CEO: Jim A Taylor
Ownership: Piedmont Aviation Services

FLEET:

Type	No	Seats	Engines
Boeing 737-200	1	C44	PW JT8D-9A

GRUMMAN G-73 FRAKES TURBO MALLARD

PAN AM AIR BRIDGE

IATA: OP   **ICAO:** none   **IATA/ARC:** 370   **RADIO:** none

CONTACTS:

Mail
1000 MacArthur Causeway
Miami, FL 33132

Telephone/FAX
Admin: +1 305 373 1120
Fax: +1 305 371 7968
Res: 1 800 359 7262

OPERATION:

Type: Scheduled passenger
Cities Served: US: FLL MPB **Caribbean:** NSB PID

HISTORY/STRUCTURE:

Founded: July 1919 (as Chalk's Flying Service)
Start Date: 1919
President: Chuck Slagle
Ownership: Flying Boats Inc

FLEET:

Type	No	Seats	Engines
Turbo Mallard	5	Y17	PWC PT6A-34

AIRBUS A300B4-203

PAN AMERICAN WORLD AIRWAYS

IATA: PA   **ICAO:** PXA   **IATA/ARC:** none   **RADIO:** Pan Am

CONTACTS:

Mail
9300 NW 36th Street
Miami, FL 33178

Internet: none

Telephone/FAX
Admin: +1 305 873 3000
Fax: +1 305 873 2480
Res: 1 800 359 7262
PR: +1 305 866 2115

OPERATION:

Type: Scheduled passenger
Cities Served: US: JFK LAX MDW MIA   **Caribbean:** SDQ SJU
Code-Share: Aeroperú, APA International, Carnival Air Lines
FFP: Worldpass

HISTORY/STRUCTURE:

Founded: 1996
Start Date: September 26, 1996
President/CEO: Martin R Shugrue
Ownership: Frost Hanna Mergers Group & private & public investors
(AMEX: PAA)

FLEET:

Type	No	Seats	Engines
A300B4-203	4	F24Y230	GE CF6-50C2
Ordered			
A300B4-203	3		

NOTES:

Pan Am is due to acquire **Carnival Air Lines** in summer 1997, and Mickey Arison will become Pan Am's largest stockholder with a 40% stake.

BOEING 727-100

PANAGRA AIRWAYS

IATA: none **ICAO:** none **IATA/ARC:** none **RADIO:** none

CONTACTS:

Mail
750 SW 34th Street, Suite 201A
Fort Lauderdale, FL 33315

Internet: http://www.panagra.com

Telephone/FAX
Admin: +1 954 359 9944
Fax: +1 954 359 3075

OPERATION:
Type: Charter passenger
Areas Served: Worldwide

HISTORY/STRUCTURE:
Founded: 1995
President: James Peabody

Start Date: March 28, 1997
Ownership: Privately held

FLEET:

Type	No	Seats	Engines
Boeing 727-100	1	F10Y108	PW JT8D-7A

DE HAVILLAND CANADA DHC-7-102 DASH 7

PARADISE ISLAND AIRLINES

IATA: BK **ICAO:** PDI **IATA/ARC:** 522 **RADIO:** Paradise Island

CONTACTS:

Mail
1550 SW 43rd Street
Fort Lauderdale, FL 33315

Telephone/FAX
Admin: +1 954 359 8043
Fax: +1 954 359 8036
Res: 1 800 428 4322

Internet: http://www.paradiseair.com

OPERATION:

Type: Scheduled passenger
Cities Served: US: FLL MIA **Caribbean:** PID

HISTORY/STRUCTURE:

Founded: 1989
President/CEO: Byron Hogue

Start Date: March 24, 1989
Ownership: Byron Hogue

FLEET:

Type	No	Seats	Engines
DHC-7-102	5	Y50	PWC PT6A-50

SAAB 340B

PENINSULA AIRWAYS (PenAir)

IATA: KS   **ICAO:** PEN   **IATA/ARC:** 339   **RADIO:** Peninsula

CONTACTS:

Mail
4851A Aircraft Drive
Anchorage, AK 99502

Telephone/FAX
Admin: +1 907 243 2485
Fax: +1 907 243 6848
Res: 1 800 448 4226

Internet: http://www.penair.com

OPERATION:

Type: Scheduled passenger
Cities Served: ADQ AED AKI AKK AKN ALZ ANC ANI AOS ATT BET CDB CYF DLG DUT EGX IGG KCG KCL KCQ KEK KGK KIB KKB KKH KKI KLL KLN KMY KNW KOY KOZ KPN KPR KPV KPY KSM KUK KWK KWP KWT KYK KZB MCG MLL NLG NUP OLH OOK ORI PIP PKA PML PTH RSH SNP STG SYB TLT TNK TOG TWA UGB UGI UNK WNA WTL
Operates as Alaska Airlines Commuter on selected routes using AS flight numbers
FFP: Alaska Airlines Mileage Plan

HISTORY/STRUCTURE:

Founded: 1955   **Start Date:** 1967 (scheduled service)
President: Orin D Seybert   **Ownership:** Seybert family

FLEET:

Type	No	Seats	Engines
PA-32-300/-301	10	Y5	LY IO-540-K1A5/-K1G5/-K1G5D
G-44 Widgeon	2	Y5	LY GO-480-B1D
G-21A Goose	3	Y6	PW R-985
PA-31 Navajo	1	Y7	LY TIO-540-A2C
PA-31 Chieftain	5	Y9	LY TIO-540-J2BD
Cessna 208	3	Y9	PT6A-114
Cessna 441	2	Y10	GA TPE331-8-401S
Metro III	5	Y19	GA TPE331-11U-611G/-612G
SAAB 340B	2	Y30	GE CT7-9

BOMBARDIER DHC-8-102 DASH 8

PIEDMONT AIRLINES

IATA: none   **ICAO:** PDT   **IATA/ARC:** 531   **RADIO:** Piedmont

CONTACTS:

Mail
5443 Airport Terminal Road
Salisbury, MD 21801

Telephone/FAX
Admin: +1 410 742 2996
Fax: +1 410 742 4069
Res: 1 800 428 4322

OPERATION:

Type: Scheduled passenger
Cities Served: US: AVL BWI CAE CHA CHO CLT CRW DCA EWN EYW FAY FLL FLO GSO HHH HPN HVN JAX JFK LYH MCO MIA ORF PBI PHF PHL RDU RIC ROA SAV SBY TLH TPA **Canada:** YYZ **Caribbean:** ELH GHB MHH TCB
All service operated as US Airways Express using only US flight numbers
FFP: US Airways Dividend Miles

HISTORY/STRUCTURE:

Founded: 1964 (as Henson Airlines) **Start Date:** October 1, 1964
President/CEO: John F Leonard   **Ownership:** US Airways Group

FLEET:

Type	No	Seats	Engines
DHC-8-102	37	Y37	PWC PW120A
DHC-8-201	10	Y37	PWC PW123

BOEING 747-100 (F)

POLAR AIR CARGO

IATA: PO **ICAO:** PAC **IATA/ARC:** 403 **RADIO:** Polar Tiger

CONTACTS:

Mail
100 Ocean Gate, 15th Floor
Long Beach, CA 90802

Telephone/FAX
Admin: +1 562 436 7471
Fax: +1 562 436 9333

Internet: none

OPERATION:

Type: Scheduled/charter cargo
Cities Served: US: ANC ATL HNL JFK LAX LCK MIA ORD SFO
México/South America: EZE GIG MAO SCL VCP
Europe: AMS HEL LHR **Asia:** BKK DEL DXB HKG KHV KIX
MEL MNL SEL SIN SYD TPE **Oceania:** AKL NAN

HISTORY/STRUCTURE:

Founded: June 1990
CEO: Ned Wallace
Ownership: Privately held

Start Date: July 1994
President: Mark S West

FLEET:

Type	No	Engines
Boeing 747-100F	14	PW JT9D-7A
Boeing 747-200F	2	PW JT9D-7Q

BOEING 727-200

PRESTIGE AIRWAYS

IATA: OI **ICAO:** none **IATA/ARC:** 335 **RADIO:** none

CONTACTS:

Mail
9815 Godwin Drive
Manassas, VA 20110

Telephone/FAX
Admin: +1 703 335 1272
Fax: +1 703 335 1354

OPERATION:

Type: Scheduled/charter passenger
Areas Served: US: MIA **México:** CUN
Operates contract and ad hoc charters from US and Caribbean

HISTORY/STRUCTURE:

Founded: 1994 (as Paradise Airways)
Start Date: March 2, 1995
President: Elijah Jackson
Ownership: NavComm Aviation II

FLEET:

Type	No	Seats	Engines
Boeing 727-200	3	Y170	PW JT8D-9A/-15

BOEING 737-400

PRO AIR

IATA: XL **ICAO:** PRH **IATA/ARC:** none **RADIO:** Prohawk

CONTACTS:

Mail
101 Elliott Ave West, Suite 500
Seattle, WA 98119

Internet: http://www.proair.com

Telephone/FAX
Admin: +1 206 623 2000
Fax: +1 206 623 6612
Res: 1 888 PROAIR7

OPERATION:

Type: Scheduled passenger
Cities Served: BWI DTT EWR IND MKE

HISTORY/STRUCTURE:

Founded: 1995
President: Craig Belmondo
Ownership: Privately held

Start Date: April 1997
CEO: Kevin Stamper

FLEET:

Type	No	Seats	Engines
Boeing 737-400	2	C8Y138	CFM56-3C1

DORNIER 328-110

PSA AIRLINES

IATA: none   ICAO: JIA   IATA/ARC: none   RADIO: Blue Streak

CONTACTS:

Mail
3400 Terminal Drive
Vandalia, OH 45377-1041

Telephone/FAX
Admin: +1 937 454 1116
Fax: +1 937 454 0653
Res: 1 800 428 4322

Internet: http://www.flypsa.com

OPERATION:

Type: Scheduled passenger
Cities Served: AZO BTV CAE CAK CHS CLE CLT CRW CVG DAY DCA EVV FNT GRR GSP HSV HVN IAD IPT ITH LAN LEX MHT PHL PIT PWM RDG RDU RIC ROA SBN TOL TRI TYS
All service operated as US Airways Express using only US flight numbers
FFP: US Airways Dividend Miles

HISTORY/STRUCTURE:

Founded: 1969 (as Vee Neal Airlines)   **Start Date:** May 19, 1980
(renamed Jetstream International, December 1, 1983)
President/CEO: Richard Pfenning   **Ownership:** US Airways Group

FLEET:

Type	No	Seats	Engines
Dornier 328-110	25	Y31/32	PWC PW119B

LOCKHEED 188 ELECTRA

REEVE ALEUTIAN AIRWAYS

IATA: RV **ICAO:** RVV **IATA/ARC:** 338 **RADIO:** Reeve

CONTACTS:

Mail
4700 West International Airport Road
Anchorage, AK 99502

Telephone/FAX
Admin: +1 907 243 1112
Fax: +1 907 249 2317
Res: 1 800 544 2248

Internet: http://alaskan.com/promos/raa.html

OPERATION:

Type: Scheduled passenger/cargo, military contract
Cities Served: ADK AKN ANC BET CDB DLG DUT PTH SDP SNP
FFP: Alaska Airlines Mileage Plan

HISTORY/STRUCTURE:

Founded: 1932 (as Reeve Airways) **Start Date:** November 15, 1932
President/CEO: Richard D Reeve **Ownership:** Reeve Corporation

FLEET:

Type	No	Seats	Engines
Lockheed Electra	3	Combi	Allison 501-D13A
Boeing 727-100QC	2	Combi	PW JT8D-7B

McDONNELL DOUGLAS MD-90-30

RENO AIR

IATA: QQ　　**ICAO:** ROA　　**IATA/ARC:** 384　　**RADIO:** Reno Air

CONTACTS:

Mail
PO Box 30059
Reno, NV 84520-3059

Telephone/FAX
Admin: +1 702 686 3835
Fax:　 +1 702 829 5754
Res:　 1 800 736 6247
PR:　 +1 702 686 3833

Internet: http://www.renoair.com

OPERATION:

Type: Scheduled/charter passenger
Cities Served: US: ABQ ANC ATL COS DEN DTW FAI GPT LAS LAX ONT ORD PDX PIE RNO SAN SEA SFB SFO SJC SNA TUS
Canada: YVR
(Seasonal: IFP PSP)
Code-Share: Hawaiian Airlines, Wings West
FFP: AAdvantage

HISTORY/STRUCTURE:

Founded: 1990
Start Date: July 1, 1992
President/CEO: Robert W Reding
Ownership: Publicly traded company (NASDAQ: RENO)

FLEET:

Type	No	Seats	Engines
MD-87	5	F12Y105	PW JT8D-219
MD-82	8	F20Y120	PW JT8D-219
MD-83	14	F20Y120	PW JT8D-219
MD-90-30	3	F20Y128	IAE V2525-D5
Ordered			
MD-83	1		

LOCKHEED L-1011 TRISTAR 1

RICH INTERNATIONAL AIRWAYS

IATA: JN **ICAO:** RIA **IATA/ARC:** none **RADIO:** Rich Air

CONTACTS:

Mail
PO Box 522067
Miami, FL 33152

Telephone/FAX
Admin: +1 305 871 5113
Fax: +1 305 871 5584

OPERATION:
Type: Charter passenger

HISTORY/STRUCTURE:
Founded: 1970
President: William Meenan
Start Date: January 1971
Ownership: Meenan and Rich family

FLEET:

Type	No	Seats	Engines
DC-8-62	2	Y189	PW JT8D-3B/-7
DC-8-63	1	Y250	PW JT8D-7
L-1011-1	10	Y341/345/362	RR RB211-22B
L-1011-500	1	Y288	RR RB211-524B4

BOEING 727-100C

RYAN INTERNATIONAL AIRLINES

IATA: 1I **ICAO:** RYN **IATA/ARC:** none **RADIO:** Ryan

CONTACTS:

Mail
6810 West Kellogg
Wichita, KS 67209

Telephone/FAX
Admin: +1 316 942 0141
Fax: +1 316 942 7949

Internet: http://www2.southwind.net/~ryan/

OPERATION:

Type: Charter passenger/cargo
Areas Served: Operates 727 freighters for Emery Worldwide and for National Fisheries in the Pacific. Passenger charters operated from Atlantic City, and winter charters operated from Cleveland, Minneapolis, and Pittsburgh. Operates 737-400/-500 aircraft for Apple Vacations/Transglobal Vacations during winter season.

HISTORY/STRUCTURE:

Founded: 1973
President/CEO: Ronald D Ryan

Start Date: March 3, 1973
Ownership: Ryan Aviation Corp

FLEET:

Type	No	Seats	Engines
Boeing 737-200	1	Y130	PW JT8D-9A
Boeing 727-100F	28	Freighter	PW JT8D-7B
Boeing 727-200F	2	Freighter	PW JT8D-7B/-15

DE HAVILLAND CANADA DHC-6-300 TWIN OTTER VISTALINER

SCENIC AIRLINES

IATA: YR   **ICAO:** YRR   **IATA/ARC:** 398   **RADIO:** Scenic

CONTACTS:

Mail
2705 Airport Drive
North Las Vegas, NV 89030

Telephone/FAX
Admin: +1 702 739 1900
Fax: +1 702 739 8065
Res: 1 800 634 6801

Internet: none

OPERATION:

Type: Scheduled/charter passenger
Cities Served: GCN LAS
Code-Share: none
FFP: none

HISTORY/STRUCTURE:

Founded: 1967   **Start Date:** June 1967
President/CEO: Clifford N Langness   **Ownership:** Aviation Services West

FLEET:

Type	No	Seats	Engines
Cessna T210	5	Y5	CO TSIO-520-R
Cessna T207A	12	Y7	CO TSIO-520-M
PA-31 Chieftain	6	Y9	LY TIO-540-J2BD
Cessna 208B	3	Y14	PWC PT6A-114A
DHC-6-300	18	Y19	PWC PT6A-27

CONVAIR 580

SIERRA PACIFIC AIRLINES

IATA: SI   **ICAO:** SPA   **IATA/ARC:** none   **RADIO:** Sierra Pacific

CONTACTS:

Mail
7700 North Business Park Drive
Tucson, AZ 85743

Telephone/FAX
Admin: +1 520 297 1143
Fax: +1 520 744 0138

OPERATION:

Type: Charter passenger, operations for US Forestry Service & US Marshalls Service

HISTORY/STRUCTURE:

Founded: 1976 (as Mountainwest Aviation)   **Start Date:** February 1976
President: Gar M Thorsrud   **Ownership:** Sierra Pacific Corp

FLEET:

Type	No	Seats	Engines
Convair 580	3	Y50	Allison 501-D13H
Boeing 737-200 (Advanced)	1	Y122	PW JT8D-17

AI(R) ATR72-212

SIMMONS AIRLINES

IATA: MQ **ICAO:** EGF **RADIO:** Eagle Flight

CONTACTS:

Mail
PO Box 612527
DFW Airport, TX 75261

Telephone/FAX
Admin: +1 972 453 4500
Fax: +1 972 425 1444
Res: 1 800 433 7300
PR: +1 817 967 1577

Internet: http://www.americanair.com

OPERATION:

Type: Scheduled passenger
Cities Served: ACT AMA AZO BMI BPT CID CLE CLL CMH CMI CRP CVG CWA DAY DBQ DFW DSM EVV FWA FYV GRB GRR HOU ICT ILE IND JFK LAN LAW LBB LIT LSE MAF MEM MKE MLI MSN OKC ORD PIA SBN SGF SHV SJT SPI SPS TOL TUL TVC
All service operated as American Eagle using only AA flight numbers
Code-Share: Canadian Airlines International
FFP: AAdvantage

HISTORY/STRUCTURE:

Founded: 1978
President/CEO: Ralph L Ricardi
Start Date: July 1, 1980
Ownership: AMR Eagle

FLEET:

Type	No	Seats	Engines
SAAB 340B	12	Y34	GE CT7-9B
SAAB 340B*Plus*	25	Y34	GE CT7-9B
ATR42-300	24	Y46	PWC PW120
ATR72-200	27	Y64	PWC PW124B/PW127

BOEING 727-200

SKY TREK INTERNATIONAL AIRLINES

IATA: none **ICAO:** none **IATA/ARC:** none **RADIO:** none

CONTACTS:

Mail
5707 Huntsman Road
Suite 101
Richmond International Airport, VA 23250
Internet: none

Telephone/FAX
Admin: +1 804 236 4000
Fax: +1 804 236 4004

OPERATION:

Type: Passenger charter

HISTORY/STRUCTURE:

Founded: 1995
President: Robert Iverson II

Start Date: 1997
Ownership: Privately held

FLEET:

Type	No	Seats	Engines
Boeing 727-200	2		PW JT8D-15

RAYTHEON BEECH 1900D

SKYWAY AIRLINES

IATA: K8 **ICAO:** SYX **IATA/ARC:** none **RADIO:** Skyway Ex

CONTACTS:

Mail
4792 South Howell Avenue
Milwaukee, WI 53207

Telephone/FAX
Admin: +1 414 747 4750
Fax: +1 414 769 4272
Res: 1 800 452 2022

OPERATION:

Type: Scheduled passenger
Cities Served: US: ATW BNA CLE CMH CVG CWA DAY DSM DTW FNT GRB GRR IND LAN LSE MCI MKG MSN OMA RFD SBN SDF STL
Canada: YYZ
All service operated as Midwest Express Connection using only YX flight numbers
FFP: Midwest Express Frequent Flyer

HISTORY/STRUCTURE:

Founded: 1993
Start Date: February 3, 1994
President: David Reeve
Ownership: Astral Aviation (subsidiary Midwest Express Holdings)

FLEET:

Type	No	Seats	Engines
Beech 1900D	15	Y19	PWC PT6A-67D

BOMBARDIER CANADAIR REGIONAL JET SERIES 100LR

SKYWEST AIRLINES

IATA: OO   ICAO: SKW   IATA/ARC: 302   RADIO: Skywest

CONTACTS:

Mail
444 South River Road
St George, UT 84770

Email: ddouglas@skywest.com
Internet: http://www.skywest-air.com

Telephone/FAX
Admin: +1 801 634 3310
Fax: +1 801 634 3305
Res: 1 800 221 1212
PR: +1 801 634 3522

OPERATION:

Type: Scheduled passenger
Cities Served: US: ABQ BFL BIL BOI BTM BUR BZN CDC COD COS CPR EKO EUG FAT GJT HLN IDA IPL JAC LAS LAX LWS MRY MSO ONT PDX PHX PIH PSC PSP RAP RNO SAN SBA SBP SFO SGU SJC SLC SMF SMX SNA SUN TUS TWF VEL WYS YUM **Canada:** YVR
All service operated as Delta Connection using only DL flight numbers
FFP: Delta SkyMiles

HISTORY/STRUCTURE:

Founded: 1972
Start Date: June 19, 1972
President/CEO: Jerry C Atkin
Ownership: SkyWest Inc (NASDAQ: SKYW)

FLEET:

Type	No	Seats	Engines
EMB-120ER Brasília	50	Y30	PWC PW118A
Canadair RJ 100LR	10	Y50	GE CF34-3A1
Ordered			
Canadair RJ 100LR	10		

LOCKHEED 382G (L-100-30) HERCULES

SOUTHERN AIR TRANSPORT

IATA: SJ **ICAO:** SJM **IATA/ARC:** 351 **RADIO:** Southern Air

CONTACTS:

Mail
PO Box 328988
Columbus, OH 43732-8988

Telephone/FAX
Admin: +1 614 751 1100
Fax: +1 614 751 9138
Info: 1 800 327 6456

Internet: http://www.southernair.com

OPERATION:

Type: Charter cargo
Areas Served: Worldwide

HISTORY/STRUCTURE:

Founded: 1947
President/CEO: William G Langton

Start Date: 1947
Ownership: James H Bastian (100%)

FLEET:

Type	No	Engines
L-100-30 Hercules	15	Allison 501-D22A
DC-8-70F	4	CFM56-2C1
Boeing 747-200F	4	PW JT9D-7J/-7Q

BOEING 737-500

SOUTHWEST AIRLINES

IATA: WN　　**ICAO:** SWA　　**IATA/ARC:** 526　　**RADIO:** Southwest

CONTACTS:

Mail
PO Box 36611
Dallas, TX 75235-1611

Telephone/FAX
Admin: +1 214 904 4000
Fax:　 +1 214 904 5097
Res:　 1 800 435 9792
Job Hot Line: +1 214 904 4803

Internet: http://www.iflyswa.com

OPERATION:

Type: Scheduled passenger
Cities Served: ABQ AMA AUS BHM BNA BOI BUR BWI CLE CMH CRP DAL DTW ELP FLL GEG HOU HRL IAH IND JAX LAS LAX LBB LIT MAF MCO MDW MCI MSY OAK OKC OMA ONT PDX PHX PVD RNO SAN SAT SDF SEA SFO SJC SLC SMF SNA STL TPA TUL TUS
FFP: Rapid Rewards

HISTORY/STRUCTURE:

Founded: 1967
Start Date: June 18, 1971
President/CEO: Herbert (Herb) D Kelleher
Ownership: Publicly traded company (NYSE: LUV)

FLEET:

Type	No	Seats	Engines
Boeing 737-200	47	Y122	PW JT8D-9A/-15
Boeing 737-500	25	Y122	CFM56-3B1
Boeing 737-300	176	Y137	CFM56-3B1
Ordered			
Boeing 737-300	19 plus 16 options		
Boeing 737-700	63 plus 67 options		

McDONNELL DOUGLAS DC-9-31

SPIRIT AIRLINES

IATA: NK **ICAO:** SWG **IATA/ARC:** 487 **RADIO:** Spirit Wings

CONTACTS:

Mail
18121 East 8 Mile Road
Eastpointe, MI 48021

Internet: none

Telephone/FAX
Admin: +1 810 779 2700
Fax: +1 810 779 9332
Res: 1 800 772 7117

OPERATION:

Type: Scheduled/charter passenger
Cities Served: ACY BOS CLE DTW FLL MCO MYR TPA

HISTORY/STRUCTURE:

Founded: 1989 (as Charter One) **Start Date:** June 1990
President: Edward W Homfeld **Ownership:** Privately held

FLEET:

Type	No	Seats	Engines
DC-9-21	1	Y75	PW JT8D-11
DC-9-30	10	Y120	PW JT8D-7B/-9A/-11
DC-9-40	2	Y130	PW JT8D-11

BOEING 727-200 (ADVANCED)

SUN COUNTRY AIRLINES

IATA: SY **ICAO:** SCX **IATA/ARC:** none **RADIO:** Sun Country

CONTACTS:

Mail
2520 Pilot Knob Road, Suite 250
Mendota Heights, MN 55120

Telephone/FAX
Admin: +1 612 681 3900
Fax: +1 612 681 3970

Internet: http://www.suncountry.com

OPERATION:

Type: Scheduled/charter passenger
Cities Served: US: BOS DFW DTW HRL IAD IAH IFP JFK MIA MSP ORD PHX SAT SLC SRQ **México/Central America/South America:** LIR SJO **Caribbean:** AUA SXM

HISTORY/STRUCTURE:

Founded: July 1, 1982
President/CEO: John J Skiba

Start Date: January 20, 1983
Ownership: New Sun

FLEET:

Type	No	Seats	Engines
Boeing 727-200 (Advanced)	10	Y180	JT8D-17/-17A/-17R/-217C
DC-10-10	3	Y374	GE CF6-6D1A
DC-10-15	2	Y374	GE CF6-50C2F

McDONNELL DOUGLAS DC-9-31

SUN JET INTERNATIONAL

IATA: JX **ICAO:** SJI **IATA/ARC:** none **RADIO:** Sunjet

CONTACTS:

Mail
4700 140th Ave N, Suite 106
Clearwater, FL 34622

Internet: none

Telephone/FAX
Admin: +1 813 530 1515
Fax: +1 813 530 1615
Res: 1 800 478 6538

OPERATION:

Type: Charter passenger
Areas Served: Operates contract charters and sub-services for other carriers

HISTORY/STRUCTURE:

Founded: 1993
Start Date: July 1993
President/CEO: David Banmiller
Ownership: John Mansour (Sun Jet Holidays)

FLEET:

Type	No	Seats	Engines
DC-9-51	2	Y133	PW JT8D-17
DC-9-81	2	Y165	PW JT8D-209
DC-9-82	1	Y165	PW JT8D-217

BOEING 727-200 (ADVANCED)

SUN PACIFIC INTERNATIONAL

IATA: none   **ICAO:** SNP   **IATA/ARC:** none   **RADIO:** Sun Pacific

CONTACTS:

Mail
2502 East Benson Highway
Tucson, AZ 85706

Telephone/FAX
Admin: +1 520 295 0455
Fax: +1 520 295 1123

OPERATION:
Type: Charter passenger

HISTORY/STRUCTURE:
Founded: 1995
President/CEO: Robert Fleming
Start Date: March 2, 1996

FLEET:

Type	No	Seats	Engines
Boeing 727-100	1	C54	PW JT8D-7B
Boeing 727-200	4	C59 or Y173	PW JT8D-9A/-15

BOEING 727-200 (ADVANCED)

SUNWORLD INTERNATIONAL AIRLINES

IATA: SM **ICAO:** SWI **IATA/ARC:** none **RADIO:** Sunworld

CONTACTS:

Mail
207 Grandview Drive
Fort Mitchell, KY 41014

Telephone/FAX
Admin: +1 606 331 0091
Fax: +1 606 578 1190

OPERATION:

Type: Charter passenger

HISTORY/STRUCTURE:

Founded: 1995
President: William Yung

Start Date: July 1996
Ownership: William Yung

FLEET:

Type	No	Seats	Engines
Boeing 727-200 (Advanced)	1	Y167	PW JT8D-15

BOEING 747-200B

TOWER AIR

IATA: FF **ICAO:** TOW **IATA/ARC:** 305 **RADIO:** Tee Air

CONTACTS:

Mail
Hangar 17
JFK International Airport
Jamaica, NY 11430

Telephone/FAX
Admin: +1 718 553 4300
Fax: +1 718 553 4312
Res: 1 800 221 2500

Internet: none

OPERATION:

Type: Scheduled passenger
Cities Served: US: JFK LAX MIA SFO **Caribbean:** SJU
Europe: ATH ORY **Asia:** TLV

HISTORY/STRUCTURE:

Founded: August 1982
Start Date: November 1, 1983
President/CEO: Morris Nachtomi
Ownership: Publicly traded company (NASDAQ: TOWR)

FLEET:

Type	No	Seats	Engines
Boeing 747-100F	2	Freighter	PW JT9D-7A
Boeing 747-200B	16	Y480 or C45Y426 or C16Y497	PW JT9D-7A/-7F/-7J/-7Q

LOCKHEED L-1011 TRISTAR 1 (F)

TRADEWINDS AIRLINES

IATA: WI   **ICAO:** TDX   **IATA/ARC:** 490   **RADIO:** Tradewinds Express

CONTACTS:

Mail
PO Box 35327
Greensboro, NC 27425

Telephone/FAX
Admin: +1 910 668 7500
Fax: +1 910 668 7517

OPERATION:

Type: Scheduled cargo
Cities Served: US: BDL GSO **Caribbean:** BQN

HISTORY/STRUCTURE:

Founded: 1969 (as Wrangler Aviation)
Start Date: 1973
President/CEO: Paul Finazzo
Ownership: Tradewinds Acquisitions

FLEET:

Type	No	Engines
L-1011-1F	1	RR RB211-22B

DOUGLAS C-118A (DC-6A) LIFTMASTER

TRANS-AIR-LINK

IATA: TY　　**ICAO:** GJB　　**RADIO:** Sky Truck

CONTACTS:

Mail
PO Box 521298
Miami, FL 33152-1298

Telephone/FAX
Admin: +1 305 871 3301
Fax:　　+1 305 871 5785

OPERATION:

Type: Scheduled/charter cargo
Cities Served: US: MIA **Caribbean:** FPO NAS STT STX SXM

HISTORY/STRUCTURE:

Founded: 1979　　**Start Date:** 1979
President/CEO: Gary J Balnicki

FLEET:

Type	No	Engines
DC-6A	2	PW R-2800-CB16
DC-6B (F)	1	PW R-2800-CB16

DOUGLAS DC-8F-55 JET TRADER

TRANS CONTINENTAL AIRLINES

IATA none   **ICAO:** TCN   **IATA/ARC** none   **RADIO:** Trans Continental

CONTACTS:

Mail
803 Willow Run Airport
Ypsilanti, MI 48198

Telephone/FAX
Admin: +1 313 484 3435
Fax: +1 313 484 3260

OPERATION:

Type: Charter cargo
Areas Served: US, South America

HISTORY/STRUCTURE:

Founded: 1994
President/CEO: Scott D Kalitta

Start Date: August 1994
Ownership: Kalitta family

FLEET:

Type	No	Engines
DC-8-50F	2	PW JT3D-3B
DC-8-62F	2	PW JT3D-3B/-7
DC-8-61F	1	PW JT3D-3B

BAe 3201 JETSTREAM SUPER 31

TRANS STATES AIRLINES

IATA: 9N   **ICAO:** LOF   **IATA/ARC:** 414   **RADIO:** Waterski

CONTACTS:

Mail
4534 North Lindbergh Boulevard,
Suite 650
St Louis, MO 63044

Telephone/FAX
Admin: +1 314 895 8700
Fax: +1 314 895 1040
Res: 1 800 221 2000
       1 800 428 4322

OPERATION:

Type: Scheduled passenger
Cities Served: ALO BDL BHM BMI BNA BOS BRL BWI CGI CID CMI COU DCA DEC EVV FAT FWA FYV GRR JFK JLN LAX LEX MEM MKE MLI MRY MSN MWA ONT ORF PAH PHL PIA PIT PSP RIC SAN SBA SBN SFO SGF SMF SPI STL SUX TBN UIN
All service operated as TW Express or US Airways Express using only TW & US flight numbers
FFP: TWA Frequent Flight Bonus, US Airways Dividend Miles

HISTORY/STRUCTURE:

Founded: May 1982 (as Resort Air)   **Start Date:** 1983
President/CEO: Hulas Kanodia   **Ownership:** Privately held

FLEET:

Type	No	Seats	Engines
Jetstream Super 31	32	Y19	GA TPE331-12UAR-701H
Jetstream 41	27	Y29	GA TPE331-14HR-805H
ATR42-300	8	Y48	PWC PW120
ATR72-200	3	Y64	PWC PW124B
Ordered			
Jetstream 41	20 options		

BOEING 727-200 (ADVANCED)

TRANS WORLD AIRLINES
IATA: TW **ICAO:** TWA **IATA/ARC:** 015 **RADIO:** TWA

CONTACTS:

Mail
One City Centre
515 North 6th Street
St Louis, MO 63101

Internet: http://www.twa.com

Telephone/FAX
Admin: +1 314 589 3000
Fax: +1 314 589 3129
Res: 1 800 221 2000
PR: +1 314 589 3213/3214

OPERATION:

Type: Scheduled passenger
Cities Served: US: ABQ ATL AUS BDL BNA BOS BWI CID CLE CLT CMH COS CVG DAY DCA DEN DFW DSM DTW EWR FLL FSD HDN HNL HOU IAD ICT IND JAN JAX JFK LAS LAX LGA LIT LNK MCI MCO MIA MKE MLI MSP MSY OKC OMA ONT ORD ORF PBI PDX PHL PHX PIT RDU RNO RSW SAN SAT SDF SEA SFO SGF SHV SJC SLC SMF SNA SRQ STL TPA TUL TYS **Canada:** YYZ **México:** CUN PVR ZIH **Caribbean:** MBJ SDQ SJU **Europe:** BCN CDG FCO LGW LIS MAD MXP **Asia:** RUH TLV **Africa:** CAI
FFP: TWA Frequent Flight Bonus

HISTORY/STRUCTURE:

Founded: July 16, 1925 (as Western Air Express)
Start Date: October 1, 1930 (as Transcontinental & Western Air)
Chairman/CEO: Gerald Gitner
Ownership: Publicly traded company (AMEX: TWA)

FLEET:

Type	No	Seats	Engines
DC-9-15	7	F8Y60	PW JT8D-7B
DC-9-30	36	F8Y90	PW JT8D-9A/-15
DC-9-40	3	F8Y90	PW JT8D-15
DC-9-50	12	F12Y95	PW JT8D-17
MD-81/82	30	F12Y130	PW JT8D-217A/-217C
MD-83	23	F12Y130/132	PW JT8D-217C/-219
Boeing 727-200	39	F12Y134	PW JT8D9A/-15
Boeing 757-200	6	F22Y158	PW2037
Boeing 767-200	12	F24Y159	PW JT9D-7R4D
Boeing 767-300	2	F30Y178	PW4060
L-1011-1	7	F28Y226	RR RB211-22B
L-1011-50/100	3	F18Y234	RR RB211-22B
Boeing 747-100	5	F29Y404	PW JT9D-7A
Boeing 747-200	2	F29Y398	PW JT9D-7A
Ordered			
MD-83	10 plus 10 options		
Boeing 757-200	14 plus 10 options		
A330-300	10 plus 20 options		

NOTES:

AIRBUS A320-231

TRANSMERIDIAN AIRLINES

IATA: T9   **ICAO:** TRZ   **IATA/ARC:** none   **RADIO:** Transmeridian

CONTACTS:

Mail
11 Bagby Street, Suite 230
Houston, TX 77002

Telephone/FAX
Admin: +1 713 615 6000
Fax: +1 713 615 6044

OPERATION:
Type: Charter passenger

HISTORY/STRUCTURE:
Founded: 1995
Start Date: October 30, 1995
President/CEO: Donald Dodson
Ownership: Prime Air (subsidiary of Translift Airways)

FLEET:

Type	No	Seats	Engines
Boeing 727-200 (Advanced)	2	Y	JT8D-15/-15A
Airbus A320-231	1	Y180	IAE V2500-A1
Several additional A320s leased in during northern winter season			

BOEING 777-200

UNITED AIRLINES

IATA: UA **ICAO:** UAL **IATA/ARC:** 016 **RADIO:** United

CONTACTS:

Mail
PO Box 66100
Chicago, IL 60666

Telephone/FAX
Admin: +1 847 700 4000
Fax: +1 847 700 7680
Res: 1 800 241 6522
PR: +1 847 700 5501

Internet: http://www.ual.com

OPERATION:

Type: Scheduled passenger/cargo
Cities Served: US: ABE ABQ ALB ANC ATL AUS BDL BHM BIL BNA BOI BOS BTV BUF BUR BWI CID CLE CLT CMH COS CVG DAY DCA DEN DFW DSM DTW EUG EWR FLL FSD GEG GRR GSO HDN HNL HPN IAD IAH ICT IND JAC JAX JFK KOA LAS LAX LGA LNK MBS MCI MCO MDT MEM MHT MIA MKE MRY MSN MSP MSY MTJ OAK OGG OKC OMA ONT ORD ORF PBI PDX PHL PHX PIT PSP PVD PWM RDU RIC RNO ROC RSW SAN SAT SDF SEA SFO SJC SLC SMF SNA STL SYR TPA TUL TUS TYS **Canada:** YVR YYC YYZ **México/Central America/South America:** CCS CNF EZE GDL GIG GRU GUA LIM MEX MVD SAL SCL SJO SYD **Caribbean:** SJU **Europe:** AMS BRU CDG DUS FRA LHR MXP ZRH **Asia:** BKK DEL GUM HKG KIX MEL MNL PEK SEL SHA TPE **Oceania:** AKL
Code-Share: Aeromar, AEROMEXICO, Air Canada, Air New Zealand, ALM, Aloha, Ansett Australia, British Midland, Cayman, Emirates, Gulfstream International, Lufthansa, SAS, Trans States, United Express (Air Wisconsin, Atlantic Coast, Mesa, UFS, WestAir)
FFP: Mileage Plus

HISTORY/STRUCTURE:

Founded: February 1, 1929 (as United Aircraft & Transport Corp)
Start Date: July 1, 1931
CEO: Gerald Greenwald
President: John A Edwardson
Ownership: UAL Corp (55% employees) (NYSE: UAL)

FLEET:

Type	No	Seats	Engines
Boeing 737-200	61	F8Y101	PW JT8D-7B/-9A/-17
Boeing 737-500	57	F8Y100	CFM56-3C1
Boeing 737-300	101	F8Y118	CFM56-3C1
Airbus A320-200	37	F12Y132	IAE V2527-A5
Boeing 727-200	51	F12Y135	PW JT8D-15
Boeing 727-200 (Advanced)	24	F12Y135	PW JT8D-15
Boeing 757-200	84	F24Y164	PW2037
Boeing 757-200 (ETOPS)	10	F24Y164	PW2037
Boeing 767-200	19	F10C33Y126 or F10C32Y126	PW JT9D-7R4D
Boeing 767-300 (ER)	23	F10C38Y158	PW4060
DC-10-10	26	F28Y259 or F38Y260	GE CF6-6D
DC-10-30/CF	6	F38Y260	GE CF6-50C2
DC-10-30F	2	Freighter	GE CF6-50C2
Boeing 777-200	16	F12C49Y231	PW4077
Boeing 747-100	13	F42Y408 or F18C70Y305	PW JT9D-7A
Boeing 747-200	9	F35C105Y124 or FF18C79Y272	PW JT9D-7J/-7R4G2
Boeing 747-400	26	F36C123Y142 or F18C80Y320	PW4056
Ordered			
Boeing 737	137 options		
Airbus A319-100	28		
Airbus A320-200	13 plus 45 options		
Boeing 757-200	6 plus 22 options		
Boeing 767	5 options		
Boeing 777	22 plus 30 options		
Boeing 747-400	22 plus 22 options		

NOTES:

BAe ATP

UNITED FEEDER SERVICE

IATA: U2   **ICAO:** UFS   **IATA/ARC:** none   **RADIO:** Feeder Flight

CONTACTS:

Mail
9275 Genaire Drive
St Louis, MO 63134

Telephone/FAX
Admin: +1 314 895 4500
Fax: +1 314 895 1040
Res: 1 800 241 6522

OPERATION:

Type: Scheduled passenger
Cities Served: AZO CAK CWA FWA GRB ORD PIA SBN YNG
All service operated as United Express using only UA flight numbers
FFP: United Mileage Plus

HISTORY/STRUCTURE:

Founded: 1993
President/CEO: Hulas Kanodia

Start Date: September 1993
Ownership: UFS Inc

FLEET:

Type	No	Seats	Engines
BAe ATP	9	Y64	PWC PW126A

BOEING 767-300F (ER)

UNITED PARCEL SERVICE

IATA: 5X   **ICAO:** UPS   **IATA/ARC:** 406   **RADIO:** UPS

CONTACTS:

Mail
1400 North Hurstbourne Parkway
Louisville, KY 40223

Telephone/FAX
Admin: +1 502 329 6500
Fax: +1 502 329 6550
Info: 1 800 743 5877
PR: +1 502 329 6522

Internet: http://www.ups.com

OPERATION:

Type: Scheduled cargo, charter passenger
Cities Served: US: ABQ ABY ALB ANC ATL AUS BDL BFI BHM BIL BOI BOS BUR BWI CID CLE CLT DEC DEN DFW DSM DTW EFD ELP EWR FAT FSD FWA GEG HNL IAD ICT JAN JAX JFK LAN LAS LAX LCK LGB LIT MCI MCO MDT MEM MHT MIA MOB MSP MSY OAK OKC OMA ONT ORD PBI PDX PHL PHX PIE PIT RDU RFD RIC RNO ROA ROC RSW SAN SAT SDF SGF SHV SJC SLC SNA STL SYR TUL TYS **Canada:** YHM YMX YYC **México:** GDL MEX **Caribbean:** SJU **Europe:** CGN EMA **Asia:** CTS HKG MNL
Other cities served by contract air carriers
Code-Share: Nippon Cargo Airlines

HISTORY/STRUCTURE:

Founded: 1907
Start Date: February 1, 1988
CEO: Kent Nelson
President: Thomas H Weidemeyer
Ownership: Trust of 18,000 current and former managers

FLEET:

Type	No	Engines
Boeing 727-100C (QF)	40	RR Tay 651-54
Boeing 727-100QC (QF)	5	RR Tay 651-54
Boeing 727-200F (Advanced)	8	PW JT8D-15/-17
Boeing 757-200PF	60	PW2040 (35) or RR RB211-535E4
DC-8-71/-73F	52	CFM56-2
Boeing 767-300F (ER)	16	GE CF6-80C2B7F
Boeing 747-100F	14	PW JT9D-7A
Ordered		
Boeing 757-200PF	\multicolumn{2}{l}{15 plus 41 options}
Boeing 767-300F (ER)	\multicolumn{2}{l}{14 plus 30 options}

NOTES:

BOEING 737-300

US AIRWAYS

IATA: US **ICAO:** USA **IATA/ARC:** 037 **RADIO:** USAir

CONTACTS:

Mail
2345 Crystal Drive
Arlington, VA 22227

Telephone/FAX
Admin: +1 703 418 7000
Fax: +1 703 418 5437
Res: 1 800 428 4322
PR: +1 703 418 5100

Internet: http://www.us-airways.com

OPERATION:

Type: Scheduled passenger
Cities Served: US: ABE ABQ ALB ATL AUS AVL BDL BGM BGR BHM BNA BOS BTV BUF BWI CAE CAK CHA CHS CLE CLT CMH CRW CVG DAB DAY DCA DEN DFW DTW ELM ERI EWR FAY FLL GRR GSO GSP HPN HSV IAD IAH ILM IND ISP ITH JAX JFK LAS LAX LEX LGA LWB MCI MCO MDT MDW MEM MHT MIA MKE MLB MSP MSY MYR ORD ORF PHL PHX PIT PNS PVD PWM RDU RIC ROA ROC RSW SAN SAT SAV SBN SDF SEA SFO SNA SRQ STL SWF SYR TOL TPA TRI TYS **Canada:** YOW YUL YYZ **México:** CUN
Caribbean: BDA GCM MBJ NAS SJU STT STX SXM
Europe: CDG FCO FRA MAD MUC
Code-Share: Deutsche BA, US Airways Express (Air Midwest, Allegheny, Chautauqua, Commutair, Mesa, Piedmont, PSA, Trans States)
FFP: US Airways Dividend Miles

HISTORY/STRUCTURE:

Founded: March 5, 1937 (as All American Airways)
Start Date: August 12, 1940
CEO: Stephen M Wolf
President: Rakesh Gangwal
Ownership: US Airways Group (NYSE: USAirGp)

FLEET:

Type	No	Seats	Engines
F28 Mk 4000	8	F4Y64	RR Spey 555-15P
Fokker 100	40	F8Y90	RR Tay 650-15
DC-9-30	62	F8Y93	PW JT8D-7B/-9A
Boeing 737-200	64	F12Y96	PW JT8D-9A/-15/-15A
Boeing 737-300	85	F12Y114	CFM56-3B1/-3B2
Boeing 737-400	54	F12Y132	CFM56-3B2
MD-81/-82	31	F8Y133/136	PW JT8D-217
Boeing 757-200	34	F24Y158	RR RB211-535E4
Boeing 767-200	12	C24Y192	GE CF6-80C2B2
Ordered			
Boeing 757	7		
A319/A320/A321	160 plus 280 options		

NOTES:

BOEING 727-200

US AIRWAYS SHUTTLE (Shuttle Inc dba)

IATA: TB **ICAO:** USS **IATA/ARC:** 857 **RADIO:** US Shuttle

CONTACTS:

Mail
LaGuardia Airport
Marine Air Terminal
Building 7 South
Flushing, NY 11371

Telephone/FAX
Admin: +1 718 397 6364
Fax: +1 718 397 6035

Internet: http://www.us-airways.com

OPERATION:

Type: Scheduled passenger
Cities Served: BOS DCA LGA
FFP: US Airways Dividend Miles

HISTORY/STRUCTURE:

Founded: October 1988 (as The Trump Shuttle)
Start Date: June 8, 1989
President/CEO: Terry Hallcom
Ownership: Citicorp

FLEET:

Type	No	Seats	Engines
Boeing 727-200	11	Y165	PW JT8D-7B/-9A

McDONNELL DOUGLAS DC-9-15F

USA JET

IATA: U7   **ICAO:** JUS   **RADIO:** Jet USA

CONTACTS:

Mail
2064 D Street
Belleville, MI 48111-1278

Internet: http://www.activaero.com

Telephone/FAX
Admin: +1 313 480 0200
Fax: +1 313 480 0202
Res: 1 800 877 5387

OPERATION:

Type: Charter cargo
Area Served: Primarily ad hoc charters in US

HISTORY/STRUCTURE:

Founded: 1994
President: Robert Phelps

Start Date: December 1994
Ownership: YIP Group

FLEET:

Type	No	Engines
Falcon 20	15	GE CF700-2D2
DC-9-15F	7	PW JT8D-7B

McDONNELL DOUGLAS DC-9-32

VALUJET AIRLINES

IATA: J7 **ICAO:** VJA **IATA/ARC:** none **RADIO:** Critter

CONTACTS:

Mail
1800 Phoenix Boulevard, Suite 126
Atlanta, GA 30349-5555

Telephone/FAX
Admin: +1 770 907 2580
Fax: +1 770 907 2586
Res: 1 800 994 8258
        1 800 825 8538

Internet: http://www.valujet.com

OPERATION:

Type: Scheduled passenger
Cities Served: ATL BOS CAK CLT CMH FLL DFW FNT IAD JAX MCO MDW MEM MSY PBI PHF PHL RDU RSW SAV SDF TPA

HISTORY/STRUCTURE:

Founded: 1992
CEO: Lewis Jordan
Ownership: Publicly traded company (NASDAQ: VJET)
Start Date: October 26, 1993
President: D Joseph Corr

FLEET:

Type	No	Seats	Engines
DC-9-30	43	Y113	PW JT8D-7B/-9A
Ordered			
MD-95	50 plus 50 options		

BOEING 737-200

VANGUARD AIRLINES

IATA: NJ   **ICAO:** VGD   **IATA/ARC:** none   **RADIO:** Vanguard Air

CONTACTS:

Mail
30 NW Rome Circle
Mezzanine Level
Kansas City International Airport
Kansas City, MO 64153
Internet: none

Telephone/FAX
Admin: +1 816 243 2100
Fax: +1 913 722 5145
Res: 1 800 826 4827

OPERATION:

Type: Scheduled passenger
Cities Served: ATL DEN DFW DSM ICT LAS LAX MCI MCO MDW MIA SFO TPA

HISTORY/STRUCTURE:

Founded: 1994
Start Date: December 2, 1994
President/CEO: John Tague
Ownership: Publicly traded company (NASDAQ: VNGD)

FLEET:

Type	No	Seats	Engines
Boeing 737-200	6	Y128	PW JT8D-7/-9A/-15
Boeing 737-300QC	2	Y149	CFM56-3B1

EMBRAER EMB-120RT BRASILIA

WESTAIR COMMUTER AIRLINES
IATA: OE **ICAO:** SDU **IATA/ARC:** 460 **RADIO:** Sundance

CONTACTS:

Mail
5588 Air Corp Way
Fresno, CA 93727

Telephone/FAX
Admin: +1 209 294 6915
Fax: +1 209 291 5784
Res: 1 800 241 6522

Internet: http://www.mesa-air.com/wac

OPERATION:
Type: Scheduled passenger
Cities Served: ACV BFL CEC CIC CLD FAT IPL IYK LAX LMT MCE MOD MRY ONT OXR PMD PSP RDD SAN SBA SBP SFO SMF SMX SNA STS VIS YUM
All service operated as United Express using only UA flight numbers
FFP: United Mileage Plus

HISTORY/STRUCTURE:
Founded: 1972 (as STOL Air)   **Start Date:** 1972
President: Rolly Bergeson   **Ownership:** Mesa Air Group

FLEET:

Type	No	Seats	Engines
Jetstream 31	21	Y19	GA TPE331-10UG-513H
EMB-120RT/ER Brasília	13	Y30	PWC PW118/118A

BOEING 737-300

WESTERN PACIFIC AIRLINES

IATA: W7   **ICAO:** KMR   **IATA/ARC:** 318   **RADIO:** Komstar

CONTACTS:

Mail
2864 South Circle Drive, Suite 1000
Colorado Springs, CO 80906

Telephone/FAX
Admin: +1 719 579 7737
Fax: +1 719 389 1999
Res: 1 800 930 3030
PR: +1 719 527 7481

Internet: http://www.westpac.com

OPERATION:

Type: Scheduled passenger
Cities Served: ATL COS DFW EWR IAD IAH IND LAX MCI MCO MDW OKC PDX PHX SAN SEA SFO TUL
Code-Share: Mountain Air Express

HISTORY/STRUCTURE:

Founded: September 1994
Start Date: April 28, 1995
President/CEO: Robert A Peiser
Ownership: Publicly traded company (NASDAQ: WPAC)

FLEET:

Type	No	Seats	Engines
Boeing 737-300	15	Y138	CFM56-3B1/-3B2
Ordered			
Boeing 737-300	6 plus 6 options		

SAAB 340B

WINGS WEST AIRLINES
IATA: RM **ICAO:** EGF **RADIO:** Eagle Flight

CONTACTS:
Mail
1 Aerovista Place, Suite B
San Luis Obispo, CA 93403

Telephone/FAX
Admin: +1 805 541 1010
Fax: +1 805 541 2881
Res: 1 800 433 7300
PR: +1 817 967 1577

Internet: http://www.americanair.com

OPERATION:
Type: Scheduled passenger
Cities Served: ABI AEX BFL BTR CLD DFW FAT FSM FYV GGG JAN LAX LCH LFT LRD MEM MRY PSP SAN SBA SBP SFO SHV SNA TXK
All service operated as American Eagle using only AA flight numbers
Code-Share: Alaska Airlines, Canadian, Hawaiian Airlines, Reno Air
FFP: AAdvantage

HISTORY/STRUCTURE:
Founded: 1979
President: Robert Cordes
Start Date: November 11, 1979
Ownership: AMR Eagle

FLEET:

Type	No	Seats	Engines
SAAB 340B	38	Y34	GE CT7-9B

McDONNELL DOUGLAS MD-11F (CF)

WORLD AIRWAYS

IATA: WO **ICAO:** WOA **IATA/ARC:** 468 **RADIO:** World

CONTACTS:

Mail
13873 Park Center Road, Suite 490
Herndon, VA 22071
Internet: http://www.worldair.com

Telephone/FAX
Admin: +1 703 834 9200
Fax: +1 703 834 9412

OPERATION:

Type: Charter passenger/cargo
Areas Served: Major contracts include sub-services for Malaysia, Garuda, and charters for US military

HISTORY/STRUCTURE:

Founded: March 29, 1948 **Start Date:** May 1948
President/CEO: Russell Ray Jr **Ownership:** WorldCorp (NYSE: WOA)

FLEET:

Type	No	Seats	Engines
DC-10-30	4	Y380	GE CF6-50C2
MD-11	6	Y409	PW4460/4462
MD-11F	3	Y410/Freighter	PW4460/4462

US Addenda

ACTION AIRLINES (XQ/AXQ/410/Action Air) PO Box 117, East Hadam, CT 06423; +1 860 448 1646, Fax: +1 860 446 0130, John Rutledge. Passenger scheduled/charter. 1 x Cessna 172, 1 x Cherokee Six, 3 x Piper Seneca, 1 x Piper Navajo, 2 x Navajo Chieftain

AIR CARGO CARRIERS (UN/SNC/Night Cargo) 4984 South Howell Avenue, Milwaukee, WI 53207; +1 414 482 1711, Fax: +1 414 482 2038, James Germek. Operates feeder services in continental US and Caribbean for major freight carriers. 5 x Shorts Skyvan, 11 x Shorts 330, 5 x Shorts 360

AIR CHARTER EXPRESS (FRG/Freight Runners) 4800 South Howell Avenue, Milwaukee, WI 53207; +1 414 744 5525, Fax: +1 414 744 4850, Charles Zens Jr. Cargo charter. 3 x Cessna 207, 1 x Cessna 401, 5 x Cessna 402, 1 x Beech 99

AIR MOLOKAI (7D/437) 333 Dairy Road, Kahului, HI 96732; +1 808 871 9550, Fax: +1 808 871 8109, Donald Johnson. Passenger scheduled/charter. 3 x Cessna 402B

AIR NEVADA (LW/ANV/568/Air Nevada) PO Box 11105, Las Vegas, NV 89111; +1 702 736 8900, Fax: +1 702 795 8116, Myron Caplan. Passenger scheduled/charter. 11 x Cessna 402

AIRPAC AIRLINES (RI/APC/856/Airpac) 7277 Perimeter Road South, King County Airport, Seattle, WA 98108; +1 206 762 8006, Fax: +1 206 762 6357, Gregory Thompson. Freight charter. 8 x Piper Seneca, 9 x Navajo Chieftain, 3 x Cessna 404, 1 x Beech 99

AIR ST THOMAS (ZP/STT/315/Paradise) PO Box 302788, St Thomas, USVI 00803; +1 809 776 2722, Fax: +1 809 776 2992, Paul Wikander. Passenger scheduled. 5 x Piper Aztec, 2 x Cessna 402, 1 x Trislander

AIR SUNSHINE (YI/RSI/806/Air Sunshine) PO Box 22237, Ft Lauderdale, FL 33335; +1 954 359 8211, Fax: +1 954 359-8229, Allen Adili. Passenger scheduled. 4 x Cessna 402, 2 x Bandeirante

AIR VEGAS (6V/389) PO Box 11008, Las Vegas, NV 89111; +1 702 736 3599, Fax: +1 702 361 8967, James Petty. Passenger scheduled/charter. 3 x Bonanza, 2 x Cessna 207, 6 x Cessna 402, 9 x Beech 99

ALASKA CENTRAL EXPRESS (9Y/AER/Ace Air) PO Box 60204, Fairbanks, AK 99706; +1 907 474 9327, Dale Erickson. Freight scheduled/charter. 3 x Cherokee Six/Lance, 2 x Cessna 207, 1 x Navajo Chieftain, 2 x Beech 1900

ALPINE AIR (5A/AIP/511/Alpine Air) PO Box 691, Provo, UT 84603; +1 801 373 1508, Fax: +1 801 373 6728, Bill Distefano. Passenger scheduled, charter freight. 1 x Piper Lance, 1 x Piper Seneca, 4 x Navajo Chieftain, 2 x Cheyenne III, 10 x Beech 99

AMERIFLIGHT (AMF/Amflight) 4700 Empire Avenue, Hangar 1, Burbank, CA 91505; +1 818 980 5005, Fax: +1 818 980 5101, Gary Richards. Cargo charter. 21 x Piper Lance, 45 x Navajo/Chieftain, 1 x King Air 200, 36 x Beech 99, 5 x Lear 35, 12 x Beech 1900, 20 x Metro III/Expediter

ARCTIC CIRCLE AIR SERVICE (CIR/Air Arctic) PO Box 190228, Anchorage, AK 99519; +1 907 243 1380, Fax: +1 907 248 0042, Ervin Terry. Passenger/cargo charter. 1 x Piper Lance, 2 x Cessna 206, 4 x Cessna 207, 2 x Cessna 402, 3 x Skyvan

ARRIVA AIR INTERNATIONAL 6001 South Power Road, Hanger 351, Mesa, AZ 85206; +1 602 988 1777, Fax: +1 602 988 1776, Steven Higgins. Cargo charter. 1 x Boeing 727-200F

BAKER AVIATION (8B/BAJ/Baker Aviation) PO Box 708, Kotzebue, AK 99752; +1 907 442 3108, Fax: +1 907 442 1745, Marjorie Baker. Passenger scheduled. 2 x Cessna 207, 2 x Cessna 402, 1 x King Air

BALTIMORE AIR TRANSPORT 701 Wilson Point Road, Suite 101, Baltimore, MD 21220; +1 410 687 3801, Fax: +1 410 687 0263. Cargo charter. 2 x Cessna 208B

BANKAIR (BKA/Bankair) 2406 Edmund Road, West Columbia, SC 29169; +1 803 794 7384, Fax: +1 803 822 8775, John Dickerson. Cargo charter. 1 x Piper Seneca, 4 x Cessna 402, 3 x Cessna 404, 9 x MU-2, 1 x Lear 25, 2 x Lear 35

BARON AVIATION SERVICES (BVN/Show Me) PO Box 518, Vichy, MO 65580; +1 314 299 4744, Fax: +1 314 299 4272, Charles Schmidt. Cargo charter/operates FedEx Feeder flights in Midwest. 2 x Beech 18, 31 x Cessna 208, 2 x DC-3

BASLER AIRLINES (BFC/Basler) PO Box 2305, Oshkosh, WI 54903; +1 414 236 7827, Fax: +1 414 236 7833. Cargo charter. 6 x DC-3, 2 x Convair 440

BELLAIR (5B) PO Box 371, Sitka, AK 99835; +1 907 747 8636, Fax: +1 907 747 6090, Kenneth Bellows. Passenger scheduled. 1 x Cessna 185, 2 x Beaver

BEMIDJI AIRLINES (CH/BMJ/872/Bemidji) PO Box 624, Bemidji, MN 56601; +1 218 751 1880, Fax: +1 218 759 3552, Larry Diffley. Passenger scheduled, cargo charter. 3 x Piper Aztec, 2 x Baron, 10 x Queen Air, 1 x King Air, 4 x Beech 99

BERING AIR (8E/BRG/Bering Air) PO Box 1650, Nome, AK 99762; +1 907 443 5464, Fax: +1 907 443 5919, James Rowe. Passenger/cargo scheduled. 4 x Cessna 207, 6 x Navajo Chieftain/T-1020, 2 x Cessna 208B, 4 x Beech 18, 1 x King Air 200

BERRY AVIATION (AHS/Tahaas) 1807 Airport Drive, San Marcos, TX 78666; +1 512 353 2379, FAX: +1 512 353 2593, Harry Berry III. Cargo charter. 4 x Metro II, 1 x Metro III

BLACKHAWK AIRWAYS (EP/BAK/744/Blackhawk) PO Box 744, Janesville, WI 53547; +1 608 756 1000, Fax: +1 608 756 5719, Richard Wixom. Cargo charter. 2 Baron, 1 x Navajo Chieftain, 3 x Beech 18, 1 x King Air 100

BORINQUEN AIR (3B/433) PO Box 37309 Airport Station, San Juan, PR 00937; +1 787 791 5060, Fax: +1 787 791 8600, Sixto Diaz-Saldana. Cargo scheduled. 1 x Aztec, 2 x Beech 18, 2 x DC-3

BUSINESS AIR (BEN/Sky Courier) RR 1 Box 1104, Bennington, VT 05201; +1 802 447 2111, Fax: +1 802 442 3582, Walter Fawcett. Cargo charter/EMS air ambulance. 3 x Baron, 1 x Navajo, 2 x Cessna 402, 2 x Cessna 404, 1 x MU-2, 11 x Bandeirante

CAMAI AIR (3C/CAM/451/Air Camai) PO Box 787, Bethel, AK 99559; +1 907 543 4040, Fax: +1 907 543 2369, Phillip Hendrickson. Passenger scheduled. 2 x Cherokee 6, 1 x Cessna 206, 4 x Cessna 207, 1 x Piper Seneca

CAPE AIR (9K/KAP/306/Cair) 660 Barnstable Road, Hyannis, MA 02601; +1 508 771 6944, Fax: +1 508 775 8815, Dan Wolf. Passenger scheduled/charter. 30 x Cessna 402C

CAPE SMYTHE AIR SERVICE (6C/CMY/879/Cape Smythe Air) PO Box 549, Barrow, AK 99723; +1 907 852 8333, Fax: +1 907 852 8332, Grant Thompson. Passenger/cargo scheduled. 2 x Cessna 185, 6 x Cessna 207, 2 x Navajo Chieftain, 4 x Piper T-1040, 3 x Beech 99, 1 x King Air 200, 1 x DC-3

CARIBAIR (B9/379) PO Box 37942, Intl Airport Station, San Juan, PR 00937; +1 787 791 1240, Fax: +1 787 791 4115, Alfredo Ramos. Passenger scheduled. 2 x Islander

CENTRAL AIR SOUTHWEST (CTL/Central Commuter) 411 Lou Holland Drive, Kansas City, MO 64116; +1 816 472 7711, Fax: +1 816 472 1682, Dewey Towner. Cargo charter. 31 x Commander 500

CENTURY AIRLINES (CTY/Century) 7002 Highland Road, Waterford, MI 48327; +1 313 666 1200, Fax: +1 313 666 1450, Norma Cryderman. Cargo charter. 2 x Lear 25

CHERRY AIR 4584 Claire Chennault Road, Dallas, TX 75248; +1 214 248 1707, Fax: +1 214 380 0046, Kenneth Donaldson. Cargo charter. 1 x Navajo Chieftain, 4 x Lear 24/25, 3 x Falcon 20

CIRCLE RAINBOW AIR PO Box 29308, Honolulu, HI 96820; +1 808 833 3507, Fax: +1 808 839 6054, Douglas Ledet. Passenger charter. 6 x Islander

COASTAL AIR TRANSPORT (DQ/CXT/457/Coastal) PO Box 2985, Christiansted, St Croix, USVI 00822; +1 809 773 6862, Michael Foster. Passenger scheduled. 1 x Cessna 402

COLUMBIA PACIFIC AIRLINES (7C) 7005-150th Place SW, Edmonds, WA 98026; +1 206 742 8720, Fax: +1 206 776 5255, Thomas Packard. Passenger scheduled/cargo charter. 1 x Piper Seneca

CONTRACT AIR CARGO 6860 South Service Drive, Waterford, MI 48327; +1 313 666 9630, Fax: +1 313 666 9614, Alan Ross. Cargo charter. 2 x Convair 340, 4 x Convair 580, 1 x DC-4

CORPORATE AIR (CPT/Air Spur) PO Box 30998, Billings, MT 59107; +1 406 248 1541, Fax: +1 406 248 7670, Linda Overstreet. Cargo charter/operates FedEx Feeder flights in Rocky Mountain area. 6 x Commander 680, 43 x Cessna 208, 10 x Beech 99, 4 x Twin Otter, 4 x Beech 1900, 3 x Shorts 330, 3 x Shorts 360

CORPORATE EXPRESS 6860 South Service Drive, Waterford, MI 48327; +1 313 666 9713, Fax: +1 313 666 9614, Michael Church. Cargo charter. 8 x DC-3

CORPORATE EXPRESS AIRLINES (3C/310) Hangar 625 A Street, Smyrna Airport, Smyrna, TN 37167; +1 615 459 8883, Fax: +1 615 459 8778, Res: 1 800 555 6565, Chuck Howell. Scheduled passenger. 6 x Jetstream Super 31

CSA AIR (IRO/Iron Air) Ford Airport, Iron Mountain, MI 49801; +1 906 774 6540, Harold Ross. Cargo charter/operates FedEx Feeder flights in Midwest. 22 x Cessna 208

DOWNEAST EXPRESS (E7/DOW/304/Downeast Express) PO Box 410, Wiscassett, ME 04578; +1 207 882 6752, Fax: +1 207 882 9262, Richard Goodrich. Scheduled/charter passenger, cargo charter. 1 x Cessna 208, 3 x Navajo/Chieftain, 1 x Beech 1300

EMPIRE AIRLINES (EM/CFS/464/Empire Air) 2115 Government Way, Coeur d'Alene, ID 83814; +1 208 667 5400, Fax: +1 208 667 8787, http://www.empirecoe.com, Mel Spade. Charter cargo/operates FedEx Feeder flights in western US. 41 x Cessna 208, 11 x F27

EXECUTIVE AIRLINES (YL/ORA/Long Island) 1300 New Highway, Farmingdale, NY 11735; +1 516 694 0600, Fax: +1 516 694 0172, Micahel Peragine. Passenger charter. 2 x Navajo Chieftain, 3 x Jetstream 31, 2 x Lear 25, 2 x Westwind

FLAMENCO AIRLINES (FK/WAF/580/Flamenco) PO Box 224, Culebra, PR 00775; +1 787 742 3885, Fax: +1 787 722 0237, Noemi Gonzalez. Passenger/cargo scheduled. 6 x Islander, 1 x Trislander, 1 x DC-3

FOUR STAR AVIATION (HK/FSC/861/Four Star) One Air Cargo Center, St Thomas, VI 00802; +1 809 776 8847, Fax: +1 809 776 5536, Curtis R White. Scheduled/charter cargo. 5 x DC-3, 4 x Convair 440

40-MILE AIR (Q5/MLA/519/Mile Air) PO Box 539, Tok, AK 99780, +1 907 883 5191, Fax: +1 907 883 5194 (main office); PO Box 61116, Fairbanks, AK 99706, +1 907 474 0018, Fax: +1 907 474 8954; fortymi@polarnet.com, Charles Warbelow. Passenger scheduled/charter. 1 x Cessna 185, 3 x Cessna 206, 2 x Cessna 207, 1 x Piper Navajo, 1 x Otter, 3 x Piper Super Cub

FRONTIER FLYING SERVICE (2F/FTA/517/Frontier Air) 3820 University Avenue, Fairbanks, AK 99709; +1 907 474 0014, Fax: +1 907 474 0774, John Hajdukovich. Passenger scheduled, cargo charter. 1 x Cessna 207, 1 x Widgeon, 6 x Navajo/Chieftain/T-1020, 2 x Beech 99, 2 x Beech 1300, 1 x DC-3

F S AIR SERVICE (FN) 6121 South Airpark Place, Anchorage, AK 99502; +1 907 346 1605, Fax: +1 907 243 1247, Floyd Salts. Passenger scheduled/charter, cargo scheduled. 3 x Navajo Chieftain, 2 x Merlin IIB, 1 x Metro III, 1 x Volpar Turboliner, 1 x CASA 212, 1 x Skyvan

GRAND AIRE EXPRESS (GAE/Grand Express) PO Box 721, Monroe, MI 48161; +1 313 457 1730, Fax: +1 313 457 1733, Tahir Cheema. Cargo charter. 7 x Aerostar, 7 x Metro II, 4 x Hansa Jet, 12 x Falcon 20

GRAND CANYON (CVU/Canyon View) PO Box 3038, Grand Canyon, AZ; 1 520 638 2463, Fax: +1 520 638 9461, John Siebold. Charter passenger. 1 x Ford 5-AT-C Tri-Motor, 6 x DHC-6-300

GRANT AVIATION (G9) PO Box 89, Emmonak, AK 99581; +1 907 949 1715, Fax: +1 907 949 1848, Mark Hiekel. Passenger scheduled/charter. 1 x Piper Saratoga, 5 x Cessna 207, 2 x Navajo Chieftain

HAGELAND AVIATION SERVICES (C6) PO Box 195, St Mary's, AK 99658; +1 907 438 2246, Fax: +1 907 438 2435, Michael Hageland. Passenger scheduled/charter. 1 x Cessna 185, 6 x Cessna 207, 1 x Cessna 402

HAINES AIRWAYS (7A) PO Box 470, Haines, AK 99827; +1 907 766 2646, Fax: +1 907 766 2614, Melanie Shallcross. Passenger scheduled/charter. 3 x Cherokee Six, 1 x Navajo Chieftain

HARBOR AIRLINES (HG/HAR/495/Harbor) 1140 North Monroe Landing Road, Oak Harbor, WA 98277; +1 206 675 8444, Fax: +1 206 675 0331, David Everett. Passenger scheduled/charter. 4 x Navajo Chieftain/T-1020

ILIAMNA AIR TAXI (LS/IAR/Iliamna Air) PO Box 109, Iliamna, AK 99606; +1 907 571 1248, Fax: +1 907 571 1244, Timothy LaPorte. Passenger scheduled/charter. 1 x Cessna 185, 1 x Bonanza, 1 x Cessna 206, 2 x Cessna 207, 1 x Baron, 4 x Beaver, 1 x Islander

ISLAND AIRLINES (IS/ISA/Island) PO Box 2495, Nantucket, MA 02584; +1 508 228 2967, Fax: +1 508 228 7575, William McGrath. Passenger scheduled/charter. 6 x Cessna 402C, 1 x Beech H18, 1 x DC-3

ISLAND EXPRESS (2S/SDY/579/Sandy Isle) 750 SW 34th Street, Ft Lauderdale, FL 33315; +1 954 359 0380, Fax: +1 954 359 7944, Ruben Acrich. Scheduled passenger. 3 x Cessna 402

KALITTA FLYING SERVICE (KFS/Kalitta) 842 Willow Run Airport, Ypsilanti, MI 48197; +1 313 484 0088, Fax: +1 313 484 9812, Donald Schilling. Cargo charter. 4 x MU-2, 1 x Hamilton Westwind, 18 x Volpar Turboliner, 17 x Lear 23/24/25, 2 x Lear 35/36, 11 x Hansa Jet, 1 x BAe 125, 1 x Jetstar 731

KENMORE AIR (5K) PO Box 82064, Kenmore, WA 98028-0064; +1 206 486 1257, +1 206 486 5471, Robert Munro. Passenger schediuled/charter. 13 x Beaver/Turbo Beaver, 5 x Otter/Turbo Otter

KETCHIKAN AIR SERVICE (6S/469) Airport Terminal Building 1600, Ketchikan, AK 99901; +1 907 225 6608, Fax: +1 907 247 5044, Michael Salazar. Passenger scheduled/charter. 1 x Cessna 185, 2 x Cessna 206, 2 x Cessna 207, 6 x Beaver/Turbo Beaver, 1 x Cessna 402, 3 x Otter/Turbo Otter

LAB FLYING SERVICE (JF/LAB/510/Lab) PO Box 272, Haines, AK 99827; +1 907 766 2222, Fax: +1 907 766 2734, Layton Bennett. Passenger scheduled/charter. 22 x Cherokee Six/Lance/Saratoga, 4 x Piper Seneca, 1 x Aerostar, 2 x Islander, 3 x Navajo Chieftain

LARRY'S FLYING SERVICE (7K/323) PO Box 2348, Fairbanks, AK 99707; +1 907 474 9169, +1 907 474 8815, Lawrence Chenaille. Passenger scheduled/charter. 3 x Cherokee Six/Lance/Saratoga, 2 x Cessna 207, 1 x Piper Aztec, 1 x Islander, 3 x Navajo Chieftain

LAS VEGAS AIRLINES (6G/540) PO Box 15105, Las Vegas, NV 89114; +1 702 647 3056, Fax: +1 702 647 1846, Donald Donohue Jr. Passenger scheduled/charter. 8 x Navajo Chieftain

LYNX AIR 1995 West Commercial Boulevard, Suite A, Ft Lauderdale, FL 33309. Cargo charter. 3 x Metro III

MARTINAIRE (MRA/Martinaire US) 8030 Aviation Place, Suite 2000, Dallas, TX 75235; +1 214 358 5858, Fax: +1 214 350 7979, Donald Wheeler. Cargo charter. 1 x Cherokee Six, 1 x Navajo Chieftain, 23 x Cessna 208B, 4 x Dornier 228, 5 x Metro III, 1 x Westwind

MERLIN EXPRESS (MEI/Package Air) PO Box 160159, San Antonio, TX 78280; +1 210 820 8677, Fax: +1 210 822 2102, Ron Stotz. Passenger/cargo charter. 3 x Metro II, 34 Metro III/Merlin IVC

METHOW AVIATION (MER/Methow) 3311 109th Street SW, Everett, WA 98204; +1 206 355 2055, Fax: +1 206 742 6868, Lavar Lufkin. Cargo charter. 5 x Beech 18, 2 x Hamilton Westwind III

MIAMI VALLEY AVIATION (MVA) 1707 Run Way, Middletown, OH 45042; +1 937 422 5050, Fax: +1 937 422 1494, James Branam. Passenger/cargo charter. 3 x Aztec, 4 x Beech 18, 3 x Lear 24/25, 6 x DC-3

MID-ATLANTIC FREIGHT (MDC/Night Ship) PO Box 35048, Greensboro, NC 27425; +1 919 668 0411, Fax: +1 919 668 4434, Don Godwin. Cargo charter. 24 x Cessna 208

MOUNTAIN AIR CARGO (MTN/Mountain) PO Box 488, Denver, NC 28037; +1 704 464 8741, Fax: +1 704 465 5281, William Simpson. Charter cargo/operates FedEx Feeder services in eastern US. 36 x Cessna 208, 2 x Shorts 330, 23 x F27

MURRAY AVIATION (MUA/Murray Air) 835 Willow Run Airport, Ypsilanti, MI 48918; +1 313 484 4800, Fax: +1 313 484 4875, Preston Murray. Cargo charter. 2 x MU-2 1 x King Air 90, 8 x CASA C-212

NEW ENGLAND AIRLINES (EJ/NEA/367/New England) Satte Airport, Westerly, RI 02891; +1 401 596 2460, Fax: +1 401 596 7366, William Bendokas. Scheduled/charter passenger. 1 x Piper Archer, 3 x Cherokee Six, 2 x Islander

NORTH STAR AIR CARGO 4340 Satellite Drive, Anchorage, AK 99502; +1 907 243 4340, Fax: +1 907 243 6545, Baxter Snider. Cargo charter. 3 x Skyvan

OLSON AIR SERVICE (4B) PO Box 142, Nome, AK 99762; +1 907 443 2229, Fax: +1 907 443 5017, Margaret Olson. Passenger scheduled/charter. 1 x Cessna 185, 1 x Centennial, 3 x Cessna 207, 1 x Evangel 4500, 2 x Cessna 402, 1 x Otter

PIEDMONT AIR CARGO/PIEDMONT AIR TRANSPORT 1184A Gaston Day School Road, Gastonia, NC 28054; +1 704 854 3004, Fax: +1 704 861 1433, Timothy Smith. Cargo charter. 1 x Baron, 1 x Cessna 402, 3 x Beech 18, 3 x DC-3, 1 x DC-6

PINE STATE AIRLINES (PE/PXX/365/Pine State) PO Box 88, Frenchville, ME 04745; +1 207 543 6334, Fax: +1 207 543 6038, Roland Martin. Scheduled passenger. 1 x Cessna 402

PLANEMASTER SERVICES (PMS/Planemaster) 32W515 West Tower Road, DuPage Airport, West Chicago, IL 60185; +1 708 513 2100, Fax: +1 708 377 3283, John McHugh. Cargo charter. 3 x Navajo Chieftain, 5 x Cessna 208, 1 x King Air 90, 1 x King Air 100, 1 x Citation

PRO MECH AIR (P3) PO Box 8660, Ketchikan, AK 99901; +1 907 225 3835, Fax: +1 907 247 3875. Kevin Hack. Passenger scheduled/charter. 3 x Cessna 185, 2 x Beaver

PROMPT AIR (PRT/Prompt Air) 5300 West 63 St, Chicago, IL 60638; +1 773 581 9010, R Alan Kaufman. Cargo charter. 7 x Cessna 210, 3 x Piper Aztec, 1 x Navajo Chieftain

RAMP 66 (PPK/Pelican) PO Box 1499, North Myrtle Beach, SC 29598; +1 803 272 5337, Fax: +1 803 272 5822, Edward Bauer. Cargo charter. 1 x Piper Lance, 3 x Bonanza, 4 x Baron, 6 x Cessna 402

REDWING AIRWAYS (RX/RWG/Redwing Air) Kirksville Municipal Airport, Route 6, Kirksville, MO 63501; +1 816 665 6607, Fax: +1 816 665 6061, James Kelsey. 1 x Cessna 320, 1 x Cessna 401, 1 x Cessna 402, 2 x Queen Air

REGIONAL EXPRESS (REC/Regional) PO Box 2775, Boise, ID 83701; +1 208 343 2524, Fax: +1 208 343 2878, Eugene Heil. Cargo charter. 1 x Cessna 401, 3 x Cessna 402, 1 x Commander 690A, 1 x Metro II

RELIANT AIRLINES (RLT/Reliant) 827 Willow Run Airport, Ypsilanti, MI 48198; +1 313 483 3266, Fax: +1 313 483 5544, Reese Zantop. Cargo charter. 13 x Falcon 20

RENOWN AVIATION (RGS/Renown) 3940 Mirchell Road, Santa Maria, CA 93455; +1 805 937 8484, Fax: +1 805 934 2007, Lawrence Sullivan. Cargo/passenger charter. 7 x Convair 240, 1 x Convair 340, 4 x Convair 580, 2 x Lockheed Electra

RHOADES INTERNATIONAL (RDS/Rhoades Express) Columbus Municipal Airport, Columbus, IN 47203; +1 812 372 1819, Fax: +1 812 378 2708, Jack Rhoades. Cargo charter. 1 x Cessna 310, 1 x Cessna 402, 6 x DC-3, 4 x Convair 240, 1 x Convair 340, 1 x Convair 440

ROYAL AIR FREIGHT (RAX/Air Royal) 2141 Airport Road, Waterford, MI 48327; +1 313 666 3070, Fax: +1 313 666 4719, William Kostich. Cargo charter. 5 x Cessna 310, 2 x Cessna 402, 1 x Navajo Chieftain, 6 x Beech 18, 2 x MU-2, 1 x Commander 690A, 5 x Bandeirante, 3 x Lear 23/24

RYAN AIR (7S/RCT/251/Arctic Transport) 1205 East International Airport Road, Suite 201, Anchorage, AK 99518; +1 907 562 2227, Fax: +1 907 563 8177, John Eckels. Passenger/cargo scheduled. 10 x Cessna 207, 3 x Cessna 402, 2 x Beech 18

SABER CARGO AIRLINES (SBR/Freighter) 4803 Express Drive, Charlotte, NC 28219; +1 704 359 8456, Fax: +1 704 359 8275, Michael Dockery. Cargo charter. 1 x Cessna 402, 1 x Beech 18, 4 x DC-3

SIERRA WEST AIRLINES (PKW/Platinum West) 4511 W Cheyenne, #401, Las Vegas, NV 89030; +1 702 638 0144, Fax: +1 702 638 0156, Deborah Robinson. Cargo charter. 4 x Metro II/Merlin IV, 5 x Metro III, 1 x Lear 25, 1 x Lear 35, 1 x Falcon 20

SKAGWAY AIR SERVICE (5U/SGY/493/Skagway Air) PO Box 357, Skagway, AK 99840; +1 907 983 2218, +1 907 983 2948, Ben Lingle. Passenger scheduled/charter. 7 x Cherokee Six/Saratoga, 1 x Piper Seneca, 1 x Islander, 1 x Piper T-1020

SOUTHCENTRAL AIR (XE/SCA/301/South Central) 135 Granite Point Court, Kenai, AK 99611; +1 907 283 7676, +1 907 283 3678, James Mason. Scheduled/charter passenger/cargo. 1 Cessna 185, 2 x Cessna 206, 1 x Cessna 207, 4 x Navajo/Chieftain, 5 x Piper T-1040

SUBURBAN AIR FREIGHT (SRB) PO Box 19090, Omaha, NE 68119; +1 402 344 4100, Fax: +1 402 344 0415. James Armstrong. Cargo charter. 1 x Commander 500, 9 x Commander 680FL, 5 x Cessna 402, 1 x Beech 99, 1 x Beech 1900, 1 x Jet Commander

SUPERIOR AVIATION (HKA/Spend Air) Ford Airport, Iron Mountain, MI 49801; +1 906 774 0400, Fax: +1 906 774 4118, Charles Henry. Cargo charter. 3 x Cessna 402, 1 x Cessna 421, 12 x Cessna 404, 1 x Cessna 441, 9 x Cessna 208, 13 Metro II/Merlin IV

TAQUAN AIR SERVICE (9Q) 1007 Water Street, Ketchikan, AK 99901; +1 907 225 2712, Fax: +1 907 225 0522, Jay Scudero. Passenger scheduled/charter. 3 x Cessna 185, 1 x Cessna 206, 1 x Cessna 208, 6 x Beaver, 4 x Otter

TAR HEEL AVIATION INC (THC/Tarheel) 278 Ellis Airport Road, Richlands, NC 28574; +1 910 324 2500, Fax: +1 910 324 3323, Jere Fountain. Cargo charter. 1 x Beech Travel Air, 1 x Baron, 2 x Navajo Chieftain, 3 x Cessna 208, 1 x Cherokee Six

TATONDUK FLYING SERVICE (3K) PO Box 61680, Fairbanks, AK 99706; +1 907 474 4697, Fax: +1 907 474 3002, Robert Everts. Passenger scheduled/charter. 1 x Cessna 206, 2 x Piper Lance

TELFORD AVIATION (TEL/Telford) Airport Road, Waterville, ME 04901; +1 207 872 5555, Fax: +1 207 872 6794, Telford Allen. Cargo charter. 2 x Navajo Chieftain, 8 x Cessna 208, 1 x Beech 99, 1 x Merlin IV

TOLAIR SERVICES (TOL/Tol Air) PO Box 37670, San Juan, PR 00937; +1 787 791 5235, Fax: +1 787 791 8385, Jorge Toledo. Cargo/passenger charter. 1 x Cherokee Six, 1 x Beech Baron, 5 x Cessna 402, 1 x Piper Navajo, 2 x Beech 18, 5 x DC-3, 2 x Convair 240, 1 x Convair 440

TRANS AIR (P6) PO Box 29239, Honolulu, HI 96820; +1 808 833 5557, Fax: +1 808 833 2636, Teimour Riahi. Passenger scheduled/charter. 3 x Cessna 402

TRANS FLORIDA AIRLINES (TFA/Trans Florida) PO Box 10150, Daytona Beach, FL 32120; +1 904 252 3053, Fax: +1 904 252 0037, Robert Willman. Passenger/cargo charter. 6 x Convair 240

TRANS NORTH AVIATION (4Q) PO Box 1445, Eagle River, WI 54521; +1 715 479 6777, Fax: +1 715 479 8178, Ronald Schaberg. Passenger scheduled/charter. 1 x Cessna 340, 1 x Piper Navajo, 2 x Cessna 421, 1 x King Air

UNION FLIGHTS (UNF/Union Flights) 6273 Freeport Boulevard, Sacramento, CA 95822; +1 916 421 8531, Fax: +1 916 421 8546, Jay Paynter. Passenger/cargo charter. 5 x Navajo/Chieftain, 9 x Cessna 208, 1 x Beech 18, 2 x Caribou

VIEQUES AIR LINK (VI/VES/381/Vieques) PO Box 487, Vieques, PR 00765; +1 787 741 3266, Fax: +1 787 741 0545, Osvaldo González. Passenger scheduled/charter. 1 x Piper Aztec, 6 x Islander, 3 x Trislander

VIKING EXPRESS (WCY/Titan Air) Aurora Municipal Airport, 43W518 Route 30, Sugar Grove, IL 60554; +1 630 466 7500, Fax: +1 630 466 7041, Robert Burwell. Cargo/passenger charter. 2 x Piper Aztec, 1 x Cessna 421, 6 x Beech 18, 1 x DC-3

WALKER'S INTERNATIONAL (XW/360) 700 SW 34th Street, Ft Lauderdale, FL 33315; +1 954 359 1405, Fax: +1 954 359 1414, Flemming Andersen. Scheduled passenger. 1 x Twin Otter

WARBELOW'S AIR VENTURES (4W/VNA/Ventaire) PO Box 60649, Fairbanks, AK 99706; +1 907 474 0518, Fax: +1 907 479 5054, wav@polarnet.com, Arthur Warbelow. Passenger scheduled/charter. 1 x Cessna 206, 2 x Cessna 207, 8 x Navajo Chieftain, 2 x Piper Super Cub

WESTAIR (PCM/Pac Valley) PO Box 7735, Fresno, CA 93747; +1 209 294 6915, Fax: +1 209 291 5784, Beth Woods. Cargo charter/operates FedEx Feeder flights in western USA. 34 x Cessna 208

WEST ISLE AIR (7Y/590) 4000 Airport Road, Anacortes, WA 98221; +1 206 293 4691, Fax: +1 206 293 0517, James Burton. Passenger scheduled/charter. 1 x Cherokee Six, 3 x Cessna 206, 1 x Cessna 207, 1 x Piper Seneca

WIGGINS AIRWAYS (WIG/035) PO Box 250, Norwood, MA 02062; +1 617 762 5690, Fax: +1 617 762 1958, David Ladd. Cargo charter/operates FedEx Feeder flights in northeastern US. 32 x Cessna 208, 4 x Beech 99, 1 x Twin Otter

WINGS OF ALASKA (SE/WAK/397/Wings Alaska) 1873 Shell Simmons Drive, Suite 119, Juneau, AK 99801; +1 907 789 0790, Fax: +1 907 789 2021, David Jacobsen. Passenger scheduled/charter. 4 x Cessna 206, 5 x Cessna 207, 6 x Beaver, 4 x Otter

WRIGHT AIR SERVICE (8V) PO Box 60142, Fairbanks, AK 99706; +1 907 474 0502, Fax: +1 907 474 0375, Robert Bursiel. Passenger scheduled/charter. 1 x Cessna 185, 3 x Helio Courier, 1 x Bonanza, 1 x Cessna 206, 2 x Cessna 207, 1 x Commander 500, 4 x Navajo/Chieftain, 2 x Cessna 208B

YUTE AIR ALASKA (4Y/UYA/Yute Air) PO Box 890, Dillingham, AK 99576; +1 907 842 5333, Fax: +1 907 842 1001, Don King. Passenger scheduled/charter, cargo charter. 1 x Cherokee Six, 3 x Cessna 206, 12 x Cessna 207, 2 x Navajo Chieftain

NOTES:

RAYTHEON BEECH 1900D

AIR ALLIANCE

IATA: 3J **ICAO:** AAQ **IATA/ARC:** 188 **RADIO:** Liason

CONTACTS:

Mail
611 6th Avenue
Québec City Airport
Ste Foy, QC G2E 5W1

Telephone/FAX
Admin: +1 418 872 7622
Fax: +1 418 872 9716

OPERATION:

Type: Scheduled/charter passenger
Cities Served: Canada: YBC YBG YGP YGR YMX YOW YQB YUL YUY YVO YWK YYY YYZ YZV **US:** BDL BOS EWR
All service operated as Air Canada Connector using only AC flight numbers
FFP: Aeroplan

HISTORY/STRUCTURE:

Founded: 1987
CEO: Robert Perrault

Start Date: March 27, 1988
Ownership: Air Canada

FLEET:

Type	No	Seats	Engines
Beech 1900D	5	Y18	PWC PT6A-67D
DHC-8-102	7	Y37	PWC PW120A

AI(R) BAe 4112 JETSTREAM 41

AIR ATLANTIC

IATA: 9A **ICAO:** ATL **IATA/ARC:** 574 **RADIO:** Air Atlantique

CONTACTS:

Mail
PO Box 248
Elmsdale, NS
B0N 1M0

Telephone/FAX
Admin: +1 709 873 5375
Fax: +1 709 873 5377
Res: 1 800 665 1177 (Canada)
Res: 1 800 426 7000 (US)

OPERATION:

Type: Scheduled/charter passenger
Cities Served: Canada: YCH YCL YDF YFC YHZ YJT YOW YQM YQX YQY YSJ YUL YYG YYT **US:** BOS
All service operated as Canadian Partner using only CP flight numbers
FFP: Canadian Plus

HISTORY/STRUCTURE:

Founded: 1985
CEO: Stephen Wetmore

Start Date: February 28, 1986
Ownership: IMP Group International

FLEET:

Type	No	Seats	Engines
Jetstream 41	5	Y29	GA TPE331-14HR-805H
DHC-8-102	3	Y37	PWC PW120A
BAe 146-200A	4	J10Y67	LY ALF502R-5

BOMBARDIER DHC-8-102 DASH 8

AIR BC

IATA: ZX   **ICAO:** ABL   **IATA/ARC:** 742   **RADIO:** Air Coach

CONTACTS:

Mail
5520 Miller Road
Richmond, BC
V7B 1L9

Telephone/FAX
Admin: +1 604 273 2464
Fax: +1 604 273 1016
Res: 1 800 663 3721
Res: 1 800 332 1080
Res: 1 800 776 3000 (US)

OPERATION:

Type: Scheduled/charter passenger
Cities Served: Canada: YBL YEG YKA YLW YMM YPR YQQ YQU YQZ YVR YWL YXE YXS YXT YYC YYJ **US:** PDX SEA
All service operated as Air Canada Connector using only AC flight numbers
FFP: Aeroplan

HISTORY/STRUCTURE:

Founded: 1980   **Start Date:** 1980
CEO: Al Thompson   **Ownership:** Air Canada

FLEET:

Type	No	Seats	Engines
DHC-8-102	13	Y37	PWC PW120A
DHC-8-311	6	Y50	PWC PW123
BAe 146-200A	5	J8Y68	LY ALF502R-5

AIRBUS A320-211

AIR CANADA

IATA: AC **ICAO:** ACA **IATA/ARC:** 014 **RADIO:** Air Canada

CONTACTS:

Mail
PO Box 14000
Postal Station St Laurent
Monteal, QC H4Y 1H4

Telephone/FAX
Admin: +1 514 422 5000
Fax: +1 514 422 7741
Res: 1 800 776 3000 (US)

Internet: http://www.aircanada.ca

OPERATION:

Type: Scheduled/charter passenger
Cities Served: Canada: YEG YFC YHZ YMX YOW YQB YQM YQR YQT YSJ YUL YVR YWG YXE YYC YYG YYT YYZ **US:** ATL BNA BOS CLT DCA DEN DFW EWR FLL HNL IAD IAH LAS LAX LGA MCO MIA MKC MSP OGG ORD PHX RDU SFO STL TPA **US (seasonal):** PBI RSW **Caribbean:** ANU BDA BGI FDF KIN MBJ NAS PAP POS PTP UVF **Europe:** CDG FRA GLA LHR MAN ZRH **Asia:** DEL HKG KIX SEL TLV
Code-Share: Air Canada Connector (Air Alliance, Air BC, Air Nova, Air Ontario, NWT Air), Air Jamaica, Alberta Citylink, All Nippon Airways, British Midland, Central Mountain Air, Continental Airlines, Finnair, Korean Air, Royal Jordanian, Swissair, United Airlines/United Express
FFP: Aeroplan

HISTORY/STRUCTURE:

Founded: April 10, 1937 (as Trans-Canada Air Lines)
Start Date: September 1, 1937
CEO: Lamar Durrent
Ownership: Publicly held (75% Canadian)

FLEET:

Type	No	Seats	Engines
Canadair RJ	26	Y50	GE CF34-3A1/3B1
DC-9-32	32	J12Y80	PW JT8D-7A
Airbus A319-100	4	J16Y96	CFM56-5A4
Airbus A320-200	34	J24Y108	CFM56-5A1
Boeing 767-200	9	J36Y159	PW JT9D-7R4D
Boeing 767-200 (ER)	14	J25Y152	PW JT9D-7R4D
Boeing 767-300 (ER)	6	J35Y168	PW PW4060
Airbus A340-300	5	J32Y252	CFM56-5C4
Boeing 747-100	3	J39Y377	PW JT9D-7
Boeing 747-200B (SCD)	3	J39Y241 or J39Y377	PW JT9D-7J
Boeing 747-400 (SCD)	3	J37Y262	PW PW4056
Ordered			
Canadair RJ		24 options	
Airbus A319-100	31		
Airbus A320-200	6		
Airbus A340-300	3	plus 3 options	

NOTES:

AIRBUS A310-300 (ET)

AIR CLUB INTERNATIONAL

IATA: HB **ICAO:** CLI **IATA/ARC:** 854 **RADIO:** Air Club

CONTACTS:

Mail
11905 Cargo Road
A-3 Office 205
Mirabel, QC J7N 1H1

Telephone/FAX
Admin: +1 514 476 3555
Fax: +1 514 476 9818

OPERATION:

Type: Charter passenger
Areas Served: Canada, Europe, Caribbean
Also operates sub-services for other carriers

HISTORY/STRUCTURE:

Founded: May 1993 **Start Date:** June 17, 1994
CEO: Claude Levesque **Ownership:** Privately held

FLEET:

Type	No	Seats	Engines
A310-300 (ET)	2	Y265	PW PW4152

BAe (HAWKER SIDDLEY) HS 748 SERIES 2A

AIR CREEBEC

IATA: YN **ICAO:** CRQ **IATA/ARC:** 219 **RADIO:** CREE

CONTACTS:

Mail
PO Box 430
Val D'Or, QC
J9P 4P4

Telephone/FAX
Admin: +1 819 825 8355
Fax: +1 819 825 0208
Res: 1 800 567 6567

OPERATION:

Type: Scheduled/charter passenger/cargo
Cities Served: YAT YCN YFA YHF YKQ YKU YLS YMO YMT YNC YNS YPO YTS YUL YVO YYU ZEM ZKE
FFP: Aeroplan

HISTORY/STRUCTURE:

Founded: June 1982
CEO: Albert Diamond
Start Date: July 1, 1982
Ownership: Privately held

FLEET:

Type	No	Seats	Engines
EMB-110P1 Bandeirante	2	Y14	PWC PT6A-34
Beech 1900D	2	Y18	PWC PT6A-67D
DHC-8-102	1	Y37	PWC PW120A
HS 748-2A	3	Y48/Combi	RR Dart 534-2
HS 748-2A	1	Freighter	RR Dart 534-2

BAe (HAWKER SIDDLEY) 748 SERIES 2A

AIR INUIT

IATA: 3H   **ICAO:** AIE   **IATA/ARC:** 875   **RADIO:** Air Inuit

CONTACTS:

Mail
1985 55 Avenue
Dorval, QC
H9P 1G9

Telephone/FAX
Admin: +1 514 636 9445
Fax: +1 514 636 8916
Res: 1 800 361 2965
Res: 1 800 661 5850 (Charters)

OPERATION:

Type: Scheduled/charter passenger/cargo
Cities Served: AKV XGR YGL YGW YIK YKG YPH YPJ YPX YQC YSK YTE YTQ YUD YUL YVP YWB YZG
Code-Share: First Air

HISTORY/STRUCTURE:

Founded: 1978   **Start Date:** 1978
CEO: Mark T Gordon   **Ownership:** Makivik Corporation

FLEET:

Type	No	Seats	Engines
DHC-6-300	4	Y18	PWC PT6A-27
DHC-8-102	1	Y37	PWC PW120A
HS 748-2A	4	Y40	RR Dart 534-2
Convair 580	4	Y49	Allison 501-D13
Convair 580 aircraft operated on behalf of Hydro Québec			

CANADA 8 – NORTH AMERICAN AIRLINES HANDBOOK

DE HAVILLAND CANADA DHC-6-300 TWIN OTTER

AIR LABRADOR (Labrador Airways)

IATA: WJ **ICAO:** LAL **IATA/ARC:** 927 **RADIO:** Lab Air

CONTACTS:

Mail
PO Box 13485
Station A
St John's, NF A1B 4B8

Telephone/FAX
Admin: +1 709 753 1240
Fax: +1 709 753 7787
Res: 1 800 563 3042

OPERATION:

Type: Scheduled/charter passenger
Cities Served: YAY YBI YDF YDI YDP YFX YHA YHG YHO YMH YMN YQX YRF YRG YSO YWK YYR YYT
FFP: Canadian Plus

HISTORY/STRUCTURE:

Founded: 1970
CEO: Roger Pike

Start Date: 1970
Ownership: Privately held

FLEET:

Type	No	Seats	Engines
DHC-2 Beaver	1		PW R-985
DHC-3 Otter	3		PW R-1340
Cessna 208	1		PWC PT6A-114
Cessna 208B	1		PWC PT6A-114
DHC-6-100	1		PWC PT6A-20
DHC-6-300	3		PWC PT6A-27
Shorts 330-300	4		PWC PT6A-45R
DHC-8-102	1	Y37	PWC 120A

CANADA

BAe (HAWKER SIDDLEY) HS 748 SERIES 2A

AIR NORTH (Air North Charter & Training dba)

IATA: 4N **ICAO:** ANT **IATA/ARC:** 287 **RADIO:** Air North

CONTACTS:

Mail
PO Box 4998
Whitehorse, YT
Y1A 4S2

Telephone/FAX
Admin: +1 403 668 2228
Fax: +1 403 668 6224
Res: 1 800 661 0407

OPERATION:

Type: Scheduled/charter passenger/cargo
Cities Served: Canada: YDA YEV YOC YXY **US:** FAI JNU

HISTORY/STRUCTURE:

Founded: 1977
Start Date: January 17, 1986 (scheduled)
CEO: Joseph T Sparling
Ownership: Joseph T Sparling & Thomas Wood

FLEET:

Type	No	Seats	Engines
PA-31-310 Navajo	1	Y/Combi	LY TIO-540-A1A
Queen Air B80	1	Y/Combi	LY IGSO-540-A1D
Beech 99	1	Y14	PWC PT6A-20
DC-3	4	Y/Combi	PW R-1830
HS 748-2A	2	Y44	RR Dart 534-2

BAe 146-200A

AIR NOVA

IATA: QK   **ICAO:** ARN   **IATA/ARC:** 983   **RADIO:** Nova

CONTACTS:

Mail
310 Goudey Drive
Enfield, NS
B2T 1E4

Telephone/FAX
Admin: +1 902 873 5000
Fax: +1 902 873 4901
Res: 1 800 776 3000 (US)

Internet: http://www.airnova.com

OPERATION:

Type: Scheduled/charter passenger
Cities Served: Canada: YDF YFC YHZ YOW YQB YQI YQM YQX YQY YSJ YSL YUL YWK YYG YYR YYT ZBF **US:** BOS EWR
All service operated as Air Canada Connector using only AC flight numbers
FFP: Aeroplan

HISTORY/STRUCTURE:

Founded: 1985
CEO: Joseph Randell

Start Date: July 14, 1986
Ownership: Air Canada

FLEET:

Type	No	Seats	Engines
DHC-8-102	12	Y37	PWC PW120A
BAe 146-200A	5	J10Y67	LY ALF502R-5

CANADA

BOMBARDIER DHC-8-301 DASH 8

AIR ONTARIO

IATA: GX **ICAO:** ONT **IATA/ARC:** 368 **RADIO:** Ontario

CONTACTS:

Mail
1 Air Ontario Drive
London, ON
N5V 3S4

Telephone/FAX
Admin: +1 519 453 8440
Fax: +1 519 453 0063
Res: 1 800 776 3000 (US)

OPERATION:

Type: Scheduled/charter passenger
Cities Served: Canada: YAM YOW YQG YQT YSB YTS YTZ YUL YWG YXU YYB YYZ YZR **US:** ABE BDL BWI CLE CMH MDT
All service operated as Air Canada Connector using only AC flight numbers
FFP: Aeroplan

HISTORY/STRUCTURE:

Founded: 1961
CEO: Stephen C Smith

Start Date: 1961
Ownership: Air Canada

FLEET:

Type	No	Seats	Engines
DHC-8-102	17	Y37	PWC PW120A
DHC-8-301	6	Y50	PWC PW123

DE HAVILLAND CANADA DHC-7-103 DASH 7

AIR TINDI

IATA: 8T   **ICAO:** none   **IATA/ARC:** 744   **RADIO:** none

CONTACTS:

Mail
PO Box 1693
Yellowknife, NWT
X1A 2P3

Telephone/FAX
Admin: +1 403 920 4177
Fax: +1 403 920 2836
Res: +1 403 920 2891

OPERATION:
Type: Scheduled/charter passenger/cargo
Cities Served: YLE YRA YSG YZF

HISTORY/STRUCTURE:
Founded: 1988
CEO: Peter Arychuk
Start Date: 1988
Ownership: Privately held

FLEET:

Type	No	Seats	Engines
Cessna A185F	2		CO IO-520-D
DHC-2 Beaver	1		PW R-985
DHC-2T Beaver	1		PWC PT6A-20
DHC-3T Otter	1		PWC PT6A-135A
Cessna 208B	1		PWC PT6A-114A
King Air E90	1		PWC PT6A-28
King Air B200C	1		PWC PT6A-42
DHC-6-100/300	5		PWC PT6A-20/27
DHC-4A Caribou	1	Freighter	PW R-2000
DHC-7-103	1	Y48/Combi	PWC PT6A-50

LOCKHEED L-1011-385-1-14 TRISTAR 150

AIR TRANSAT

IATA: TS **ICAO:** TSC **IATA/ARC:** 649 **RADIO:** Transat

CONTACTS:

Mail
11600 Cargo Road A1
Mirabel International Airport
Mirabel, QC J7N 1G9

Telephone/FAX
Admin: +1 514 476 1011
Fax: +1 514 476 1038
Res: 1 800 470 1011

OPERATION:
Type: Charter passenger
Cities Served: Canada: YHZ YMX YQB YUL YVR YYC YYZ
US (some seasonal): FLL LAS MCO PIE PSP
México (some seasonal): ACA CUN MZT PVR SJD ZLO
Caribbean (some seasonal): CMW FDF HOG MBJ POP SCU SDQ SXM VRA **South America (some seasonal):** ADZ CTG **Europe:** CDG LGW MAN
Europe (seasonal): AMS ATH BFS BHX BOD BRU BSL CIA CWL DUB EDI EXT FRA GLA LBA LIS MAD MRS NCE NCL NTE PIK SNN STN SXB SXF TLS

HISTORY/STRUCTURE:
Founded: December 1986   **Start Date:** November 14, 1987
CEO: Philippe Sureau   **Ownership:** Transat AT Inc

FLEET:

Type	No	Seats	Engines
Boeing 757-200	5	Y228	RR RB211-535E4
L 1011-1	2	J19Y343	RR RB211-22B
L 1011-100	2	J19Y343	RR RB211-22B
L 1011-150	4	J19Y343	RR RB211-22B
L 1011-500	2	J19Y296	RR RB211-524B4-02

DE HAVILLAND CANADA DHC-6-300 TWIN OTTER

AKLAK AIR

IATA: 6L   **ICAO:** AKK   **IATA/ARC:** 709   **RADIO:** Aklak

CONTACTS:

Mail
PO Box 1190
Inuvik, NWT
X0E 0T0

Telephone/FAX
Admin: +1 403 979 3555
Fax: +1 403 979 3388
Res: +1 403 979 3777

OPERATION:

Type: Scheduled/charter passenger
Cities Served: YEV YPC YSY YUB

HISTORY/STRUCTURE:

Founded: 1977   **Start Date:** 1977
Ownership: Inuvialuit Joint Venture Company

FLEET:

Type	No	Seats	Engines
Beech 99	2	Y15	PWC PT6A-27
DHC-6-300	1	Y19/Combi	PWC PT6A-27

BAe 3112 JETSTREAM 31

ALBERTA CITYLINK

IATA: none **ICAO:** none **IATA/ARC:** none **RADIO:** none

CONTACTS:

Mail
PO Box 161
Medicine Hat, AB
T1A 7E8

Telephone/FAX
Admin: +1 403 527 3328
Fax: +1 403 527 4721
Res: 1 800 332 1080

OPERATION:

Type: Scheduled passenger
Cities Served: YLL YQL YXH YYC
Code-Share: Air BC, Air Canada
FFP: Aeroplan

HISTORY/STRUCTURE:

Founded: 1996
CEO: Les Little

Start Date: July 15, 1996
Ownership: Affiliated with Bar XH Aviation

FLEET:

Type	No	Seats	Engines
Jetstream 31	4	Y19	GA TPE331-10UG-513H
Jetstream 31	2	Y19	GA TPE331-12UAR-705H

CONVAIR 580 (F)

ALL CANADA EXPRESS

IATA: none **ICAO:** CNX **IATA/ARC:** none **RADIO:** Canex

CONTACTS:

Mail
#603 50 Burnhamthorpe Road West
Mississauga, ON
L5B 3C2

Telephone/FAX
Admin: +1 905 896 7175
Fax: +1 905 896 1549

OPERATION:

Type: Charter cargo
Cities Served: Canada: YVR YYC YYZ **US:** BFI
Operates service on behalf of UPS

HISTORY/STRUCTURE:

Founded: 1992
CEO: John MacKenzie

Start Date: 1992
Ownership: Privately held

FLEET:

Type	No	Engines
Convair 580F	1	Allison 501-D13
Boeing 727-100F	2	PW JT8D-7B
Boeing 727-200F (Advanced)	2	PW JT8D-17R

BEECH 1900C-1 AIRLINER

ATHABASKA AIRWAYS

IATA: 9T **ICAO:** ABS **IATA/ARC:** 909 **RADIO:** Athabaska

CONTACTS:

Mail	Telephone/FAX
PO Box 100	Admin: +1 306 764 1404
Prince Albert, SK	Fax: +1 306 763 1313
S6V 5R4	Res: 1 800 667 9356

OPERATION:
Type: Scheduled/charter passenger
Cities Served: YBE YBR YNL YPA YQR YSF YVC YWG YXE ZFD ZWL

HISTORY/STRUCTURE:
Founded: 1955 **Start Date:** 1955
CEO: Jim Glass **Ownership:** Privately held

FLEET:

Type	No	Seats	Engines
Cessna A185F	4		CO IO-520-D
DHC-2 Beaver	1		PW R-985
Cessna 310R	4		CO IO-520-M
Cessna 402C	2		CO TSIO-520-VB
Piper PA-31-350	2		LY TIO-540-J2BD
DHC-3 Otter	1		PW R-1340
DHC-3T Otter	1		PWC PT6A-135A
Cessna 404	1		CO GSTIO-520-M
Cessna 441	1		GA TPE331-8-401S
DHC-6-100/200	3		PWC PT6A-20
Beech 1900C-1	1	Y19	PWC PT6A-65B
Beech 1900D	2	Y18	PWC PT6A-67B

FAIRCHILD SA227-CC METRO 23

BEARSKIN AIRLINES

IATA: JV **ICAO:** BLS **IATA/ARC:** 632 **RADIO:** Bearskin

CONTACTS:

Mail
1475 W Walsh Street
Thunder Bay, ON
P7E 4X6

Telephone/FAX
Admin: +1 807 577 1141
Fax: +1 807 474 2610
Res: 1 800 465 5039

OPERATION:

Type: Scheduled/charter passenger
Cities Served: KIF MSA SUR WNN XBE XKS YAC YAG YAM YAX YER YFH YGQ YHD YIB YLH YMG YNO YOW YPL YPM YQK YQT YRL YSB YSP YTL YTS YVZ YWG YWP YXL YXZ YYB ZPB ZRJ ZSJ
FFP: Aeroplan

HISTORY/STRUCTURE:

Founded: July 1963
CEO: Harvey Friesen

Start Date: 1963
Ownership: Privately held

FLEET:

Type	No	Seats	Engines
PA-23 Aztec	3		LY IO-540-C4B5
King Air A100	4	Y12	PWC PT6A-28
Beech 99	8	Y14	PWC PT6A-28
Metro III	5	Y19	GA TPE331-11U-612G
Metro 23	2	Y19	GA TPE331-12U-701G

BOEING 727-200 COMBI (ADVANCED)

BRADLEY AIR SERVICES (First Air)

IATA: 7F **ICAO:** FAB **IATA/ARC:** 245 **RADIO:** First Air

CONTACTS:

Mail
3257 Carp Road
Carp, ON
K0A 1L0

Telephone/FAX
Admin: +1 613 839 3340
Fax: +1 613 839 5690
Res: 1 800 267 1247

OPERATION:

Type: Scheduled/charter passenger/cargo
Cities Served: Canada: YBB YCB YCO YCY YFB YFR YFS YGT YHI YHK YHY YIO YLC YLE YOW YRA YRB YRT YSG YSR YTE YUL YUX YVM YVP YXP YXY YYH YZF YZS **Cargo:** DAY YMX YOW YVR YYC
Greenland: SFJ
Code-Share: Air Inuit, Greenlandair
FFP: Aeroplan

HISTORY/STRUCTURE:

Founded: 1946 **Start Date:** 1946
CEO: Kamal Hanna **Ownership:** Makivik Corporation

FLEET:

Type	No	Seats	Engines
Cessna A185F	1		CO IO-520-D
DHC-2 Beaver	2		PW R-985
Beech 99	1		PWC PT6A-20
King Air A100	1		PWC PT6A-28
DHC-6-300	10		PWC PT6A-27
Gulfstream 1C	1		RR Dart 529-8X
HS 748-2A	8	Y43/Combi	RR Dart 534/535-3
DHC-7-150	1	Ice Patrol Surveyor	PWC PT6A-50
Boeing 727-100C	3	Y125/Combi/Freighter	PW JT8D-7B
Boeing 727-200F	2	Freighter	PW JT8D-7B/-15
Boeing 727-200C (Advanced)	1	Y180/Combi/Freighter	PW JT8D-15

DOUGLAS DC-4 (C-54G) SKYMASTER

BUFFALO AIRWAYS

IATA: none **ICAO:** BFL **IATA/ARC:** none **RADIO:** Buffalo

CONTACTS:

Mail
PO Box 1479
Hay River, NWT
X0E 0R0

Telephone/FAX
Admin: +1 403 873 6112
Fax: +1 403 873 8393

OPERATION:

Type: Scheduled/charter passenger/cargo
Cities Served: YFS YHY YZF

HISTORY/STRUCTURE:

Founded: 1970
CEO: Joe McBryan

Start Date: 1970
Ownership: Privately held

FLEET:

Type	No	Seats	Engines
Cessna A185E	2		CO IO-520-D
Travel Air B95	1		LY O-360-A1A
PA-31-350 Chieftain	2		LY TIO-540-J2BD
Norseman V	1		PW R-1340
Douglas DC-3	10		PW R-1830
PBY-5A Canso	3	Air Tanker	PW R-1830-92
CL-215-1A10	4	Air Tanker	PW R-2800-CA3
Curtiss C-46	2	Freighter	PW R-2800
DC-4	4	Freighter/Air Tanker	PW R-2800

SAAB 340B*PLUS*

CALM AIR INTERNATIONAL

IATA: MO   **ICAO:** CAV   **IATA/ARC:** 622   **RADIO:** Calm Air

CONTACTS:

Mail
90 Thompson Drive
Thompson, MB
R8N 1Y8

Telephone/FAX
Admin: +1 204 778 6471
Fax: +1 204 778 6954
Res: 1 800 839 2256

OPERATION:

Type: Scheduled/charter passenger
Cities Served: XLB XPK XSI XTL YBK YBT YCS YEK YFO YGO YGX YHO YLR YOH YQD YQT YRT YTH YUT YVQ YWG YXN YYL YZS ZJN ZTM
All service operated as Canadian Partner using only CP flight numbers
FFP: Canadian Plus

HISTORY/STRUCTURE:

Founded: 1960
Start Date: 1976 (scheduled service)
CEO: Arnold Morberg
Ownership: Canadian Regional Airlines (45%)

FLEET:

Type	No	Seats	Engines
PA-31-350 Chieftain	1	Y9	LY TIO-540-J2BD
King Air 200	2	Y10	PWC PT6A-41
DHC-6-100	1	Y19	PWC PT6A-20
DHC-6-200	1	Y19	PWC PT6A-20
SAAB 340B	2	Y34	GE CT7-9B
HS 748-2A	4	Y42	RR Dart 534-2

BOEING 757-200

CANADA 3000 AIRLINES

IATA: 2T **ICAO:** CMM **IATA/ARC:** 570 **RADIO:** Elite

CONTACTS:

Mail
27 Fasken Drive
Toronto, ON
M9W 1K6

Telephone/FAX
Admin: +1 416 674 0257
Fax: +1 416 674 0256

OPERATION:

Type: Charter passenger
Cities Served: Canada: YEG YHZ YMX YOW YUL YVR YWG YYC YYJ YYT YYZ **US:** FLL HNL LAS LAX MCO OGG RSW **México:** CUN MZT PVR SJD **México (seasonal):** ACA CZM HUX ZIH ZLO
Caribbean (many seasonal): ANU GCM GND MBJ NAS POP SDQ SKB UVF **Central America (seasonal):** BZE LIR SJO **Europe:** AMS LGW MAN
Europe (seasonal): BHX BRU CDG CPH DUS EMA GLA HAM KEF MUC

HISTORY/STRUCTURE:

Founded: April 1, 1988 (as Air 2000 Airlines)
Start Date: December 1, 1988
CEO: Angus Kinnear
Ownership: Privately held

FLEET:

Type	No	Seats	Engines
Airbus A320-200	6	Y168	CFM56-5A3
Boeing 757-200	7	Y228	RR RB211-535E4
Ordered			
Airbus A330-200	2	plus 1 option	

McDONNELL DOUGLAS DC-10-30

CANADIAN AIRLINES INTERNATIONAL

IATA: CP **ICAO:** CDN **IATA/ARC:** 018 **RADIO:** Canadian

CONTACTS:

Mail
615 18th Street SE
Calgary, AB
T2E 6J5

Telephone/FAX
Admin: +1 403 294 2000
Fax: +1 403 294 2066
Res: 1 800 665 1177
Res: 1 800 426 7000 (US)

Internet: http://www.cdnair.ca

OPERATION:

Type: Scheduled/charter passenger
Cities Served: Canada: YCB YEG YEV YFB YFO YHZ YMX YOW YPR YRB YRT YTH YUL YVQ YVR YXS YXT YXY YYC YYZ YZF
US: BOS DFW HNL LAS LAX LGA MIA MCO ORD SFO TPA
México/South America: EZE GRU MEX MTY **Europe:** FCO LHR
Asia: BKK HKG MNL NGO NRT PEK TPE
Code-Share: Air Alma, Air Atlantic, Air New Zealand, Air St-Pierre, ALITALIA, American, American Eagle, British Airways, Calm Air International, Canadian Regional, Inter-Canadien, Japan Airlines, Malaysia, Mandarin Airlines, Philippines, QANTAS
FFP: Canadian Plus

HISTORY/STRUCTURE:

Founded: July 1, 1942 (as Canadian Pacific Air Lines)
CEO: Kevin Benson **Ownership:** Canadian Airlines Corp

FLEET:

Type	No	Seats	Engines
Boeing 737-200C (Advanced)	2	Y112/Combi	PW JT8D-17/17A
Boeing 737-200/200C (Advanced)	42	J12Y88	PW JT8D-9A/17/17A
Airbus A320-200	12	J24Y108	CFM56-5A1
Boeing 767-300 (ER)	11	J30Y180	GE CF6-80C2B6/2B6F
DC-10-30	9	J28Y228	GE CF6-50C2/C2B
Boeing 747-400	4	J48Y379	GE CF6-80C2B1F
Ordered			
Airbus A320-200	10		

FOKKER F28 FELLOWSHIP MK1000

CANADIAN REGIONAL AIRLINES

IATA: KI **ICAO:** CDR **IATA/ARC:** **RADIO:** Canadian Regional

CONTACTS:

Mail
8050 22nd Street NE
Calgary, AB
T2E 7H6

Telephone/FAX
Admin: +1 403 294 3090
Fax: +1 403 266 6825
Res: 1 800 665 1177
Res: 1 800 426 7000 (US)

OPERATION:

Type: Scheduled/charter passenger
Cities Served: Canada: YAM YBL YCD YCG YEG YGK YHY YKA YLW YMM YOJ YOP YOW YPE YQD YQG YQL YQQ YQR YQT YQU YSB YSM YTH YVR YWG YXC YXE YXJ YXS YXU YYC YYD YYE YYF YYJ YYZ YZP **US:** PDX SEA
All service operated as Canadian Partner using only CP flight numbers
FFP: Canadian Plus

HISTORY/STRUCTURE:

Founded: 1966 (as Lethbridge Air Services)
CEO: Mary Jordan   **Ownership:** Canadian Airlines Corp

FLEET:

Type	No	Seats	Engines
DHC-8-102	10	Y37	PWC PW120A
ATR42-300	6	Y44	PWC PW120
DHC-8-301	14	Y50	PWC PW123
F28 Mk1000	16	Y65 or J10Y45	RR Spey 555-15/15N

AIRBUS A320-231

CANAIR CARGO

IATA: WW **ICAO:** CWW **IATA/ARC:** **RADIO:** Canair

CONTACTS:

Mail
2450 Derry Road E
Hangar #2, Suite #120
Mississauga, ON L5S 1B2

Telephone/FAX
Admin: +1 905 676 7790
Fax: +1 905 676 7803

OPERATION:

Type: Charter passenger/cargo

HISTORY/STRUCTURE:

Founded: 1990
CEO: Dan Goliger

Start Date: 1990
Ownership: Privately held

FLEET:

Type	No	Seats	Engines
Cessna 310R	1		CO IO-520-MB
Convair 580	3		Allison 501-D13D
Convair 580F	5	Freighter	Allison 501-D13D
Boeing 737-200F (Advanced)	2	Freighter	PW JT8D-9A
Boeing 737-200C (Advanced)	1	Freighter	PW JT8D-9A
Boeing 737-200C	2	Freighter	PW JT8D-9A
Boeing 737-200C	1	Y122/Combi	PW JT8D-9A
Two Airbus A320s leased during northern winter season			

RAYTHEON BEECH 1900D

CENTRAL MOUNTAIN AIR

IATA: 9M **ICAO:** GLR **IATA/ARC:** 634 **RADIO:** Glacier

CONTACTS:

Mail
PO Box 998
Smithers, BC
V0J 2N0

Telephone/FAX
Admin: +1 250 847 4780
Fax: +1 250 847 3744
Res   1 800 663 3905

OPERATION:

Type: Scheduled/charter passenger
Cities Served: YCD YCG YDL YDQ YKA YLW YOH YQU YVR YXC YXJ YXS YXT YYC YYD YYE YYF
All service operated as Air Canada Connector using only AC flight numbers
FFP: Aeroplan

HISTORY/STRUCTURE:

Founded: 1987   **Start Date:** 1987
CEO: Neil Blackwell **Ownership:** Privately held

FLEET:

Type	No	Seats	Engines
CATPASS 200	1	EMS	PWC PT6A-41
CATPASS 200	1	Y11	PWC PT6A-41
Beech 1900C-1	4	Y19	PWC PT6A-65B
Beech 1900D	3	Y18	PWC PT6A-67D
Ordered			
Beech 1900D	8	plus 10 options	

DE HAVILLAND CANADA DHC-2 BEAVER

HARBOUR AIR

IATA: H3   **ICAO:** none   **IATA/ARC:** none   **RADIO:** Harbour

CONTACTS:

Mail
4760 Inglis Drive
Richmond, BC
V7B 1W4

Telephone/FAX
Admin: +1 604 278 3478
Fax: +1 604 278 9897
Res: 1 800 665 0212

Internet: http://www.harbour-air.com

OPERATION:

Type: Scheduled/charter passenger
Cities Served: CXH YAJ YAQ YAV YBQ YBW YGG YKK YPI YTB YVR YWH YZP ZMT ZQS ZSW

HISTORY/STRUCTURE:

Founded: 1981   **Start Date:** 1981
CEO: Greg McDougall   **Ownership:** Privately held

FLEET:

Type	No	Seats	Engines
Cessna A185F	6		CO IO-520-D
DHC-2 Beaver	19		PW R-985
DHC-3 Otter	1		PW R-1340
DHC-3T Otter	2		PWC PT6A-135A
DHC-6-100/200/300	6		PWC PT6A-20/-27

SIKORSKY S-76A MK II

HELIJET AIRWAYS

IATA: JB   **ICAO:** JBA   **IATA/ARC:** 613   **RADIO:** Helijet

CONTACTS:

Mail
4520 Agar Drive
Richmond, BC
V7B 1A3

Telephone/FAX
Admin: +1 604 273 4688
Fax: +1 604 273 5301
Res: 1 800 665 4354

Internet: none

OPERATION:

Type: Scheduled/charter passenger
Cities Served: CXH YVR YWH

HISTORY/STRUCTURE:

Founded: September 1986
CEO: Daniel Sitnam

Start Date: November 27, 1986
Ownership: W M Helijet Airways

FLEET:

Type	No	Seats	Engines
S-76A	4	Y12	Allison 250-C30S

Other helicopters carry the titles of Vancouver Helicopters, a charter division of Helijet Airways

AI(R) ATR42-300

INTER-CANADIEN

IATA: none **ICAO:** ICN **IATA/ARC:** none **RADIO:** Inter-Canadien

CONTACTS:

Mail
795 Stuart Graham Blvd N
Dorval, QC
H4Y 1E4

Telephone/FAX
Admin: +1 514 631 9802
Fax: +1 514 631 2699
Res: 1 800 665 1177

OPERATION:

Type: Scheduled/charter passenger
Cities Served: YBC YBX YGL YGP YGR YGV YGW YHR YNA YOW YQB YUL YUY YVO YWK YYY YYZ YZV
All service operated as Canadian Partner using only CP flight numbers
FFP: Canadian Plus

HISTORY/STRUCTURE:

Founded: 1946 (as Air Rimouski) **Ownership:** Canadian Regional
CEO: Michel Gagne

FLEET:

Type	No	Seats	Engines
ATR42-300	4	Y44	PWC PW120
Fokker F28 Mk 1000	2	J10Y45	RR Spey 555-15/15N
Aircraft interchange frequently with those of Canadian Regional			

BOEING 727-200

KELOWNA FLIGHTCRAFT AIR CHARTER

IATA:　　　　　ICAO: KFA　　　IATA/ARC:　　　　RADIO: Flightcraft

CONTACTS:

Mail
1-5655 Kelowna Airport Road
Kelowna, BC
V1V 1S1

Internet: http://www.greyhound.ca

Telephone/FAX
Admin: +1 250 765 1481
Fax:　　+1 250 765 1489
Res:　　1 800 661 8747 (Greyhound Air)
Res:　　1 800 505 3225 (Charters)

OPERATION:

Type: Charter passenger/cargo
Cities Served: Greyhound Cities: YEG YHM YLW YOW YVR YWG YYC YYZ **Freighters:** Operates primarily throughout the domestic Purolator network, but other domestic courier, ad hoc, and overseas work is undertaken.
FFP: Greyhound Travel Rewards (Greyhound Air only)

HISTORY/STRUCTURE:

Founded: 1970　　　　　　　　**Start Date:** 1974
CEO: Barry Lapointe　　　　　**Ownership:** Barry Lapointe & Jim Rogers

FLEET:

Type	No	Seats	Engines
Cessna 340	1		CO TSIO-520-N
Cessna 402B	2		CO TSIO-520E
Duke A60	1		LY TIO-541-E1B4
IAI 1124 Westwind	1		GA TFE731-3-1G
DC-3	1	Freighter	PW R-1830
Convair 580	12	Pax/Combi/Freighter	Allison 501-D13
Convair 5800	2	Freighter	Allison 501-D22G
Boeing 727-100F	8	Freighter	PW JT8D-7B/9
Boeing 727-200F	2	Freighter	PW JT8D-7B
Boeing 727-200	1	Y168 (Greyhound)	PW JT8D-7B
Boeing 727-200 (A)	6	Y170 (Greyhound)	PW JT8D-9A

DE HAVILLAND CANADA DHC-6-300 TWIN OTTER

KENN BOREK AIR

IATA: 4K   **ICAO:** KBA   **IATA/ARC:** 652   **RADIO:** Borek Air

CONTACTS:

Mail
290 McTavish Road NE
Calgary, AB
T2E 7G5

Telephone/FAX
Admin: +1 403 291 3300
Fax: +1 403 250 6908

OPERATION:

Type: Scheduled/charter passenger/cargo
Cities Served: YFB YGZ YIO YLC YRB YSR YTE YXP
Also conducts extensive worldwide charter and leasing operations

HISTORY/STRUCTURE:

Founded: 1971
CEO: Kenn Borek

Start Date: 1971
Ownership: Privately held

FLEET:

Type	No	Seats	Engines
Cessna A185	2		CO IO-520-D
Baron B55	1		CO IO-470-L
Beech 99	3		PWC PT6A-20
King Air B90/C90	2		PWC PT6A-20
King Air 100/A100	5		PWC PT6A-28
King Air 200	3		PWC PT6A-41
DHC-6-100/200/300	25		PWC PT6A-20/-27
EMB-110P1 Bandeirante	2		PWC PT6A-34
Douglas C-117D	1	Freighter	Wright R-1820

DE HAVILLAND CANADA DHC-2 BEAVER

LA RONGE AVIATION (Air Sask Aviation)

IATA: 7W **ICAO:** ASK **IATA/ARC:** 094 **RADIO:** Air Sask

CONTACTS:

Mail
PO Box 320
La Ronge, SK
S0J 1L0

Telephone/FAX
Admin: +1 306 425 2774
Fax: +1 306 425 2700
Res: 1 800 665 7275

OPERATION:

Type: Scheduled/charter passenger
Cities Served: YPA YQR YSF YVC YXE ZFD ZWL
Code-Share: Northern Dene Airways

HISTORY/STRUCTURE:

Founded: 1958
CEO: Pat Campling Sr

Start Date: 1958
Ownership: Privately held

FLEET:

Type	No	Seats	Engines
Cessna A185F	4		CO IO-520-D
DHC-2 Beaver	3		PW R-985
Baron E55	1		CO IO-470-L
Baron 58	1		CO IO-520-C
PA-31-310 Navajo	2		LY TIO-540-A2C
PA-31-325 Navajo	1		LY TIO-540-F2BD
PA-31-350 Chieftain	2		LY TIO-540-J2BD
DHC-3 Otter	2		PW R-1340
Beech 99A	1		PWC PT6A-27
DHC-6-100	3		PWC PT6A-20
Jetstream 31	2	Y19	GA TPE331-10UG-513H

DORNIER 228-202

MINISTIC AIR (Kistigan)

IATA: none **ICAO:** MNS **IATA/ARC:** none **RADIO:** Ministic

CONTACTS:

Mail
PO Box 42008
Winnipeg, MB
R3J 3X7

Telephone/FAX
Admin: +1 204 832 8550
Fax: +1 204 889 4731

OPERATION:

Type: Scheduled/charter passenger
Cities Served: YIV YRS YST YWG ZSJ

HISTORY/STRUCTURE:

Founded: 1981
CEO: George Brotherston

Start Date: 1981
Ownership: George Brotherston (98%)

FLEET:

Type	No	Seats	Engines
Cessna U206	3		CO IO-520-F
Commander 500	1		LY O-540-A2B
PA-31-310 Navajo	2		LY TIO-540-A1A
PA-31-350 Chieftain	2		LY TIO-540-J2BD
Commander 681	1		GA TPE331-1-151K
King Air 100	1		PWC PT6A-28
Dornier 228-202	2		GA TPE331-5-252D
Beech 1900D	1	Y18	PWC PT6A-67D

DE HAVILLAND CANADA DHC-6-200 TWIN OTTER

NAKINA OUTPOST CAMPS & AIR SERVICE

IATA: none   **ICAO:** none   **IATA/ARC:** none   **RADIO:** none

CONTACTS:

Mail
PO Box 126
Nakina, ON
P0T 2H0

Telephone/FAX
Admin: +1 807 329 5341
Fax: +1 807 329 5876

OPERATION:

Type: Scheduled/charter passenger
Cities Served: YOG YQN

HISTORY/STRUCTURE:

Founded: 1973
CEO: Don Bourdignon

Start Date: 1973
Ownership: Don & Millie Bourdignon

FLEET:

Type	No	Seats	Engines
DHC-2 Beaver	1		PW R-985
DHC-2T Beaver	1		PWC PT6A-20
DHC-3T Otter	1		PWC PT6A-135A
Cessna 208B	2		PWC PT6A-114A
DHC-6-200	1		PWC PT6A-20
Shorts 330-100	1		PWC PT6A-45R

CATPASS 200 (BEECH SUPER KING AIR)

NORTHERN THUNDERBIRD AIR (NT Air)

IATA: none **ICAO:** NTA **IATA/ARC:** none **RADIO:** Thunderbird

CONTACTS:

Mail
PO Box 1510
Prince George, BC
V2L 4V5

Telephone/FAX
Admin: +1 250 963 9611
Fax: +1 250 963 8422
Res: 1 800 963 9611

OPERATION:

Type: Scheduled/charter passenger/cargo
Cities Served: YCQ YKA YLW YVR YXS YYD YZY

HISTORY/STRUCTURE:

Founded: 1971
CEO: Vernon Martin

Start Date: 1971
Ownership: Privately held

FLEET:

Type	No	Seats	Engines
Cessna U206F	1		CO IO-520-F
Commander 500	2		LY IO-540-E1B5
PA-31-350 Chieftain	2		LY TIO-540-J2BD
King Air A100	1		PWC PT6A-28
CATPASS 200	2		PWC PT6A-41
DHC-6-300	1		PWC PT6A-27

BEECH 99 AIRLINER

NORTHWESTERN AIR LEASE

IATA: none **ICAO:** none **IATA/ARC:** none **RADIO:** Polaris

CONTACTS:

Mail
PO Box 23
Fort Smith, NWT
X0E 0P0

Telephone/FAX
Admin: +1 403 872 2216
Fax: +1 403 872 2214

OPERATION:
Type: Scheduled/charter passenger
Cities Served: YSM YZF

HISTORY/STRUCTURE:
Founded: 1965
CEO: Terry Harrold

Start Date: 1965
Ownership: Privately held

FLEET:

Type	No	Seats	Engines
Cessna 337G	1	Y4	CO IO-360-G
Cessna 401	1	Y4	CO TS10-520-E
Aerostar 600	1	Y6	LY IO-540-G1B5
Beech 99	2	Y15	PWC PT6A-20
Jetstream 31	1	Y19	GA TPE331-10UGR-514H

CESSNA 208B GRAND CARAVAN

NORTH-WRIGHT AIR

IATA: HW **ICAO:** NWL **IATA/ARC:** none **RADIO:** Northwright

CONTACTS:

Mail
Bag Service 2200
Norman Wells, NWT
X0E 0V0

Telephone/FAX
Admin: +1 403 587 2288
Fax: +1 403 587 2962
Res: 1 800 661 0702

OPERATION:

Type: Scheduled/charter passenger
Cities Served: YCK YEV YGH YLE YVQ YWJ YZF ZFN
FFP: Canadian Plus

HISTORY/STRUCTURE:

Founded: 1986
CEO: Warren Wright

Start Date: 1987
Ownership: Privately held

FLEET:

Type	No	Seats	Engines
Helio H295	1		LY GO-480-G1D6
Cessna 207	1		CO IO-520-F
Cessna 337C/337D	2		CO IO-360-C/D
PC-6/B1-H2 Porter	1		PWC PT6A-20
BN-2A-26 Islander	1		LY O-540-E4C5
PA-31-350 Chieftain	1		LY TIO-540-J2BD
Cessna 208B	1		PWC PT6A-114
Beech 99	1		PWC PT6A-20
DHC-6-100	1		PWC PT6A-20

BOEING 737-200C (ADVANCED)

NWT AIR (Northwest Territorial Airways dba)

IATA: NV **ICAO:** NWT **IATA/ARC:** 668 **RADIO:** Territorial

CONTACTS:

Mail
Postal Service 9000
Yellowknife, NWT
X1A 2R3

Telephone/FAX
Admin: +1 403 669 6600
Fax: +1 403 873 4274
Res: 1 800 661 0789

Internet: http://www.nwtair.nt.ca

OPERATION:

Type: Scheduled/charter passenger/cargo
Cities Served: YCB YEG YEV YFB YRT YWG YZF
Scheduled services operated as Air Canada Connector using only AC flight numbers
FFP: Aeroplan

HISTORY/STRUCTURE:

Founded: 1962 **Start Date:** 1962
CEO: Mark Winders **Ownership:** Air Canada

FLEET:

Type	No	Seats	Engines
Boeing 737-200C (Advanced)	3	Y11/Combi	PW JT8D-9A
L-100-30 Hercules	1	Freighter	AN 501-D22A

SHORTS SD3-60 VARIANT 300

PACIFIC COASTAL AIRLINES

IATA: 8P **ICAO:** PCO **IATA/ARC:** 905 **RADIO:** Pasco

CONTACTS:

Mail
4440 Cowley Crescent
Richmond, BC
V7B 1B8

Telephone/FAX
Admin: +1 604 273 8666
Fax:　 +1 604 273 6864
Res:　 1 800 663 2872

OPERATION:

Type: Scheduled/charter passenger
Cities Served: YPW YRN YVR YZT ZEL
FFP: Canadian Plus

HISTORY/STRUCTURE:

Founded: 1979
CEO: Daryl Smith

Start Date: 1979
Ownership: Air BC/Powell Air

FLEET:

Type	No	Seats	Engines
DHC-2 Beaver	3	Y6	PW R-985
DHC-3 Otter	1	Y9	PW R-1340
G-21A Goose	4	Y7	PW R-985
Beech 99	4	Y14	PWC PT6A-27/28
Shorts 360-300	3	Y30	PWC PT6A-65AR

FAIRCHILD SA226-TC METRO II

PERIMETER AIRLINES

IATA: UW **ICAO:** PAG **IATA/ARC:** 711 **RADIO:** Perimeter

CONTACTS:

Mail
626 Ferry Road
Winnipeg, MB
R3H 0T7

Telephone/FAX
Admin: +1 204 786 7031
Fax: +1 204 783 5587
Res: 1 800 665 8986

OPERATION:

Type: Scheduled/charter passenger/cargo
Cities Served: YBR YBV YCR YDN YGO YIV YNE YOH YRS YST YWG ZGI

HISTORY/STRUCTURE:

Founded: 1960
CEO: William J Wehrle

Start Date: 1960
Ownership: Perimeter Aviation

FLEET:

Type	No	Seats	Engines
Travel Air D95A/E95	3		LY IO-360-B1B
Baron 95-B55	1		CO IO-470-1
Duke B60	1		LY IGSO-480-A1E
Queen Air A65	1		LY IGSO-480-A1E6
Metro II	13		GA TPE331-1OUA-511G
Lear 35A	1		GA TFE731-2-2B
BAe 125/800A	1		GA TFE731-5R-1H

CANADA

FAIRCHILD SA226-AT MERLIN IV

PROVINCIAL AIRLINES (Interprovincial)

IATA: AG **ICAO:** PAL **IATA/ARC:** 967 **RADIO:** none

CONTACTS:

Mail
Hangar #2
PO Box 29030
St John's, NF A1A 5B5

Telephone/FAX
Admin: +1 709 576 1800
Fax: +1 709 576 1802
Res: 1 800 563 2800

OPERATION:

Type: Scheduled/charter passenger/cargo
Cities Served: YAY YBI YBX YDF YDI YDP YFX YHA YHG YHO YJT YMH YMN YQX YRF YRG YSO YYR YYT ZUM
Scheduled passenger service operated as Interprovincial under a commercial agreement with Air Nova
FFP: Aeroplan

HISTORY/STRUCTURE:

Founded: August 1972
CEO: Thomas W Collingwood
Start Date: 1980 (scheduled)
Ownership: Privately held

FLEET:

Type	No	Seats	Engines
BN-2A-21 Islander	1		LY IO-540-K1B5
PA-31-310 Navajo	5		LY TIO-540-A1A
PA-31-350 Chieftain	2		LY TIO-540-J2BD
Metro II	2		GA TPE331-1OUA-511G
Merlin IV	1	Freighter	GA TPE331-3UW-303G
King Air 200	4	Surveillance	PWC PT6A-41
DHC-6-300	2		PWC PT6A-27
Metro III	3		GA TPE331-11U-601G
Convair 580F	1	Freighter	Allison 501-D13D

LOCKHEED L-1011-385-1-15 TRISTAR 100

ROYAL AVIATION

IATA: QN **ICAO:** ROY **IATA/ARC:** 498 **RADIO:** Roy

CONTACTS:

Mail
685 BL Stuart Graham North
Dorval, QC
H4Y 1E4

Telephone/FAX
Admin: +1 514 739 7000
Fax: +1 514 739 7993

OPERATION:

Type: Charter passenger
Cities Served: Canada: Main Bases: YEG YHZ YMX YUL YVR YWG YYC YYZ **Canada (seasonal):** YDF YFC YOW YQG YQM YQR YQT YQX YQY YSJ YTH YXE YXS YXU YXY YYJ YYT YZF
USA (some seasonal): EWR FLL LAS MCO PIE
Mexico (some seasonal): CUN LTO MZT SJD ZIH ZLO
Caribbean (some seasonal): ANU HOG MBJ POP VRA
Europe (seasonal): AMS BHX CDG GLA LGW MAN MUC SXF VIE ZRH

HISTORY/STRUCTURE:

Founded: August 3, 1979
CEO: Michel LeBlanc
Start Date: April 29, 1992
Ownership: Groupe Royal Aviation

FLEET:

Type	No	Seats	Engines
Boeing 727-200 (Advanced)	5	Y186	PW JT8D-15/17/17A
Airbus A310-300	2	Y256	
L-1011-100	2	J19Y343	RR RB211-22B

AIRBUS A320-232

SKYSERVICE

IATA: none **ICAO:** SSV **IATA/ARC:** 884 **RADIO:** Skyfinder

CONTACTS:

Mail
9785 Ryan Avenue
Dorval, QC
H9P 1A2

Telephone/FAX
Admin: +1 514 636 1626
Fax: +1 514 636 3300

OPERATION:

Type: Charter passenger
Cities Served: Canada: YYZ **US (seasonal):** LAS RNO
México (seasonal): ACA CUN HUX LTO SJD ZLO
Caribbean (seasonal): ANU AUA MBJ NAS UVF VRA
Europe (seasonal): ATH BCN BFS CIA MXP PSR SUF VCE

HISTORY/STRUCTURE:

Founded: 1986 **Start Date:** 1989
CEO: L Russell Payson **Ownership:** Privately held

FLEET:

Type	No	Seats	Engines
PA-31-T1 Navajo	1		PWC PT6A-28
Cessna 500	1		PWC JT15D-1
Lear 35/35A	4		GA TFE731-2-2B
BAe 125/800A	1		GA TFE731-5R-1H
Airbus A320-200	1	Y179	IAE V2527-A5
Airbus A330-300	1	J32Y331	PW PW4168

EMBRAER EMB-110P1 BANDEIRANTE

SKYWARD AVIATION

IATA: K9   **ICAO:** SGK   **IATA/ARC:** 470   **RADIO:** Skyward

CONTACTS:
Mail
PO Box 1207
Thompson, MB
R8N 1P1

Telephone/FAX
Admin: +1 204 778 7088
Fax: +1 204 677 5946
Res: 1 800 665 0638

OPERATION:
Type: Scheduled/charter passenger
Cities Served: XLB XSI XTL YEK YGO YRT YST YTH YXN YYQ ZAC ZGI ZTM

HISTORY/STRUCTURE:
Founded: 1986   **Start Date:** 1986
CEO: F P Behrendt   **Ownership:** Privately held

FLEET:

Type	No	Seats	Engines
Cessna 206	2		CO IO-520-F
Cessna 207	1		CO IO-520-F
Cessna 310R	2		CO IO-520-M
Cessna 402B/402C	2		CO TSIO-520-VB/E
Cessna 414	1		CO TSIO-520-J
Cessna 421C	1		CO GTSIO-520-L
Cessna 500	1		PWC JT15D-1
EMB-110P1 Bandeirante	4		PWC PT6A-34

DE HAVILLAND CANADA DHC-7-102 DASH 7

VOYAGEUR AIRWAYS

IATA: 4V   **ICAO:** VAL   **IATA/ARC:** 908   **RADIO:** Voyageur

CONTACTS:
Mail
PO Box 1734
CFB North Bay
Hornell Heights, ON
P0H 1P0

Telephone/FAX
Admin: +1 705 476 1750
Fax: +1 705 476 6773
Res: 1 800 461 1636

OPERATION:
Type: Charter passenger/cargo; operates emergency medical service in Canada/US

HISTORY/STRUCTURE:
Founded: 1968   **Start Date:** 1968
CEO: Max Shapiro   **Ownership:** Voyageur Airport Services

FLEET:

Type	No	Seats	Engines
King Air 100/A100	10		PWC PT6A-28
King Air 200C	1	EMS	PWC PT6A-42
Cessna 500/501	2	EMS	PWC JT15D-1A
DHC-7-102	4	EMS/Y48	PWC PT6A-50

BAe (HAWKER SIDDLEY) 748 SERIES 2B

WASAYA AIRWAYS

IATA: WG   **ICAO:** WSG   **IATA/ARC:** 093   **RADIO:** Wasaya

CONTACTS:

Mail
PO Box 308
Pickle Lake, ON
P0V 3A0

Telephone/FAX
Admin: +1 807 928 2244
Fax: +1 807 928 2595
Res: 1 800 423 3393

OPERATION:

Type: Scheduled/charter passenger/cargo
Cities Served: KIF SUR WNN XBE XKS YAX YBS YPL YQT YTL YWP YXL

HISTORY/STRUCTURE:

Founded: 1986 (as Kelner Airways)   **Start Date:** 1986
CEO: Terry DeLuce   **Ownership:** Privately held

FLEET:

Type	No	Seats	Engines
Cessna 208B	4	Y9	PWC PT6A-114A
Cessna 208B	1	Freighter	PWC PT6A-114
CATPASS 200	2	Y13	PWC PT6A-41
HS 748-2A/B	6	Y/Combi	RR Dart 534/535/536/550-2

DE HAVILLAND CANADA DHC-6-100 TWIN OTTER

WEST COAST AIR

IATA: 8O **ICAO:** none **IATA/ARC:** 222 **RADIO:** Coast Air

CONTACTS:

Mail
900 - 1188 W Georgia Street
Vancouver, BC
V6E 4A2

Telephone/FAX
Admin: +1 604 606 6800
Fax: +1 604 606 6820
Res: 1 800 347 2222

OPERATION:

Type: Scheduled/charter passenger
Cities Served: CXH YWH

HISTORY/STRUCTURE:

Founded: 1995
CEO: Al Baydala

Start Date: January 25, 1996
Ownership: Privately held

FLEET:

Type	No	Seats	Engines
DHC-6-100	3		PWC PT6A-20
DHC-6-200	1		PWC PT6A-20

BOEING 737-200C (ADVANCED)

WESTJET

IATA: M3   **ICAO:** WJA   **IATA/ARC:** none   **RADIO:** Westjet

CONTACTS:

Mail
35 McTavish Place NE
Calgary, AB
T2E 7J7

Telephone/FAX
Admin: +1 403 735 2600
Fax: +1 403 571 4649
Res: 1 800 538 5696

Internet: www.westjet.com

OPERATION:

Type: Scheduled passenger
Cities Served: YEG YLW YQR YVR YXE YYC YYJ

HISTORY/STRUCTURE:

Founded: 1995
CEO: Clive Beddoe

Start Date: February 29, 1996
Ownership: Privately held

FLEET:

Type	No	Seats	Engines
Boeing 737-200 (Advanced)	3	Y120	PW JT8D-7B/9A
Boeing 737-200C (Advanced)	2	Y120	PW JT8D-7B/9A
Ordered			
Boeing 737-200	1		

BEECH KING AIR A100

WILDERNESS AIRLINE

IATA: 6W **ICAO:** WLD **IATA/ARC:** **RADIO:** Wilderness

CONTACTS:

Mail
4540 Agar Drive
Richmond, BC
V7B 1A4

Telephone/FAX
Admin: +1 604 276 2635
Fax:　 +1 604 276 9586
Res:　 1 800 665 9453

Internet: none

OPERATION:

Type: Scheduled/charter passenger
Cities Served: Canada: QBC YAA YVR **(seasonal):** YBL YRD ZEL

HISTORY/STRUCTURE:

Founded: 1975
CEO: David Kahl

Start Date: 1975
Ownership: Privately held

FLEET:

Type	No	Seats	Engines
Cessna A185F	1	Y4	CO IO-520-D
Cessna U206F	1	Y4	CO IO-520-F
DHC-2 Beaver	1	Y7	PW R-985
BN-2A-20 Islander	1	Y9	LY IO-5400-K1B5
King Air A100	2	Y11	PWC PT6A-28
King Air 200	1	Y13	PWC PT6A-41
Beech 1900C	1	Y19	PWC PT6A-65B

Canada Addenda

AIR ALMA (4L/AAJ/248/Air Alma) CP 577, 345 Chemin de L'Aeroport, Alma, QC G8B 5W1; +1 418 668 5566, Fax: +1 418 668 7711, Res: 1 800 463 9660, Jacques Simard. Passenger scheduled/
charter. 1 x Piper Navajo, 1 x Bell 222, 1 x Cessna 404, 3 x Bandeirante, 1 x Lear 24A

AIR CHARTER/AIR MONTRÉAL (AMO) 9785 Ryan Ave, Dorval, QC H9P 1H2; +1 514 631 2111, Fax: +1 514 631 8335, Res: 1 800 561 4270, Reginald Overing. Passenger/cargo charter. 2 x Navajo Chieftain, 1 x Merlin III, 2 x Metro II, 1 x Cessna 550, 2 x Metro III

AIR 500 (BRM) 2450 Derry Road East, Hangar #9, Mississauga, ON L5S 1B2; +1 905 673 1500, Dennis Chadala. Cargo charter. 3 x MU-2, 1 x Cessna 500, 1 x Cessna 550

AIR GEORGIAN (Simo Air & Air Georgian) (GGN) Oro-Barrie Regional Airport, Oro, ON L0L 2E0; +1 705 487 7777, Fax:+1 705 487 2220, Paul Mulrooney. Passenger/cargo charter. 2 x Cessna 208, 7 x Cessna 208B, 1 x King Air 200, 1 x Beech 1900C-1

AIR NUNAVUT (YH/ BFF/898/Air Baffin) PO Box 1239, Iqaluit, NWT X0A 0H0; +1 819 979 4018, Fax: +1 819 979 4318, Res: +1 819 979 4018, Jeff Mahoney. Passenger scheduled/charter. 1 x Piper Navajo, 1 x Navajo Chieftain, 1 x CATPASS 200

AIR SATELLITE (QR/ASJ) Aéroport De Baie-Comeau, Pointe Lebel, QC; +1 418 589 8923, Fax: +1 418 589 7416, Res: 1 800 463 8512, Edith Fournier. Passenger scheduled/charter. 1 x Cessna 337, 1 x Piper Aztec, 3 x Cessna 310R, 1 x Cessna 335, 1 x Islander, 4 x Cessna 402, 1 x Trislander, 1 x Bandeirante

AIRSPEED AVIATION (5S/SPD) RR #7, Abbotsford International Airport, Abbotsford, BC V2S 5W6; +1 604 852 9245, Fax: +1 604 850 2756, John Giesbrecht. Passenger scheduled/charter. 2 x Cessna 414

AIR WAVE TRANSPORT (AWV) 245 Britannia Road East, Mississauga, ON L4Z 2Y7; +1 905 568 4222, Fax: +1 905 890 4507, Chris Dunn. 2 x Navajo Chieftain, 2 x Gulfstream I

AVIATION BOREAL CP 1572, Val C'Or, QC J9P 5Y8; +1 819 825 0405, Fax: +1 819 825 0405, Jean-Marie Arsenault. 1 x Navajo, 1 x Navajo Chieftain, 2 x DC-3

AVIATION QUEBEC LABRADOR (QLA) CP 575, Sept Îles, QC G4R 4K7; +1 418 962 7901, Fax: +1 418 962 9202, Res: 1 800 361 8620, Jacques Cleary. Passenger scheduled/charter. 2 x Piper Aztec, 2 x Navajo Chieftain, 1 x Otter, 3 x Bandeirante

BAXTER AVIATION (6B) PO Box 1110, Nanaimo, BC V9R 6E7; +1 250 754 1066, Fax: +1 250 754 1075, Res: 1 800 661 5599, Tom Baster. Passenger scheduled/charter. 2 x Cessna A185F, 9 x Beaver

COAST WESTERN AIRLINES PO Box 1827, Sechelt, BC V0N 3A0; +1 604 885 4711, Fax: +1 604 885 1083. Passenger scheduled/charter. 1 x Cessna 180, 2 x Beaver

COMMERCIAL AVIATION (BJ) PO Box 460, Hearst, ON P0L 1N0; +1 705 362 8505, Fax: +1 705 362 7437, Res: 1 800 394 0767, Charters: 1 888 362 8505, Michel Boucher. Passenger scheduled/charter. 1 x Cessna 172, 2 x Navajo Chieftain, 1 x Piper Cheyenne II

CONFORTAIR (V7/COF) CP 1622, Sept Îles, QC G4R 5C7; +1 418 968 4660, Fax: +1 418 962 0190, Res: 1 800 353 4660. Passenger scheduled/charter. 1 x Piper Aztec, 3 x Navajo Chieftain, 1 x Jetstream 31

CONTACT AIR (V8) PO Box 5175, Fort McMurray, AB T9H 3G2; +1 403 743 8218, Fax: +1 403 743 8225, Ray McKenzie. Passenger scheduled/charter. 1 x Cessna 172, 1 x Cessna 177, 1 x Cessna A185F, 1 x Cessna 207A, 2 x Beaver, 2 x Navajo Chieftain, 1 x Beech 99, 2 x King Air 100/A100

CORPORATE EXPRESS (CPB/Penta) 1441 Aviation Park NE, Calgary, AB T2E 8M7, +1 403 274 9801; Fax: +1 403 274 9807, Gordon Peariso. Passenger charter/contract. 4 x Jetstream 31

COVAL AIR (CVL) PO Box 1451, Campbell River, BC V9W 5C7; +1 250 287 8371, Fax: +1 250 287 8366, D Denney. Passenger/cargo scheduled/charter. 2 x Cessna A185F, 1 x Cessna 206, 2 x Beaver, 1 x Islander, 2 x Otter, 1 x Twin Otter

ENTERPRISE AIR 1000 Stevenson Road North, Oshawa, ON L1J 5P5; +1 905 721 0054, Fax: +1 905 721 0349, Walter Clow. 2 x Cessna 310, 1 x Beech 18, 1 x DC-3

HANNA'S AIR SALTSPRING (4H) 215 Vesuvius Road, Salt Spring Island, BC V8K 2S3; +1 250 537 9359, Fax: +1 250 537 9980, Res: 1 800 665 2359, Randy Hanna. Passenger scheduled/charter. 2 x Cessna 185

HAWKAIR AVIATION SERVICES Site 116, Comp 5, Bristol Road, RR #4, Terrace, BC V8G 4V2; +1 250 635 4295, Fax: +1 250 635 4295, Paul Hawkins. Cargo charter. 2 x Bristol 170

JACKSON AIR SERVICE (U8/JCX) PO Box 1000, Flin Flon, MB R8A 1N7; +1 204 687 8247, Fax: +1 204 687 7694, Reservations: 1 800 838 6359, Bill Jackson. Passenger scheduled/charter. 3 x Cessna 185, 1 x Cessna 206, 2 x Beaver, 1 x Navajo Chieftain, 2 x Otter

K D AIR (XC/KDC) RR #2, S-225, C-11, Port Alberni, BC V9Y 7L6; +1 250 752 5884, Fax: +1 250 752 5750, Reservations: 1 800 665 4244, K Banke. Passenger scheduled/charter. 1 x Cessna 172, 1 x Piper Navajo, 1 x Navajo Chieftain

KEYSTONE AIR SERVICES (BZ/KEE/921) PO Box 2140, Swan River, MB R0L 1Z0; +1 204 734 9351, Fax: +1 204 734 9181, Reservations: 1 800 665 3975, Clifford Arlt. Passenger scheduled/charter. 1 x Seneca, 1 x Piper Navajo, 2 x Navajo Chieftain

KNIGHTHAWK AIR EXPRESS (KNX) #1601 55 York Street, Toronto, ON M5J 1R7; +1 416 214 4880, Fax: +1 416 214 4883, Hugh MacMillan. Cargo charter. 1 x Piper Navajo, 1 x Beech 99, 1 x Beech 1900C, 4 x Falcon 20

LITTLE RED AIR SERVICE (LRA) PO Box 584, Fort Vermilion, AB T0H 1N0; +1 403 927 4630, Fax: +1 403 927 3667, Henry Grandjambe. Passenger/cargo scheduled/charter. 4 x Cessna 206, 1 x Islander, 1 x Navajo Chieftain, 1 x Cessna 421, 1 x King Air 90, 2 x King Air 100

MORNINGSTAR AIR EXPRESS (MEI/Morningstar) 29 Airport Road, Edmonton, AB T5G 0W6; +1 403 471 3022, Fax: +1 403 479 3856, Aaron A Perdue. Charter cargo. 2 x Cessna 208B, 1 x Metro II, 1 x HS 125/700A, 1 x Challenger, 5 x Boeing 727-100F (operated for FedEx)

NAVAIR CHARTER (FCV) 9556 Hampden Road, Sidney, BC V8L 5V5; +1 250 656 3937, Fax: +1 250 656 3936, Bernie L'Hirondelle. Cargo charter. 1 x Islander, 5 x Piper Navajo, 1 x Navajo Chieftain, 5 x MU-2, 1 x Metro II

NORTH AMERICAN AIRLINES (NTM) Box 630, 1441 Aviation Park NE, Calgary, AB T2E 8M7; +1 403 275 7700, Fax: +1 403 275 5947, D G Hollier. Passenger/cargo charter. 2 x Piper Navajo, 2 x Navajo Chieftain, 1 x King Air 100, 1 x Metro II, 4 x Metro III, 1 x Lear 35, 1 x Gulfstream I

NORTH VANCOUVER AIRLINES (VL/NRV) #311 5360 Airport Road S, Richmond, BC V7B 1B4; +1 604 278 1608, Fax: +1 604 278 2608, Reservations: 1 800 228 6608, Zoltan Kunn. Passenger/cargo scheduled/charter. 2 x Piper Navajo, 1 x Navajo Chieftain, 2 x King Air 100

NORTHERN DENE AIRWAYS PO Box 2106, Prince Albert, SK S6V 6K1; +1 306 764 0550, Fax: +1 306 953 0070, Dave Webster. Passenger/cargo scheduled/charter. 1 x Cessna 172, 1 x Cessna 180, 1 x Cessna 185F, 3 x Baron, 1 x Piper Navajo, 4 x Navajo Chieftain, 1 x King Air A90

PEM-AIR (PD/PEM/329) RR #6, Pembroke Municipal Airport, Pembroke, ON K8A 6W7; +1 613 687 8139, Fax: +1 613 687 5166, Reservations: 1 800 267 3131, Jason O'Brien. Passenger scheduled/charter. 1 x Cessna 172, 3 x Navajo Chieftain, 3 x King Air 100

POINTS NORTH AIR BAG 7000, La Ronge, SK S0J 1L0; +1 306 633 2137, Fax: +1 306 633 2152, George Eikel. Passenger/cargo charter. 1 x Cessna A185, 1 x Beaver, 1 x Cessna 402C, 3 x Otter, 1 x DC-3

PROPAIR (PRO) BG GR 20, RR #1, Rouyn Airport, Rouyn, QC J9X 5B7; +1 819 762 0811, Fax: +1 819 762 1852, Jean Pronovost. Passenger/cargo charter. 1 x Cessna 182, 1 x Cessna A185F, 3 x Beaver, 4 x Otter, 3 x King Air A100, 2 x King Air 200, 1 x Merlin IV, 1 x Metro II

SAMARITAN AIR SERVICE (HLO) 2450 Derry Road East, Hangar #6, Mississauga, ON L5S 1B2; +1 905 672 2226, Fax: +1 905 672 2229, Adam Keller. Passenger charter. 1 x Beech 18, 2 x MU-2, 1 x Lear 24B, 1 x Lear 25C, 2 x Jetstream 31

SEAIR 4640 Inglis Drive, Richmond, BC V7B 1W4; +1 604 273 8900, Fax: +1 604 273 7351, Res: 1 800 447 3247, Peter Clarke. Passenger scheduled/charter. 1 x Cessna 180, 2 x Cessna 185, 3 x Beaver/Turbo Beaver

SHUSWAP AIR (3S/SFC) PO Box 1887, Salmon Arm, BC V1E 4P9; +1 250 832 8830, Fax +1 250 832 2825, Reservations: 1 800 663 4074, Stepen Raffel. Passenger scheduled/charter. 1 x Cessna 172, 1 x Cessna 182, 1 x King Air 100.

SKY FREIGHTERS PO Box 226, Errington, BC V0R 1N0. 4 x Douglas C-117D

SUMMIT AIR CHARTERS PO Box 134, Atlin, BC V0W 1A0; +1 250 651 7600, Fax: +1 250 651 7537, Res: 1 800 661 1944, James Tait. Passenger/cargo charter. 1 x Cessna 185, 3 x Cessna 207, 2 x Skyvan

SUNWEST INTERNATIONAL AVIATION SERVICES (Chinook) 230 Aviation Place NE, Calgary, AB T2E 7G1; +1 403 275 8121, Fax: +1 403 275 4637, Gordon Laing. Passenger/cargo charter. 1 x Cessna 182, 3 x Piper Navajo, 1 x Navajo Chieftain, 1 x King Air B100, 4 x Metro II, 1 x Cessna 550, 1 x Lear 35

THUNDER AIRLINES (THU) 310 Hector Dougall Way, Thunder Bay, ON P7E 6M6; +1 807 475 4211, Fax: +1 807 475 5841, Ken Bittle. Passenger/cargo scheduled/charter. 1 x Navajo Chieftain, 3 x Cessna 208B, 3 x King Air A100, 1 x Metro, 1 x Shorts 330

TIMBERLINE AIR 46190A Airport Road, Chilliwack, BC V2P 1A5; +1 604 792 4614, Fax: +1 604 792 0822, Reservations: 1 800 668 1626, Denise Fast. Passenger/cargo scheduled/charter, Canada/USA. 1 x Piper Navajo, 1 x Cessna 208, 2 x King Air 100

TRANS-CAPITAL AIR Hangar #1, Toronto City Centre Airport, Toronto, ON M5V 1A1; +1 416 203 1144, Fax: +1 416 203 1120, Victor Pappalardo. Passenger charter. 2 x Dash 7

TRANS-CÔTE (7T) CP 298, Lourdes de Blanc Sablon, QC G0C 1W0; +1 418 461 2663, Fax: +1 418 461 2228, Paul A Joncas. Passenger charter. 3 x Piper Navajo, 1 x King Air A100

TRANSFAIR CP 9, Longue Pointe de Mingan, QC G0G 1V0; +1 418 949 2261, Fax: +1 418 949 2304, Jean Paul Fafard. Cargo charter. 1 x Cessna 180, 1 x Douglas DC-3, 1 x Convair 240

V KELNER AIRWAYS PO Box 1060 Station A, Goose Bay, Labrador, NF P7C 4T9; +1 709 896 8470, Fax: +1 709 896 8475, Frank Kelner. Passenger/cargo scheduled/charter. 3 x Cessna 208B, 3 x PC-12

VANCOUVER ISLAND AIR (FT) PO Box 727, Campbell River, BC V9W 6J3; +1 250 287 2433, Fax: +1 250 286 3269, Larry Langford. Passenger/cargo scheduled/charter. 3 x Beaver, 3 x Beech 18

WEST WIND AVIATION (WEW) Hangar #10, John G Diefenbaker Airport, Saskatoon, SK S7L 6S1; +1 306 652 9121, Fax: +1 306 652 3958, Dennis Goll. Passenger/cargo charter. 5 x Cessna 401, 1 x Cessna 402C, 1 x King Air 100, 1 x Cessna 500, 1 x King Air 200, 1 x King Air B200, 1 x Jetstream 31, 2 x HS 748

WESTERN EXPRESS (WES) Box 24259 APO, Vancouver International Airport, Richmond, BC V7B 1Y4; +1 604 273 1500, Fax: +1 604 273 0504, Res: 1 800 701 9009, D Oliver. Cargo scheduled/charter. 1 x Merlin IIB, 2 x Merlin IVA, 1 x F-27F

WILLISTON LAKE AIR SERVICES PO Box 490, Mackenzie, BC V0J 2C0; +1 250 997 5557, Fax: +1 997 5595, D Magnuson. Passenger/cargo charter. 1 x Piper Seneca, 2 x Navajo Chieftain

NOTES:

DE HAVILLAND CANADA DHC-7-103 DASH 7

GRØNLANDSFLY (GREENLANDAIR)

IATA: GL   **ICAO:** GRL   **IATA/ARC:** 631   **RADIO:** Greenlandair

CONTACTS:

Mail
PO Box 1012
DK-3900 Nuuk
Greenland
Email: glsales@greennet.gl
Internet: http://www.greenland-guide.dk/gla/

Telephone/FAX
Admin: +299 2 88 88
Fax: +299 2 88 36

OPERATION:

Type: Scheduled/charter passenger
Cities Served: Greenland: AGM CNP GOH JAV JCH JEG JFR JGO JGR JHS JJU JNN JNS JSU JUV KUS NAQ OBY SFJ THU UAK UMD
Europe: REK
Service to Canada operated in cooperation with First Air (Bradley Air Services); service to Copenhagen operated by SAS-Scandinavian

HISTORY/STRUCTURE:

Founded: November 7, 1960
Start Date: 1963
Chairman: Jonathan Motzfeldt
Ownership: Greenland government (37.5%), SAS-Scandinavian (37.5%), Danish government (25%)

SIKORSKY S-61N

FLEET:

Type	No	Seats	Engines
MD 500D	4	Y4	Allison 250-C20B
AS350B2	6	Y6	Turboméca Arriel 1D1
Bell 407	1	Y6	Allison 250-C47
Beech 200	1	Y7	PWC PT6A-41
Bell 212	4	Y9	PWC PT6T-3B
DHC-6-300	2	Y18/Combi	PWC PT6A-27
Sikorsky S-61N	4	Y25	GE CT58-140-2
DHC-7-103	4	Y50	PWC PT6A-50
(Additional helicopters leased during northern summer season)			

GREENLAND Addendum

SULUIT AIR PO Box 860, DK-3900 Nuuk, Greenland; +299 26 666, Fax: +299 26 961, Per Rosing-Petersen. Charter passenger. 1 x Cessna 208 (Amphibian)

NOTES:

AI(R) ATR42-320

AIR SAINT-PIERRE

IATA: PJ   **ICAO:** SPM   **IATA/ARC:** 638   **RADIO:** Saint Pierre

CONTACTS:

Mail
BP 4225
9 rue Albert Briand
F-95700 Saint-Pierre et Miquelon

Telephone/FAX
Admin: +508 41 47 18
Fax: +508 41 23 36

Internet: none

OPERATION:

Type: Scheduled passenger
Cities Served: FSP **Canada:** YHZ YMX YQY YYT
All scheduled service operated as Canadian Partner using only CP flight numbers
Code-Share: Canadian Airlines International
FFP: Canadian Plus

HISTORY/STRUCTURE:

Founded: 1961   **Start Date:** 1961
CEO: Remy L Briand   **Ownership:** Briand family

FLEET:

Type	No	Seats	Engines
PA-23 Aztec	1	Y5	LY IO-540-C4B5
PA-31-350 Chieftain	1	Y7	LY TIO-540-J2BD
ATR42-320	1	Y48	PWC PW121

McDONNELL DOUGLAS DC-9-32

AERO CALIFORNIA

IATA: JR   **ICAO:** SER   **IATA/ARC:** 078   **RADIO:** Aerocalifornia

CONTACTS:

Mail
Aquiles Serdan 1995
La Paz, BCS 23000

Telephone/FAX
Admin: +52 112 59 002
Fax: +52 112 35 343
Res: +52 5 207 1392 (Mexico City)
Res: 1 800 237 6225 (US/Can)

Internet: none

OPERATION:

Type: Scheduled passenger
Cities Served: México: AGU CEN CJS CLQ CUL CUU CVM DGO GDL HMO LAP LMM LTO MAM MEX MTY MZT PBC SJD SLP TIJ TPQ TRC ZLO **US:** LAX TUS

HISTORY/STRUCTURE:

Founded: 1960
CEO: Raul A Archiga E

Start Date: 1960
Ownership: Privately held

FLEET:

Type	No	Seats	Engines
DC-9-14	5	C8Y73	PW JT8D-7A/-7B
DC-9-15	6	C8Y73	PW JT8D-7A/-7B
DC-9-32	5	C6Y100	PW JT8D-9A
Ordered			
DC-9-83	2		

MÉXICO

McDONNELL DOUGLAS DC-9-14

AEROCARIBE

IATA: QA **ICAO:** CBE **IATA/ARC:** 723 **RADIO:** Aerocaribe

CONTACTS:

Mail
Avenida Coba 5, Local B1 y B3
Plaza América
77500 Cancún, QR

Xola 535, 28 Fl, Col del Valle
México, DF 03100

Telephone/FAX
Admin: +52 98 87 4002
Fax   +52 98 84 9996

Admin: +52 5 682 0230
Fax: +52 5 543 3382
Res: +52 98 84 2000 (Cancún)
Res: 01 800 50 220 (México)
Res: 1 800 531 7921 (US/Canada)

Email: qamse@mail.interaccess.com.mx

OPERATION:

Type: Scheduled/charter passenger
Cities Served: México: ACA CME CTM CUN CZA CZM HUX MEX MID MTY OAX PCM PQM TGZ VER VSA **Caribbean/Central America:** BZE FRS GUA HAV
Some scheduled service operated using MX flight numbers
Code-Share: AEROMEXICO, Mexicana

HISTORY/STRUCTURE:

Founded: 1972 (as Aerolíneas Bonanza)
Start Date: July 12, 1975
CEO: Jaime Valenzuela
Ownership: CINTRA Holdings

FLEET:

Type	No	Seats	Engines
BN-2A-III	2	Y16	LY O-540-E4C5
Fairchild F-27J	3	Y44	RR Dart 532-7
Fairchild FH-227B/D	3	Y50	RR Dart 532-7
DC-9-14	4	Y85	PW JT8D-7B
Ordered			
Cessna 208	2		
DC-9-15	1		

BOEING 727-200 (ADVANCED)

AEROEXO (Aeroejecutivo)

IATA: SX **ICAO:** AJO **IATA/ARC:** 456 **RADIO:** Aeroexo

CONTACTS:

Mail
Avenida Humberto Lobo 660
Cold del Valle
San Pedro Garza Garcia, NL 66220

Telephone/FAX
Admin: +52 8 366 4400
Fax: +52 8 338 1889
Res: 01 800 006 22 (México)
Res: 1 800 237 6396 (US/Can)

Internet: none

OPERATION:

Type: Scheduled/charter passenger
Cities Served: México: CUN GDL MEX MTY TIJ **US:** LAS
Charter operations to US, Caribbean
Code-Share: Aerolíneas Bonanza
FFP: Pasajero Leal

HISTORY/STRUCTURE:

Founded: November 1975 (as Aeroejecutivo)
Start Date: 1975
CEO: Eduardo Morales
Ownership: Privately held (affiliated with AVIACSA)

FLEET:

Type	No	Seats	Engines
Boeing 727-200 (Advanced)	2	Y164	PW JT8D-15A

McDonnell Douglas DC-9-15

AEROLINEAS INTERNACIONALES

IATA: N2   **ICAO:** AIN   **IATA/ARC:** 440   **RADIO:** Aerolineas Internacionales

CONTACTS:

Mail
Blvd Vicente Guerrero 46
Col Lomas de la Selva
Cuernavaca, MOR 62270

Telephone/FAX
Admin: +52 73 11 5120
Fax: +52 73 11 5270
Res: 01 800 99 091 (México)

Internet: http://www.iwm.com.mx/foroemp/aerint.html

OPERATION:

Type: Scheduled/charter passenger
Cities Served: México: ACA AGU CUL CVJ GDL HMO MEX MTY REX TIJ
FFP: Exclusive Card

HISTORY/STRUCTURE:

Founded: June 24, 1993   **Start Date:** March 25, 1994
CEO: Jorge Luis Rodriguez   **Ownership:** Privately held

FLEET:

Type	No	Seats	Engines
DC-9-15	1	Y90	PW JT8D-7A
Boeing 727-100	2	Y118	PW JT8D-7B
Boeing 727-200 (Advanced)	1	Y150	PW JT8D-17

FAIRCHILD SA227-AC METRO III

AEROLITORAL (Servicios Aéreos Litoral)

IATA: 2Z   **ICAO:** SLI   **IATA/ARC:** 642   **RADIO:** Aerolitoral

CONTACTS:

Mail
Carretera Miguel Aleman Km 22.8
Apodaca, NL 66601

Telephone/FAX
Admin: +52 8 386 2070
Fax: +52 8 386 1601
Res : +52 8 369 0757 (Monterrey)
Res : +01 800 90 999 (México)
Res: +1 800 247 6639 (US/Can)

Email: aerolitoral1@infosel.net.mx
Internet: http://www.aerolitoral.com

OPERATION:

Type: Scheduled passenger
Cities Served: México: AGU BJX CEN CJS CUL CUU DGO GDL GUB GYM HMO LAP LMM LOV LTO MAM MLM MTY MXL MZT PDS PVR QRO SJD SLP TAM TPQ TRC VER VSA ZIH ZLO
US: ELP PHX SAT TUS
Code-Share: AEROMEXICO, Mexicana

HISTORY/STRUCTURE:

Founded: May 1989   **Start Date:** July 1989
CEO: Carlos Trevino   **Ownership:** CINTRA Holdings

FLEET:

Type	No	Seats	Engines
Metro III	14	Y19	GA TPE331-12
Metro 23	13	Y19	GA TPE331-12

AI(R) ATR42-320

AEROMAR (Transportes Aéreos Aeromar)

IATA: VW **ICAO:** ROM **IATA/ARC:** 942 **RADIO:** Aeromar

CONTACTS:

Mail
Hangar 7, Zona E Aviación General
Aeropuerto Internacional
Ciudad de México, México, DF 15620

Telephone/FAX
Admin: +52 5 627 0205
Fax: +52 5 756 0174
Res: +52 5 627 0207 (Mexico City)
Res: 01 800 70 429 (México)
Res: +1 210 829 7482 (US)

Internet: none

OPERATION:
Type: Scheduled passenger
Cities Served: México: AGU BJX CLQ CVM DGO GDL HUX LZC MEX MLM MTY PAZ PBC QRO SCX SLP UPN ZCL ZLO **US:** IAH SAT
Code-Share: AEROMEXICO, Mexicana, United Airlines

HISTORY/STRUCTURE:
Founded: 1987 **Start Date:** November 7, 1987
CEO: Juan I Steta **Ownership:** Privately held

FLEET:

Type	No	Seats	Engines
ATR42-320	6	Y46/Y48	PWC PW121
ATR42-500	2	Y48	PWC PW 127E
Ordered			
ATR42-500	3		

McDONNELL DOUGLAS DC-9-83 (MD-83)

AEROMEXICO (Aerovías de México dba)

IATA: AM **ICAO:** AMX **IATA/ARC:** 139 **RADIO:** Aeromexico

CONTACTS:

Mail
Avendia Paseo de la Reforma 445
México, DF 06500

Telephone/FAX
Admin: +52 5 133 4000
Fax: +52 5 133 4628
Res: +52 5 228 9910 (Mexico City)
Res: 01 800 90 999 (México)
Res: 1 800 247 3737 (US/Can)

Internet: http://www.wotw.com/aeromexico

OPERATION:

Type: Scheduled passenger
Cities Served: México: ACA AGU BJX CEN CJS CPE CUL CUN CUU DGO GDL GYM HMO LAP LMM MAM MEX MID MTY MZT OAX PVR REX SJD TAP TIJ TRC VER VSA ZIH **USA:** ATL DFW IAH JFK LAX MIA MSY PHX SAN **South America:** LIM GRU **Europe:** CDG MAD
Code-Share: Aerocaribe/Aerocozumel, Aerolitoral, Aeromar, Aeroperú, Air France, America West, Delta Air Lines, Mexicana
FFP: Club Premier

HISTORY/STRUCTURE:

Founded: 1934 (as Aeronaves de México)
Start Date: May 15, 1934
CEO: Alfonso Pasquel
Ownership: CINTRA Holdings

FLEET:

Type	No	Seats	Engines
DC-9-31	3	J12Y90	PW JT8D-17
DC-9-32	15	J12Y90	PW JT8D-17
DC-9-82	10	J12Y133	PW JT8D-217A/-217C
DC-9-83	3	J12Y135	PW JT8D-219
DC-9-87	2	J12Y102	PW JT8D-219
MD-88	10	J12Y125	PW JT8D-219
Boeing 757-200	6	J12Y179	PW 2037
Boeing 767-200ER	2	J42Y324	PW 4060
Boeing 767-300ER	1	J21Y188	PW 4060
DC-10-15	1	J40Y236	GE CF6-50C2F

NOTES:

BOEING 727-200 (ADVANCED)(F)

AEROMEXPRESS

IATA: QO **ICAO:** MPX **IATA/ARC:** 976 **RADIO:** Aeromexpress

CONTACTS:

Mail
Avenida Texcoco esq Av Tahel S/N
Col Penon de los Banos
México, DF 15620

Telephone/FAX
Admin: +52 5 237 0203
Fax: +52 5 237 2226
Info: 01 800 70 693 (México)

Internet: none

OPERATION:

Type: Scheduled/charter cargo
Cities Served: México/Central America: BJX GDL MEX MID SJO
US: DFW LAX MIA
Code-Share: AEROMEXICO, Mexicana, Aerocozumel/Aerocaribe, Aerolitoral, Aeroperú

HISTORY/STRUCTURE:

Founded: 1989
CEO: Javier Elizalde

Start Date: December 1, 1989
Ownership: CINTRA Holdings

FLEET:

Type	No	Engines
Boeing 727-200F	2	PW JT8D-17

BOEING 707-300C (H)

AERO POSTAL DE MEXICO

IATA: none   **ICAO:** PTX   **IATA/ARC:** none   **RADIO:** Aeropostal

CONTACTS:

Mail	**Telephone/FAX**
Hangar 3, Zona C	Admin: +52 5 756 4263
Terminal de Aviación General	Fax: +52 5 756 4432
Aeropuerto Internacional Ciudad de México	
México, DF 15620	

OPERATION:

Type: Charter cargo

HISTORY/STRUCTURE:

Founded: 1991
Start Date: 1992
Ownership: Privately held

FLEET:

Type	No	Engines
C-130A Hercules	2	Allison T56-A-9D
Boeing 707-300C	1	PW JT3D-3 (Q)
Ordered		
Boeing 707-300C	1	

BOEING 727-200

ALLEGRO (Líneas Aéreas Allegro)

IATA: LL   **ICAO:** GRO   **IATA/ARC:** 902   **RADIO:** Allegro

CONTACTS:

Mail
José Benitez 2709
Col Obispado
Monterrey, NL 64060

Telephone/FAX
Admin: +52 8 333 9938
Fax: +52 8 333 9940
Res: +52 5 264 8454 (México)

Internet: none

OPERATION:

Type: Scheduled/charter passenger
Cities Served: CUN MEX
Charter operations to US, Canada, Caribbean, Central and South America

HISTORY/STRUCTURE:

Founded: 1992
CEO: Fernando Padilla

Start Date: December 26, 1992
Ownership: Privately held

FLEET:

Type	No	Seats	Engines
DC-9-14	1	Y90	PW JT8D-7B
DC-9-83	5	Y165	PW JT8D-219
Boeing 727-200	3	Y165	JT8D-17
Three DC-9-83s leased to Aero Lloyd (Germany) December-April			

BOEING 727-200 (ADVANCED)

AVIACSA (Aviación de Chiapas SA)

IATA: 6A **ICAO:** CHP **IATA/ARC:** none **RADIO:** Aviacsa

CONTACTS:

Mail
Hangar No 13, Zona D
Aeropuerto Internacional Ciudad de México
Aviación General
México, DF 15520

Internet: none

Telephone/FAX
Admin: +52 5 756 0650
Fax: +52 5 700 3852
Res: +52 5 448 8900 (Mexico City)
Res: 01 800 006 22 (México)
Res: 1 800 237 6396 (US/Can)

OPERATION:

Type: Scheduled/charter passenger
Cities Served: México: CTM CUN MID MEX OAX TAP TGZ
Charter operations to US, Caribbean
Code-Share: Aerolíneas Bonanza
FFP: Pasajero Leal

HISTORY/STRUCTURE:

Founded: May 1990
Start Date: September 1990
CEO: Eduardo Morales
Ownership: Privately held (affiliated with AEROEXO)

FLEET:

Type	No	Seats	Engines
Boeing 727-100	2	Y118	PW JT8D-7B
Boeing 727-200 (Advanced)	4	Y164	PW JT8D-15
Ordered			
DC-9-21	4	(ex-ValuJet)	

MÉXICO

BOEING 707-300C (H)

MAS AIR (Transportes Mas de Carga)

IATA: MY **ICAO:** MAA **IATA/ARC:** 865 **RADIO:** Mas Air

CONTACTS:

Mail
Almacen 22, Aduana Interior
Aeropuerto Internacional
Ciudad de México, México, DF 15520

Telephone/FAX
Admin: +52 5 786 9555
Fax: +52 5 786 9543

Internet: none

OPERATION:
Type: Scheduled/charter cargo
Cities Served: México: GDL **US:** LAX MIA
Charter service to BOG CCS EZE JFK LIM MVD SCL VCP

HISTORY/STRUCTURE:
Founded: September 13, 1990
Start Date: April 29, 1992
CEO: Cristian Ureta
Ownership: Promotor Aéreo Latinamericano (75%), International Aviation Services (25%)

FLEET:

Type	No	Capacity	Engines
Boeing 707-300C	1		PW JT3D-3C
DC-8-71F	1		CFM56-121

BOEING 727-200 (ADVANCED)

MEXICANA DE AVIACION

IATA: MX   **ICAO:** MXA   **IATA/ARC:** 132   **RADIO:** Mexicana

CONTACTS:

Mail
Xola 535, Col del Valle
México, DF 03100

Telephone/FAX
Admin: +52 5 440 3000
Fax: +52 5 523 2364
Res: +52 5 325 0990 (Mexico City)
Res: 01 800 50 220 (México)
Res: 1 800 531 7921 (US/Can)
PR: +52 5 687 8430

Internet: http://www.mexicana.com

OPERATION:

Type: Scheduled passenger
Cities Served: US: DEN EWR LAX MCO MIA ORD SAT SFO SJC **Canada:** YMX YYZ **México** ACA BJX CME CUN CZM GDL HMO HUX MEX MID MLM MTT MTY MXL MZT NLD OAX PVR PXM SJD SLW TAM TIJ VER VSA ZCL ZIH ZLO **Central America/South America:** BOG EZE GUA LIM SCL SJO **Caribbean:** HAV
Code-Share: Aerocaribe/Aerocozumel, Aerolitoral, Aeromar, AEROMEXICO, SERVIVENSA, United Airlines
FFP: Frecuenta

HISTORY/STRUCTURE:

Founded: 1921   **Start Date:** July 12, 1921
CEO: Fernando Flores   **Ownership:** CINTRA Holdings

FLEET:

Type	No	Seats	Engines
Fokker 100	10	Y108	RR Tay 650
Airbus A320-231	12	Y156	IAE V2500-A1
Boeing 727-264 (Advanced)	23	Y156	PW JT8D-17/-17R
Boeing 757-2Q8	2	Y201	PW2040

MÉXICO

BOEING 727-200 (F)

MEXICARGO

IATA: GJ **ICAO:** MXC **IATA/ARC:** 624 **RADIO:** Mexicargo

CONTACTS:

Mail
Norte 192 No 640
Col Pensador Méxicano
México, DF 15510

Telephone/FAX
Admin: +52 5 760 0999
Fax: +52 5 760 0793

Email: mexcgo@mail.iwm.com.mx
Internet: none

OPERATION:

Type: Charter cargo
Cities Served: México: GDL HMO LAP MEX TIJ **US:** MIA SAT

HISTORY/STRUCTURE:

Founded: August 18, 1991   **Start Date:** February 1996
CEO: Marco A Mediola   **Ownership:** Privately held

FLEET:

Type	No	Engines
Boeing 727-200F	1	PW JT8D-7B

MÉXICO

BOEING 737-200 (ADVANCED)

TAESA (Transportes Aéreos Ejecutivos SA)
IATA: GD **ICAO:** TEJ **IATA/ARC:** 838 **RADIO:** TAESA

CONTACTS:

Mail
Aviación General
Zona de Hangares C, No 27
Aeropuerto Intl Cd de México
PO Box 9-212
México, DF 15001

Telephone/FAX
Admin: +52 5 227 0727
Fax: +52 5 227 4044
Res: +52 5 227 0700 (Mexico City)
Res: 01 800 90 463 (México)
Res: 1 800 32 TAESA (US/Can)
PR: +52 5 227 4017

Internet: http://www.wotw.com/wow/mexico/city/taesa.html

OPERATION:
Type: Scheduled/charter passenger/cargo, FBO
Cities Served: México: ACA BJX CUN CJS CUL GDL HMO MID MEX MTY MLM PVR TAP TLC ZCL **US:** EGE LRD OAK ORD
FFP: Viajero Frecuente

HISTORY/STRUCTURE:
Founded: 1988 **Start Date:** April 27, 1988
CEO: Alberto Abed **Ownership:** Abed family

FLEET:

Type	No	Seats	Engines
DC-9-14/-15	5	Y90	PW JT8D-7A
Boeing 737-200 (Advanced)	2	Y130	PW JT8D-15
Boeing 737-300	3	Y148	CFM56-3C-1/3B-2
Boeing 737-500	2	Y133	CFM56-3C-1
Boeing 727-100	2	Y131 or Y128	PW JT8D-7B/-7E
Boeing 727-100C	3	Freighter	PW JT8D-7B/-9A
Boeing 757-200	1	Y228	RR RB211-535E4
DC-10-30	2	Y355 or Y356	GE CF6-50C2
DC-10-30F	1	Freighter	GE CF6-50C2
Ordered	**No**	**Ordered**	**No**
Boeing 737-300	5	Boeing 757-200	1
Boeing 727-200	2	Boeing 767-300ER	1

ILYUSHIN IL-18D

AEROCARIBBEAN

IATA: none **ICAO:** CRN **IATA/ARC:** none **RADIO:** AeroCaribbean

CONTACTS:
Mail
Calle 23, Numero 64
Vedado, Havana, Cuba

Telephone/FAX
Admin: +53 7 335016/334543
Fax: +53 7 335016

Internet: http://www.cubaweb.cu

OPERATION:
Type: Charter passenger/freight

HISTORY/STRUCTURE:
Founded: 1982 **Start Date:** 1982
CEO: Julian Alvarez Infiesta **Ownership:** Cuban government

FLEET:

Type	No	Seats	Engines
DC-3	2	Y28	PW R-1830
Antonov An-24B	1	Y44	IV AI-24-II
Antonov An-26	4	Freighter	IV AI-24-VT
Fairchild F-27F	1	Y44	RR Dart 529-7E
Yakovlev Yak-40	5	Y30/Freighter	IV AI-25
Ilyushin Il-14M	1	Y40	SH ASh-82T
Ilyushin Il-18D/V	5	Y100/Freighter	IV AI-20M

YAKOVLEV YAK-40

AEROGAVIOTA

IATA: none   **ICAO:** GTV   **IATA/ARC:** none   **RADIO:** Gaviota

CONTACTS:

Mail
Avenida 47, Numero 2814
Reparto Kolhy
Havana, Cuba

Telephone/FAX
Admin: +53 7 813068
Fax: +53 7 332621

Internet: none

OPERATION:

Type: Charter passenger/freight

HISTORY/STRUCTURE:

Founded: 1994
Start Date: 1994
Ownership: Cuban government

FLEET:

Type	No	Seats	Engines
Mil Mi-8	1	Y32/Cargo	IZ TV2-117A
Antonov An-26/26B	8	Freighter	IV AI-24-VT
Yakovlev Yak-40	3	Y32	IV AI-25
All operated by Cuban Air Force			

McDONNELL DOUGLAS MD-88

AIR ARUBA

IATA: FQ **ICAO:** ARU **IATA/ARC:** 276 **RADIO:** Aruba

CONTACTS:

Mail
PO Box 1017
Oranjestad, Aruba

Telephone/FAX
Admin: +2978 30005
Fax: +2978 25867/30006
Res: 1 800 882 7822
PR: 1 800 858 8028

Internet: http://www.interknowledge.com/air-aruba

OPERATION:

Type: Scheduled/charter passenger
Cities Served: Caribbean: AUA BON CUR **South America:** BOG CCS GRU MDE **US:** BWI EWR MIA TPA
Code-Share: ALM, AVIANCA, KLM, SAM, Surinam Airways
FFP: yes

HISTORY/STRUCTURE:

Founded: September 1986   **Start Date:** August 18, 1988
CEO: Henri Coffi   **Ownership:** Privately held

FLEET:

Type	No	Seats	Engines
DC-9-31	1	C8Y90	PW JT8D-9A
DC-9-83	1	C8Y135	PW JT8D-219
MD-88	2	C8Y135	PW JT8D-219

CARIBBEAN

CESSNA 208 CARAVAN I

AIR CARAIBES

IATA: WS   **ICAO:** ISB   **IATA/ARC:** none   **RADIO:** Island Bird

CONTACTS:

Mail
Aéroport du Raizet
F-97139 Abymes, Guadeloupe

Telephone/FAX
Admin: +590 82 12 25
Fax: +590 83 54 66
Res: +590 82 12 25

Internet: none

OPERATION:

Type: Scheduled/charter passenger
Cities Served: PTP SBH SFG

HISTORY/STRUCTURE:

Founded: 1987
Start Date: 1987
CEO: Lionel Guerin
Ownership: Union Stars Aviation (50%), Hayot family (50%)

FLEET:

Type	No	Seats	Engines
Beech King Air C90	1	Y6	PWC PT6A-20A
Beech King Air 200	2	Y9/Y11	PWC PT6A-21/-41
Cessna Citation	1	Y7	PWC JT15D-4B
BN-2A	2	Y9	LY O-540-E4C5
Cessna 208	3	Y9	PWC PT6A-114
DHC-6-300	1	Y18	PWC PT6A-27
Dornier 228-200	3	Y19	GA TPE331-5-252D

NAMC YS-11A-500

AIR CARIBBEAN

IATA: C2 **ICAO:** none **IATA/ARC:** 189 **RADIO:** none

CONTACTS:

Mail
PO Box 1021
Port of Spain, Trinidad

Internet: none

Telephone/FAX
Admin: +1 809 623 2500
Fax: +1 809 623 8182
Res: 1 809 623 2500

OPERATION:

Type: Scheduled passenger/cargo
Cities Served: POS TAB

HISTORY/STRUCTURE:

Founded: November 26, 1991
Start Date: August 8, 1993
CEO: Leslie Lucky-Samaroo
Ownership: Luxsam Holdings (50%), Medishi Investments (50%)

FLEET:

Type	No	Seats	Engines
YS-11A-500	4	Y60	RR Dart 542-10
YS-11A-600	1	Freighter	RR Dart 542-10
Ordered			
Boeing 737-200	1		

AI(R) ATR42-300

AIR GUADELOUPE

IATA: TX **ICAO:** AGU **IATA/ARC:** 427 **RADIO:** Air Guadeloupe

CONTACTS:

Mail
Aéroport du Raizet
F-97139 Abymes, Guadeloupe

Internet: none

Telephone/FAX
Admin: +590 91 5344
Fax: +590 83 7003
Res: +590 91 5344

OPERATION:

Type: Scheduled passenger/charter
Cities Served: Caribbean: DOM DSD FDF GBJ LSS PAP PTP SBH SDQ SFG SJU SXM **South America:** CAY

HISTORY/STRUCTURE:

Founded: 1969 (as Société Antillaise de Transport Aérien/Air Guadeloupe)
Start Date: 1994
CEO: François Paneole
Ownership: Société Nouvelle Air Guadeloupe (51% Guadeloupe Investissement Aeronautique; 49% Société d'Economie Mixte)

FLEET:

Type	No	Seats	Engines
DHC-6-300	2	Y19	PWC PT6A-27
Dornier 228-200	4	Y19	GA TPE331-5/-5A
ATR42-300	2	Y50	PWC 120
ATR72-200	1	Y70	PWC 124B

AIRBUS A320-214

AIR JAMAICA

IATA: JM **ICAO:** AJM **IATA/ARC:** 201 **RADIO:** Juliette Mike

CONTACTS:

Mail
72-76 Harbour Street
Kingston, Jamaica

Telephone/FAX
Admin: +1 809 922 3460
Fax:　 +1 809 922 0107
Res:　 1 800 523 5585

Internet: http://www. airjamaica.com

OPERATION:

Type: Scheduled passenger
Cities Served: Caribbean: ANU BGI GCM KIN MBJ NAS **US:** ATL BWI EWR FLL JFK LAX MCO MIA ORD PHL **Europe:** LHR
Code-Share: Air Canada, Air Jamaica Express
FFP: Seventh Heaven

HISTORY/STRUCTURE:

Founded: 1968
Start Date: April 1, 1969
CEO: Gordon Stewart
President: Albert P Chappell
Ownership: Air Jamaica Holdings (75% individual investors, 25% Jamaican government)

FLEET:

Type	No	Seats	Engines
DC-9-82	2	FY144	PW JT8D-217
Boeing 727-200 (Advanced)	2	F8Y140	PW JT8D-15
A320-214	2	CY150	CFM56-5B4
A310-324(ET)	6	F18Y200	PW 4152
Ordered			
A320-200	2		
Two DC-9-83s wet-leased from Great American			

CARIBBEAN

DORNIER 228-202

AIR JAMAICA EXPRESS

IATA: JM   **ICAO:** AJM   **IATA/ARC:** 201   **RADIO:** Juliette Mike

CONTACTS:

Mail
Kingston Tinson Pen Aerodrome
Kingston 11, Jamaica

Telephone/FAX
Admin: +1 809 923 9498
Fax: +1 809 937 3807
Res: 1 800 523 5585

Internet: http://www.airjamaica.com

OPERATION:

Type: Scheduled passenger
Cities Served: KTP MBJ NEG POT
Code-Share: Air Jamaica

HISTORY/STRUCTURE:

Founded: 1973 (as Jamaica Air Taxi)   **Start Date:** February 20, 1996
CEO: Gordon Stewart   **Ownership:** Air Jamaica Holdings

FLEET:

Type	No	Seats	Engines
BN-2A-III	1	Y17	LYO-540-E4C5
Dornier 228-200	3	Y19	GA TPE331-5/-5A

CARIBBEAN

AI(R) ATR42-300

AIR MARTINIQUE

IATA: PN **ICAO:** MTQ **IATA/ARC:** 871 **RADIO:** Air Martinique

CONTACTS:

Mail
Aéroport du Lamentin
F-97232 Le Lamentin, Martinique

Telephone/FAX
Admin: +596 51 08 09
Fax: +596 51 59 27
Res: +596 51 08 09

Internet: none

OPERATION:

Type: Scheduled passenger
Cities Served: CIW FDF PAP PTP SFG SLU SVD SXM UNI

HISTORY/STRUCTURE:

Founded: 1974 (as Compagnie Antillaise d'Affrêtments Aériens-CAAA)
Start Date: October 20, 1993 (Société Nouvelle Air Martinique)
CEO: Guy Aurore
Ownership: Privately held

FLEET:

Type	No	Seats	Engines
Dornier 228-200	3	Y19	GA TPE331-5-252D
ATR42-300	2	Y48/Y50	PWC PW120

McDONNELL DOUGLAS DC-9-82 (MD-82)

ALM ANTILLEAN AIRLINES

IATA: LM   **ICAO:** ALM   **IATA/ARC:** 119   **RADIO:** Antillean

CONTACTS:

Mail
Aeropuerto Hato
Curaçao, Netherlands Antilles

Telephone/FAX
Admin: +599 933 8888
Fax: +1 305 594 1030
Res: 1 800 327 7230

Internet: http://www.empg.com/alm

OPERATION:

Type: Scheduled/charter passenger
Cities Served: Caribbean: AUA BON CUR KIN PAP POS SXM SJU SDQ
US: ATL FLL MIA **South America:** CCS PBM VLN
Code-Share: American, KLM

HISTORY/STRUCTURE:

Founded: 1964 (as Antilliaanse Luchtvaart Maatschappij NV)
Start Date: August 1, 1964
CEO: Kitland Chong
Ownership: Netherlands Antilles government

FLEET:

Type	No	Seats	Engines
DHC-8-300	2	Y50	PWC 123
DC-9-82	3	Y146	PW JT8D-217/-217C

BOMBARDIER DHC-8-301 DASH 8

BAHAMASAIR

IATA: UP **ICAO:** BHS **IATA/ARC:** 111 **RADIO:** Bahamas

CONTACTS:

Mail
PO Box N4881
Nassau, Bahamas

Internet: none

Telephone/FAX
Admin: +1 809 377 8451
Fax: +1 305 718 9115
Res: 1 800 222 4262

OPERATION:

Type: Scheduled passenger
Cities Served: Caribbean: ASD ATC AXP CRI ELH FPO GGT GHB IGA LGI MHH MYG NAS PLS RSD SAQ SML TBI TCB ZSA **US:** MCO MIA PBI
Code-Share: Congo Air, Sky Unlimited

HISTORY/STRUCTURE:

Founded: 1973
Start Date: June 7, 1973
Chairman: Lester Turncuest
GM: William Curtis
Ownership: Bahamasair Holdings (Bahamas government)

FLEET:

Type	No	Seats	Engines
Shorts 360 (200)	1	Y36	PWC PT6A-65AR
DHC-8-300	7	Y50	PWC PW123
Boeing 737-200	1	Y120	PW JT8D-9A

CARIBBEAN

AIRBUS A321-131

BWIA INTERNATIONAL

IATA: BW **ICAO:** BWA **IATA/ARC:** 106 **RADIO:** West Indian

CONTACTS:

Mail
Administration Building
Golden Grove Road
PO Box 604
Piarco International Airport
Trinidad
Internet: none

Telephone/FAX
Admin: +1 809 669 3000
Fax: +1 809 664 3535
Res: 1 800 538 2942

OPERATION:

Type: Scheduled passenger
Cities Served: Caribbean: ANU BGI GND KIN POS SLU SXM TAB
US: JFK MIA **Canada:** YYZ **South America:** CCS GEO **Europe:** FRA LHR
FFP: BWIA Frequent Flyer

HISTORY/STRUCTURE:

Founded: 1939 (as British West Indian Airways)
Start Date: November 27, 1940
Chairman: Ken Gordon
CEO: Gilles Filliatreault
Ownership: Private investors (51%); Trinidad & Tobago government (33.5%), employees (15.5%)

FLEET:

Type	No	Seats	Engines
DC-9-83	7	C8Y125	PW JT8D-219
A321-100	2	C16Y154	IAE V2530-A5
L-1011-500	5	C28Y210	RR RB211-524B4

BOEING 737-200 (ADVANCED)

CAYMAN AIRWAYS

IATA: KX   **ICAO:** CAY   **IATA/ARC:** 378   **RADIO:** Cayman

CONTACTS:

Mail
PO Box 1101
Georgetown
Grand Cayman, Cayman Islands
Internet: http://www.caymans.com/~caymans/cayman_airways.html

Telephone/FAX
Admin: +1 809 949 8200
Fax: +1 809 949 7607
Res: 1 800 422 9626

OPERATION:

Type: Scheduled passenger
Cities Served: Caribbean: CYB GCM KIN **US:** ATL IAH MCO MIA TPA
Code-Share: United

HISTORY/STRUCTURE:

Founded: 1955 (as Cayman Brac Airways)
Start Date: July 1968
Chairman: Leonard Ebanks
Ownership: Cayman Islands government

FLEET:

Type	No	Seats	Engines
Boeing 737-200 (Advanced)	2	Y122	PW JT8D-15A/-17A

TUPOLEV TU-154M

CUBANA

IATA: CU **ICAO:** CUB **IATA/ARC:** 136 **RADIO:** Cubana

CONTACTS:

Mail
Calle 23 Numero 64
Vedado, Havana 1040C, Cuba
Internet: http://www.cubaweb.cu/turismo/cubana

Telephone/FAX
Admin: +53 736 775
Fax: +53 736 190

OPERATION:

Type: Scheduled/charter passenger/freight. Cubana also operates many flights for the Cuban military.
Cities Served: Caribbean: AVI BCA BYM CMW CCC FDF GAO GER HAV HOG MOA MZO PTP SCU VRA VTU **Canada:** YMX **México/Central America/South America:** BOG CUN CCS EZE GIG GRU GYE LIM MEX PTY SCL SJO UIO **Europe:** BCN BRU FCO LGW LIS LPA MAD ORY SCQ SVO SXF VIT

HISTORY/STRUCTURE:

Founded: October 8, 1929 (as Compañía Nacional Cubana de Aviación Curtiss)
Start Date: October 30, 1930
Administrator: Heriberto Prieto Musa   **Ownership:** Cuban government

FLEET:

Type	No	Seats	Engines
Mil Mi-8	5	Y32/Cargo	IZ TV2-117A
Antonov An-24B	2	Y50	IV AI-24-II
Antonov An-24RV	6	Y50	IV AI-24-VT
Antonov An-26	12	Freighter	IV AI-24-VT
Antonov An-26B	7	Freighter	IV AI-24-VT
Yakovlev Yak-40	8	Y32	IV AI-25
Yakovlev Yak-42D	4	Y120	LO D-36
Tupolev Tu-154B-2	4	Y156	KU NK-8-2U
Tupolev Tu-154M	3	Y156	SO D-30-KU-154
Ilyushin Il-62M	14	C4Y156	SO D-30-KU
Ilyushin Il-76MD	2	Freighter	SO D-30-KP
Cubana uses DC-10-30s operated by AOM France on many European flights			

BOEING 727-200

HALISA AIR (Haitian Aviation Line SA)

IATA: WD **ICAO:** HBC **IATA/ARC:** 851 **RADIO:** Halisa

CONTACTS:

Mail
7270 NW 12th St
Miami, FL 33126, USA

Internet: none

Telephone/FAX
Admin: +1 305 477 2400
Fax: +1 305 758 1476
Res: +1 305 477 2400

OPERATION:

Type: Scheduled/charter passenger
Cities Served: Caribbean: PAP **US:** MIA

HISTORY/STRUCTURE:

Founded: 1995
CEO: Ronald Madsen

Start Date: April 1995
Ownership: Privately held

FLEET:

Type	No	Seats	Engines
Boeing 727-200	1	Y169	PW JT8D-7B
(leased from/operated by Falcon Air Express)			

CARIBBEAN

DE HAVILLAND CANADA DHC-6-300 TWIN OTTER VISTALINER

ISLAND AIR

IATA: G5 **ICAO:** none **IATA/ARC:** none **RADIO:** none

CONTACTS:

Mail
PO Box 2433
George Town
Grand Cayman, Cayman Islands

Telephone/FAX
Admin: +1 809 949 0241
Fax: +1 809 949 7044

Internet: none

OPERATION:

Type: Scheduled/charter passenger
Cities Served: CYB GCM LYB

HISTORY/STRUCTURE:

Founded: 1989
CEO: Mervyn Cumber

Start Date: 1989
Ownership: Privately held

FLEET:

Type	No	Seats	Engines
BN-2A-26	1	Y8	LY O-540-E4C5
PA-31 Navajo	1	Y7	LY TIO-540-J2BD
DHC-6-300	1	Y19	PWC PT6A-27

BOEING 727-200 (ADVANCED)

LAKER AIRWAYS (BAHAMAS)

IATA: 7Z   **ICAO:** LBH   **IATA/ARC:** 569   **RADIO:** Laker Bahamas

CONTACTS:

Mail
1170 Lee Wagner Boulevard, Suite 200
Fort Lauderdale, FL 33315

Telephone/FAX
Admin: +1 954 359 0199
Fax: +1 954 359 7698
Res: +1 954 359 0199

Internet: none

OPERATION:

Type: Charter passenger, primarily on behalf of Princess Vacations between the Bahamas and the US

HISTORY/STRUCTURE:

Founded: 1992
Start Date: May 18, 1992
CEO: Sir Freddie Laker
Ownership: Sir Freddie Laker (34%), Sir Jack Hayward (33%), Oscar Wyatt (33%)

FLEET:

Type	No	Seats	Engines
Boeing 727-200 (Advanced)	2	Y175	PW JT8D-15

BOMBARDIER DHC-8-110 DASH 8

LIAT

IATA: LI **ICAO:** LIA **IATA/ARC:** 140 **RADIO:** LIAT

CONTACTS:

Mail
PO Box 819
V C Bird International Airport
Coolidge
Antigua

Telephone/FAX
Admin: +1 809 462 0700
Fax: +1 809 462 3455
Res: +1 809 462 0700

Internet: http://www.turq.com/antigua/liat.html

OPERATION:

Type: Scheduled passenger
Cities Served: Caribbean: ANU AXA BBQ BGI BQU CRU DCF DOM EIS FDF GND MNI NEV POS PTP SJU SKB SLU STI STT STX SVD SXM TAB UNI **South America:** CCS GEO
Code-Share: Airlines of Carriacou, Dominair

HISTORY/STRUCTURE:

Founded: September 20, 1956 (as Leeward Islands Air Transport Services)
Start Date: September 20, 1974
Chairman: Fred Jarvis
Ownership: 11 Caribbean governments (30.8%), BWIA (29.2%), private investors (26.7%), employees (13.3%)

FLEET:

Type	No	Seats	Engines
DHC-6-300	6	Y19	PWC PT6A-27
DHC-8-100	9	Y37	PWC PW120A/121

BEECH 1900C-1 AIRLINER

TURKS & CAICOS AIRWAYS

IATA: QW **ICAO:** TCI **IATA/ARC:** 254 **RADIO:** Turk National

CONTACTS:

Mail
PO Box 114
Providenciales, Turks & Caicos Islands

Telephone/FAX
Admin: +1 809 946 4255
Fax: +1 809 941 5781

Internet: none

OPERATION:

Type: Scheduled passenger
Cities Served: CAP GDT MDS NAS NCA PLS POP XSC

HISTORY/STRUCTURE:

Founded: 1978 (as Turks & Caicos National Airline)
Start Date: August 29, 1992
CEO: C D Moser
Chairman: A V Butterfield Sr
Ownership: Aerocorp

FLEET:

Type	No	Seats	Engines
PA-23 Aztec F	2	Y5	LY IO-540-C4B5
BN-2A	2	Y9	LY O-540-E4C5
Beech 1900C	1	Y19	PWC PT6A-65B
Ordered			
EMB-120 Brasília	2		

DE HAVILLAND CANADA DHC-6-300 TWIN OTTER

WINAIR (Windward Islands Airways International)

IATA: WM **ICAO:** WIA **IATA/ARC:** 295 **RADIO:** Winair

CONTACTS:

Mail
PO Box 2088
Philipsburg
St Maarten, Netherlands Antilles
Internet: none

Telephone/FAX
Admin: +599 5 52568
Fax: +599 5 54229
Res: +599 5 54237/54210/52002

OPERATION:

Type: Scheduled/charter passenger
Cities Served: AXA EIS EUX NEV SAB SBH SKB STT

HISTORY/STRUCTURE:

Founded: August 24, 1961 (as Windward Islands Airways)
Start Date: August 5, 1962
CEO: Eugene Holiday
Chairman: M Ferrier
Ownership: Netherlands Antilles government

FLEET:

Type	No	Seats	Engines
DHC-6-300	3	Y19	PWC PT6A-27

Caribbean Addenda

ABACO AIR PO Box 492, Marsh Harbour, Abaco, Bahamas; +1 242 367 2266, Fax: +1 242 367 3256, Andrew Kelly. Passenger charter. 2 Commander 500, 1 x BN-2 Islander

AEROCHAGO (G3/AHG/198/Aerochago) Aeropuerto Las Americas, Zona de Carga, Santo Domingo, Dominican Republic; +1 809 549 0709, Fax: +1 809 549 0708, Col Pedro Rodriguez. Cargo charter. 1 x Convair 240

AEROTAXI (CNI/Seraer) Calle 27 Numero 102E/Nym, Vedado, Havana, Cuba; +53 732 2515, Fax: +53 733 3082, Benigno Miranda. Passenger charter. 27 x An-2, 1 x DC-3

AIR ANGUILLA PO Box 110, The Valley, Anguilla, Leeward Islands; +1 809 497 2643; Fax: +1 809 497 2982, Restormel Franklin. Passenger charter. 2 x BN-2 Islander

AIR HAITI (HJA/Air Haiti) Champ du Mars, Port-au-Prince, Haiti; +509 23 40 10, Fax: +509 23 89 38. Cargo charter. 2 x Super C-46C

AIR SAINT BARTHÉLÉMY (OJ/BTH/981/Air Barth) St Jean, F-97133 Saint Barthélémy, Guadeloupe; + 590 27 71 90, Fax: +590 27 67 03, Eric Coury. Passenger scheduled/charter using aircraft leased from Air Guadeloupe and Air Saint Martin as needed

AIR SAINT MARTIN (S6/ASM/707/Air Saint Martin) Immeuble Le Lieu No 1 & 11, F-97139 Abymes, Guadeloupe; +590 82 96 63, Fax: +590 91 49 69, Raphael Koury. Passenger scheduled/charter. 7 x Cessna 208B, 2 x Reims/Cessna F406

AIR TAXI Avenida Nuñez de Caceres 2, Los Prados, Apartado Postal 229-9, Santo Domingo, Dominican Republic; +1 809 541 5333; Fax: +1 809 541 8038, Jimmy Butler. Passenger charter. 3 x BN-2 Islander

AIRLINES OF CARRIACOU (C4/COU/484/Air Carriacou) PO Box 221, St George's, Grenada; +1 809 444 3549, Fax: +1 809 444 2898, Curll N Searles. Passenger scheduled (all flights carry only LIAT's code). 3 x BN-2 Islander

APA INTERNATIONAL AIR (7P/APY/917/APA International) PO Box 524039, Miami, FL 33152-4039, USA; +1 305 526 3304, Fax: +1 305 871 4012, Rafael Trujillo. Scheduled passenger under code-share with Pan Am, scheduled/charter cargo using wet-leased equipment from US carriers

AVIA AIR (8R/ARB/Aviair) PO Box 69, Queen Beatrix Airport, Aruba, Netherlands Antilles; +297 834 600, Fax: +297 826 355, Efy Tromp. Passenger scheduled/charter. 3 x Cessna 402B, 2 x Bandeirante

CARDINAL AIRLINES (NN/DCF/855/Cardinal Air) 26 King George V Street, Roseau, Dominica; +1 809 449 8922, Fax: +1 809 449 8923, John Tomlinson. Passenger scheduled. 2 x Beech C99

CARIB AVIATION (DEL) PO Box 318, St John's, Antigua; +1 809 462 3452, Fax: +1 809 462 3125, Frank Delisle. Charter passenger. 3 x P.68C, 3 x BN-2 Islander, 1 x Queen Air

CARIBAIR (B9/379) PO Box 37942, International Airport Station, San Juan, PR 00937; +1 787 791 1240, Fax: +1 787 791 0036, Alfredo Ramos. Passenger scheduled. 2 x BN-2 Islander

CARIBAIR Avenida Luperon, Aeropuerto Internacional de Herrera, Santo Domingo, Dominican Republic; +1 809 567 2394, Fax: +1 809 567 7033, Rafael Rosado Fermin. Passenger charter. 1 x Bell 206B, 1 x PA-32 Lance, 2 x PA-34 Seneca, 2 x PA-31 Navajo, 1 x BN-2 Islander

EAGLE AIR SERVICES PO Box 838, Castries, St Lucia; +1 758 452 1900, Fax: +1 758 452 9683, Ewart Hinkson. Passenger charter. 2 x BN-2 Islander

FLY BVI PO Box 3347, Road Town, British Virgin Islands; 1 800 435 9284 (US), +1 809 495 1747, Fax: +1 809 495 1973, Nikki Abrams. Passenger charter. 3 x PA-23 Aztec, 1 x BN-2 Islander, 1 x Cessna 404, 2 x Cessna 172

HAITI AIR FREIGHT (9F/HLS/671) PO Box 590626, Miami, FL 33159, USA; +1 305 871 5814, Fax: +1 305 871 1879, Smith Augustin. Cargo charter. 2 x Convair 440, 1 x DC-6B

HELENAIR (2Y/HCL) PO Box 253, Castries, St Lucia; +1 758 452 7196; Fax: +1 758 451 7360, Joaquin A Willie. Passenger scheduled/charter. 2 x PA-31 Navajo, 3 x BN-2 Islander, 1 x Beech 99A

INTERISLAND AIRWAYS PO Box 191, Providenciales, Turk & Caicos Islands; +1 809 941 5481, Fax: +1 809 941 5481, Lyndon R Gardiner. Passenger charter. 4 x PA-23 Aztec, 1 x Cessna 421

MUSTIQUE AIRWAYS (Q4/MAW/Mustique) PO Box 1232, Kingstown, St Vincent; +1 809 458 4380, Fax: +1 809 456 4586, Jonathan Palmer. Passenger scheduled. 2 x Baron 58, 1 x Cessna 402C, 5 x BN-2 Islander

NEVIS EXPRESS Airport, Newcastle, Nevis, St Kitts & Nevis; +1 809 469 9755, Fax: +1 809 469 9751, Allen Haddadi. Passenger charter. 2 x BN-2 Islander

REGION AIR (RL/Spice) Point Salines Intl Airport, St George's, Grenada; +1 809 444 1117; Fax: +1 809 444 1114. Scheduled/charter passenger. 1 x Cessna 402B, 1 x BN-2 Islander

SAPSA (SERVICIOS AEREOS PROFESIONALES) Avenida Luperon, Aeropuerto Domestico de Herrera, Santo Domingo, Dominican Republic; +1 809 540 4570; Fax: +1 809 540 4667, José Miguel Patin Hernandez. Passenger charter. 2 x BN-2 Islander, 3 x DHC-6-100/200/300 Twin Otter, 2 x Shorts 360

SVG AIR PO Box 39, Kingstown, St Vincent; +1 809 456 5610, Fax: +1 809 458 4697, Paul Gravel. Passenger charter. 1 x Commander 500S, 1 x BN-2 Islander

TAINO AIR PO Box F4006, Freeport Intl Airport, Bahamas; +1 242 352 8885, Fax: +1 242 352 5175, John Doherty. Passenger charter. 1 x Commander 500, 2 x Cessna 402C

TCI SKYKING (RU) PO Box 398, Turks & Caicos Islands; +1 809 941 3292, Fax: +1 809 941 5127, Harold Chares. Passenger scheduled/charter. 2 x PA-23 Aztec, 3 x Cessna 402B/C, 1 x Cessna 404, 1 x Shorts 360

TRADO (TAD/Trans Dominican) Aeropuerto Intl Las Americas, Santo Domingo, Dominican Republic; +1 809 549 0591, Fax: +1 809 542 0169, Amin Canaan. Passenger/cargo charter. 1 x Convair 440, 1 DC-6B (F), 1 x DC-7C (F)

TRANS ISLAND AIR (TRD/Trans Island) South Ramp, Grantley Adams International Airport, Christ Church, Barbados; +1 246 428 1654, Fax: +1 246 428 0916, Herbert Yearwood. Passenger charter. 2 x Cessna 402C, 3 x BN-2 Islander, 1 x Bandeirante

NOTES:

CITY & AIRPORT DECODE

A

ABE	Allentown, PA
ABI	Abilene, TX
ABQ	Albuquerque, NM
ABR	Aberdeen, SD
ABY	Albany, GA
ACA	Acapulco, México
ACK	Nantucket, MA
ACT	Waco, TX
ACV	Eureka/Arcata, CA
ACY	Atlantic City Intl, NJ
ADK	Adak Island, AK
ADQ	Kodiak, AK
ADZ	San Andres, Colombia
AED	Aleneva, AK
AEX	Alexandria, LA
AGM	Tasilaq, Greenland
AGS	Augusta, GA
AGT	Ciudad del Este, Brazil
AGU	Aguascalientes, México
AHN	Athens, GA
AIA	Alliance, NE
AKI	Akiak, AK
AKK	Akhiok, AK
AKL	Auckland, New Zealand
AKN	King Salmon, AK
AKV	Akulivik, QC
ALB	Albany, NY
ALM	Alamogordo, NM
ALO	Waterloo, IA
ALS	Alamosa, CO
ALW	Walla Walla, WA
ALZ	Alitak, AK
AMA	Amarillo, TX
AMS	Amsterdam, Netherlands
ANC	Anchorage, AK
ANI	Aniak, AK
ANU	Antigua, West Indies
AOO	Altoona, PA
AOS	Amook, AK
APF	Naples, FL
ARN	Stockholm-Arlanda, Sweden
ART	Watertown, NY
ASD	Andros Town, Bahamas
ASE	Aspen, CO
ASU	Asunción, Paraguay
ATC	Arthur's Town, Bahamas
ATH	Athens, Greece
ATL	Atlanta, GA
ATT	Atmautluak, AK
ATW	Appleton, WI
ATY	Watertown, SD
AUA	Aruba, Aruba
AUG	Augusta, ME
AUS	Austin, TX
AVI	Ciego de Avila, Cuba
AVL	Asheville, NC
AVP	Wilkes-Barre/Scranton, PA
AXA	Anguilla, Leeward Is
AXP	Spring Point, Bahamas
AZO	Kalamazoo, MI

B

BAQ	Barranquilla, Colombia
BBQ	Barbuda, West Indies
BBR	Basse Terre, French Antilles
BCA	Baracoa, Cuba
BCN	Barcelona, Spain
BDA	Bermuda-Kindley Field
BDL	Bradley Intl, CT
BDR	Bridgeport, CT
BEH	Benton Harbor, MI
BET	Bethel, AK
BFD	Bradford, PA
BFF	Scottsbluff, NE
BFI	Seattle-Boeing Field, WA
BFL	Bakersfield, CA
BFS	Belfast, UK
BGI	Barbados, Barbados
BGM	Binghamton, NY
BGR	Bangor, ME
BHB	Bar Harbor, ME
BHM	Birmingham, AL
BHX	Birmingham, UK
BIL	Billings, MT
BIS	Bismarck, ND
BJI	Bemidji, MN
BJX	León/Guanajuato, México
BKK	Bangkok, Thailand
BKW	Beckley, WV
BKX	Brookings, SD
BLF	Bluefield, WV
BLI	Bellingham, WA
BMG	Bloomington, IN
BMI	Bloomington, IL
BNA	Nashville, TN
BOD	Bordeaux, France
BOG	Bogotá, Colombia
BOI	Boise, ID
BOM	Mumbai, India
BON	Bonaire, Netherlands Antilles
BOS	Boston, MA
BPT	Beaumont/Pt Arthur, TX
BQK	Glynco Jetport, GA
BQN	Aguadilla, PR
BQU	Port Elizabeth, Windward Islands
BRD	Brainerd, MN
BRL	Burlington, IA
BRO	Brownsville, TX
BRU	Brussels, Belgium
BRW	Barrow, AK
BSL	Basle-Mulhouse, France
BTM	Butte, MT
BTR	Baton Rouge, LA
BTV	Burlington, VT
BUD	Budapest, Hungary
BUF	Buffalo, NY
BUR	Burbank, CA
BWD	Brownwood, TX
BWI	Baltimore, MD
BYM	Bayamo, Cuba
BZE	Belize City, Belize
BZN	Bozeman, MT

C

CAE	Columbia, SC
CAI	Cairo, Egypt
CAK	Akron/Canton, OH
CAP	Cap-Haïtien, Haiti
CAY	Cayenne, French Guiana
CBE	Cumberland, MD
CCC	Cayo Coco, Cuba
CCS	Caracas, Venezuela
CDB	Cold Bay, AK
CDC	Cedar City, UT
CDG	Paris-Charles de Gaulle, France
CDR	Chadron, NE
CDV	Cordova, AK
CEC	Crescent City, CA
CEN	Ciudad Obregon, México
CEZ	Cortez, CO
CGI	Cape Girardeau, MO
CGN	Cologne/Bonn, Germany
CGX	Meigs Field, IL
CHA	Chattanooga, TN
CHO	Charlottesville, VA
CHS	Charleston, SC
CIA	Rome-Ciampino, Italy
CIC	Chico, CA
CID	Cedar Rapids, IA
CIU	Chippewa County, MI
CIW	Canouan Island, Windward Islands
CJS	Ciudad Juárez, México
CKB	Clarksburg, WV
CLD	Carlsbad, CA

CLE	Cleveland, OH
CLL	College Station, TX
CLM	Port Angeles, WA
CLO	Cali, Colombia
CLQ	Colima, México
CLT	Charlotte, NC
CME	Ciudad del Carmen, México
CMH	Columbus, OH
CMI	Champaign, IL
CMW	Camaguey, Cuba
CMX	Hancock, MI
CNF	Belo Horizonte, Brazil
CNM	Carlsbad, NM
CNP	Nerlerit Inaat, Greenland
CNW	Waco-Connolly, TX
COD	Cody, WY
COS	Colorado Springs, CO
COU	Columbia, MO
CPE	Campeche, México
CPH	Copenhagen, Denmark
CPR	Casper, WY
CRI	Crooked Island, Bahamas
CRP	Corpus Christi, TX
CRU	Carriacou, Windward Islands
CRW	Charleston, WV
CSG	Columbus, GA
CTG	Cartegena, Colombia
CTM	Chetumal, México
CTS	Sapporo-Chitose, Japan
CUL	Culiacán, México
CUN	Cancún, México
CUR	Curaçao, Netherlands Antilles
CUU	Chihuahua, México
CVG	Cincinnati, OH
CVJ	Cuernavaca, México
CVM	Ciudad Victoria, México
CVN	Clovis, NM
CWA	Central Wisconsin, WI
CWF	Lake Charles, LA
CWL	Cardiff, UK
CXH	Coal Harbour, BC
CYB	Cayman Brac, West Indies
CYF	Chefornak, AK
CYS	Cheyenne, WY
CZA	Chichen Itza, México
CZM	Cozumel, México

D

DAB	Daytona Beach, FL
DAL	Love Field, Dallas, TX
DAY	Dayton, OH
DBQ	Dubuque, IA
DCA	Washington-National, DC
DCF	Can Field, West Indies
DDC	Dodge City, KS
DEC	Decatur, IL
DEL	Delhi, India
DEN	Denver, CO
DFW	Dallas/Fort Worth, TX
DGO	Durango, México
DHN	Dothan, AL
DIK	Dickinson, ND
DLG	Dillingham, AK
DLH	Duluth, MN
DOM	Dominica, West Indies
DPS	Denpasar, Bali, Indonesia
DRO	Durango, CO
DRT	Del Rio, TX
DSD	La Desirade, French Antilles
DSM	Des Moines, IA
DTW	Detroit-Metro Wayne County, MI
DUB	Dublin, Ireland
DUJ	Dubois, PA
DUS	Düsseldorf, Germany
DUT	Dutch Harbor, AK
DVL	Devils Lake, ND
DXB	Dubai, UAE

E

EAT	Wenatchee, WA
EAU	Eau Claire, WI
EDI	Edinburgh, UK
EEK	Eek, AK
EEN	Keene, NH
EFD	Ellington Field, TX
EGE	Vail, CO
EGX	Egegik, AK
EIS	Tortola, British Virgin Islands
EKO	Elko, NV
ELD	El Dorado, AR
ELH	North Eleuthera, Bahamas
ELM	Elmira/Corning, NY
ELP	El Paso, TX
EMA	East Midlands, UK
ENA	Kenai, AK
ERI	Erie, PA
ESC	Escanaba, MI
EUG	Eugene, OR
EUX	St Eustatius, Netherlands Antilles
EVV	Evansville, IN
EWR	Newark Intl, NJ
EXT	Exeter, UK
EYW	Key West, FL
EZE	Buenos Aires-Pistarini, Argentina

F

FAI	Fairbanks, AK
FAR	Fargo, ND
FAT	Fresno, CA
FAY	Fayetteville, NC
FCA	Kalispell, MT
FCO	Rome-Fiumicino, Italy
FDF	Fort-de-France, Martinique
FHU	Fort Huachuca/Sierra Vista, AZ
FKL	Franklin, PA
FLG	Flagstaff, AZ
FLL	Fort Lauderdale, FL
FLO	Florence, SC
FMN	Farmington, NM
FNL	Fort Collins/Loveland, CO
FNT	Flint, MI
FOD	Fort Dodge, IA
FOE	Topeka Forbes AFB, KS
FPO	Freeport, Bahamas
FRA	Frankfurt, Germany
FRM	Fairmont, MN
FRS	Flores, Guatemala
FSD	Sioux Falls, SD
FSM	Fort Smith, AR
FSP	St Pierre & Miquelon
FUK	Fukuoka, Japan
FWA	Fort Wayne, IN
FYV	Fayetteville, AR

G

GAL	Galena, AK
GAO	Guantanamo, Cuba
GBD	Great Bend, KS
GBJ	Marie Galante, French Antilles
GCC	Gillette, WY
GCK	Garden City, KS
GCM	Grand Cayman Island, West Indies
GCN	Grand Canyon, AZ
GDL	Guadalajara, México
GDT	Grand Turk, Turks & Caicos Is
GDV	Glendive, MT
GDX	Magadan, Russia
GEG	Spokane, WA
GEO	Georgetown, Guyana
GER	Nueva Gerona, Cuba
GFK	Grand Forks, ND
GGG	Longview, TX
GGT	George Town, Bahamas
GGW	Glasgow, MT
GHB	Governors Harbour, Bahamas
GIG	Rio de Janeiro-Intl, Brazil
GJT	Grand Junction, CO

GLA	Glasgow, UK
GLH	Greenville, MS
GND	Grenada, Windward Islands
GNU	Goodnews Bay, AK
GNV	Gainesville, FL
GOH	Nuuk, Greenland
GON	New London/Groton, CT
GPT	Gulfport/Biloxi, MS
GPZ	Grand Rapids, MN
GRB	Green Bay, WI
GRI	Grand Island, NE
GRR	Grand Rapids, MI
GRU	São Paulo-Guarulhos, Brazil
GSO	Greensboro/High Pt/Winston-Salem, NC
GSP	Greenville/Spartanburg, SC
GTF	Great Falls, MT
GTR	Golden Triangle Regional, Columbus, MS
GUA	Guatemala City, Guatemala
GUB	Guerrero Negro, México
GUC	Gunnison, CO
GUM	Guam, Guam
GUP	Gallup, NM
GVA	Geneva, Switzerland
GYE	Guayaquil, Ecuador
GYM	Guaymas, México

H

HAV	Havana, Cuba
HDN	Steamboat Springs-Hayden, CO
HEL	Helsinki, Finland
HGR	Hagerstown, MD
HHH	Hilton Head Island, SC
HIB	Hibbing/Chisholm, MN
HII	Lake Havasu City, AZ
HKG	Hong Kong, China
HKY	Hickory, NC
HLN	Helena, MT
HMO	Hermosillo, México
HNL	Honolulu, HI
HNM	Hana, Maui, HI
HOB	Hobbs, NM
HOG	Holguín, Cuba
HOM	Homer, AK
HON	Huron, SD
HOT	Hot Springs, AR
HOU	Houston, TX
HPB	Hooper Bay, AK
HPN	Westchester County, NY
HRL	Harlingen, TX
HSV	Huntsville/Decatur, AL
HTS	Huntington, WV
HUF	Terre Haute, IN
HUX	Huatulco, México
HVN	New Haven, CT
HVR	Havre, MT
HYA	Hyannis, MA
HYS	Hays, KS

I

IAD	Washington-Dulles Intl, DC
IAH	Houston-Intercontinental, TX
ICT	Wichita, KS
IDA	Idaho Falls, ID
IFP	Bullhead City, AZ
IGA	Inagua, Bahamas
IGG	Igiugig, AK
IGM	Kingman, AZ
ILE	Killeen, TX
ILI	Iliamna, AK
ILM	Wilmington, NC
ILN	Wilmington, OH
IMT	Iron Mountain, MI
IND	Indianapolis, IN
INL	International Falls, MN
INT	Winston-Salem/Smith-Reynolds, NC
IPL	El Centro/Imperial, CA
IPT	Williamsport, PA
IQT	Iquitos, Perú
ISN	Williston, ND
ISO	Kinston, NC
ISP	Long Island MacArthur, NY
IST	Istanbul, Turkey
ITH	Ithaca, NY
ITO	Hilo, HI
IYK	Inyokern, CA

J

JAC	Jackson Hole, WY
JAN	Jackson, MS
JAV	Ilulissat, Greenland
JAX	Jacksonville, FL
JBR	Jonesboro, AR
JCH	Qasigiannguit, Greenland
JEG	Aasiaat, Greenland
JFK	New York-Kennedy Intl, NY
JFR	Paamiut, Greenland
JGO	Qeqertarsuaq, Greenland
JGR	Gronnedal Heliport, Greenland
JHM	Kapalua, Maui, HI
JHS	Sisimiut, Greenland
JHW	Jamestown, NY
JJU	Qaqortoq, Greenland
JLN	Joplin, MOJMS Jamestown, ND
JNN	Nanortalik, Greenland
JNS	Narsaq, Greenland
JNU	Juneau, AK
JON	Johnstone Island, US
JST	Johnstown, PA
JSU	Maniitsoq, Greenland
JUV	Upernavik, Greenland

K

KCG	Fisheries, AK
KCL	Chignik, AK
KCQ	Chignik, AK
KEF	Keflavík, Iceland
KEK	Ekwok, AK
KGK	Koliganek, AK
KHH	Kaohsiung, Taiwan
KHV	Khabarovsk, Russia
KIB	Ivanof Bay, AK
KIF	Kingfisher Lake, ON
KIN	Kingston, Jamaica
KIX	Osaka-Kansai, Japan
KKB	Kitoi Bay, AK
KKH	Kongiganak, AK
KKI	Akiachak, AK
KLL	Levelock, AK
KLN	Larsen Bay, AK
KMY	Moser Bay, AK
KNV	Knights Inlet, BC
KNW	New Stuyahok, AK
KOA	Kona, Hawaii, HI
KOY	Olga Bay, AK
KOZ	Ouzinkie, AK
KPN	Kipnuk, AK
KPR	Port Williams, AK
KPV	Perryville, AK
KPY	Port Bailey, AK
KSA	Kosrae, Caroline Is
KSM	Saint Marys, AK
KTN	Ketchikan, AK
KTP	Tinson, Jamaica
KUK	Kasigluk, AK
KUL	Kuala Lumpur, Malyasia
KUS	Kulusuk, Greenland
KVC	King Cove, AK
KVL	Kivalina, AK
KWA	Kwajalein, Marshall Is
KWK	Kwigillngok, AK
KWN	Quinhagak, AK
KWP	West Point, AK
KWT	Kwethluk, AK
KYK	Karluk, AK
KZB	Zachar Bay, AK

L

LAF	Lafayette, IN
LAM	Los Alamos, NM
LAN	Lansing, MI

LAP	La Paz, México
LAR	Laramie, WY
LAS	Las Vegas, NV
LAW	Lawton, OK
LAX	Los Angeles, CA
LBA	Leeds/Bradford, UK
LBB	Lubbock, TX
LBE	Latrobe, PA
LBF	North Platte, NE
LBL	Liberal, KS
LCH	Lake Charles, LA
LCK	Columbus (Rickenbacker), OH
LEB	Lebanon, NH
LEX	Lexington, KY
LFT	Lafayette, LA
LGA	New York-LaGuardia, NY
LGB	Long Beach, CA
LGI	Deadmans Cay, Long Is, Bahamas
LGW	London-Gatwick, UK
LHR	London-Heathrow, UK
LIH	Lihue, Kauai, HI
LIM	Lima, Perú
LIR	Liberia, Costa Rica
LIS	Lisbon, Portugal
LIT	Little Rock, AR
LMM	Los Mochis, México
LMT	Klamath Falls, OR
LNK	Lincoln, NE
LNS	Lancaster, PA
LNY	Lanai City, Lanai, HI
LOV	Monclova, México
LPA	Las Palmas, Gran Canaria, Spain
LPB	La Paz, Bolivia
LRD	Laredo, TX
LRM	Casa de Campo, Dominican Republic
LRU	Las Cruces, NM
LSE	La Crosse, WI
LSS	Terre-de-Haut, Guadeloupe
LTO	Loreto, México
LWB	Greenbrier, WV
LWS	Lewiston, ID
LWT	Lewistown, MT
LYH	Lynchburg, VA
LZC	Lazaro Gardenas, México

M

MAD	Madrid, Spain
MAF	Midland/Odessa, TX
MAJ	Majuro, Marshall Is
MAM	Matamoros, México
MAN	Manchester, UK
MAO	Manaus, Brazil
MAR	Maracaibo, Venezuela
MBJ	Montego Bay, Jamaica
MBL	Mainstee, MI
MBS	Saginaw, MI
MCE	Merced, CA
MCG	McGrath, AK
MCI	Kansas City, MO
MCK	McCook, NE
MCN	Macon, GA
MCO	Orlando Intl, FL
MCW	Mason City, IA
MDE	Medellín, Colombia
MDS	Middle Caicos, Turks & Caicos Is
MDT	Harrisburg Intl, PA
MDW	Midway, IL
MEI	Meridian, MS
MEL	Melbourne, Australia
MEM	Memphis, TN
MEX	Mexico City, México
MFE	McAllen, TX
MFR	Medford, OR
MGA	Managua, Nicaragua
MGM	Montgomery, AL
MGW	Morgantown, WV
MHH	Marsh Harbour, Bahamas
MHK	Manhattan, KS
MHR	Sacramento-Mather, CA
MHT	Manchester, NH
MIA	Miami, FL
MID	Mérida, México
MKC	Kansas City, MO
MKE	Milwaukee, WI
MKG	Muskegon, MI
MKK	Molokai/Hoolehua, HI
MKL	Jackson, TN
MLB	Melbourne, FL
MLI	Moline, IL
MLL	Marshall, AK
MLM	Morelia, México
MLS	Miles City, MT
MLU	Monroe, LA
MNI	Montserrat, Montserrat
MNL	Manila, Philippines
MOA	Moa, Cuba
MOB	Mobile, AL
MOD	Modesto, CA
MOT	Minot, ND
MPB	Miami-Watson Island, FL
MQT	Marquette, MI
MRS	Marseille, France
MRY	Monterey, CA
MSA	Muskrat Dam, ON
MSL	Muscle Shoals, AL
MSN	Madison, WI
MSO	Missoula, MT
MSP	Minneapolis/St Paul, MN
MSS	Massena, NY
MSY	New Orleans, LA
MTH	Marathon, FL
MTJ	Montrose, CO
MTO	Mattoon, IL
MTT	Minatitlán, México
MTY	Monterrey, México
MUC	Munich, Germany
MVD	Montevideo, Uruguay
MVN	Mt Vernon, IL
MVY	Martha's Vineyard, MA
MWA	Marion, IL
MWH	Moses Lake, WA
MXL	Mexicali, México
MXP	Milan-Malpensa, Italy
MYG	Mayaguana, Bahamas
MYR	Myrtle Beach, SC
MYU	Mekoryuk, AK
MZO	Manzanillo, Cuba
MZT	Mazatlán, México

N

NAN	Nadi, Fiji
NAQ	Qaanaaq, Greenland
NAS	Nassau, Bahamas
NCA	North Caicos, Turks & Caicos Is
NCE	Nice, France
NCL	Newcastle, UK
NEG	Negril, Jamaica
NEV	Nevis, Leeward Islands
NGO	Nagoya, Japan
NLD	Nuevo Laredo, México
NLG	Nelson Lagoon, AK
NME	Nightmute, AK
NRT	Tokyo-Narita, Japan
NSB	Bimini North, Bahamas
NTE	Nantes, France
NUP	Nunapitchuk, AK

O

OAJ	Jacksonville, NC
OAK	Oakland, CA
OAX	Oaxaca, México
OBY	Ittoqqortoormiit, Greenland
OFK	Norfolk, NE
OGG	Kahului, Maui, HI
OGS	Ogdensburg, NY
OKC	Oklahoma City, OK
OLF	Wolf Point, MT
OLH	Old Harbor, AK
OMA	Omaha, NE
OME	Nome, AK
ONT	Ontario, CA
OOK	Toksook Bay, AK
ORD	Chicago-O'Hare International, IL

ORF	Norfolk/Virginia Beach/Williamsburg, VA
ORH	Worcester, MA
ORI	Port Lions, AK
ORY	Paris-Orly, France
OSH	Oshkosh, WI
OTH	North Bend, OR
OTM	Ottumwa, IA
OTZ	Kotzebue, AK
OWB	Owensboro, KY
OXR	Oxnard, CA

P

PAH	Paducah, KY
PAP	Port-au-Prince, Haiti
PAZ	Poza Rica, México
PBC	Puebla, México
PBI	West Palm Beach, FL
PCM	Playa del Carmen, México
PDS	Piedras Negras, México
PDT	Pendleton, OR
PDX	Portland, OR
PEK	Beijing, China
PEN	Penang, Malaysia
PFN	Panama City, FL
PGA	Page, AZ
PGV	Greenville, NC
PHF	Newport News/Wmbg, VA
PHL	Philadelphia, PA
PHX	Phoenix, AZ
PIA	Peoria, IL
PIB	Laurel Pine Belt Regional Airport, MS
PID	Nassau Paradise Island, Bahamas
PIE	St Petersburg Intl, FL
PIH	Pocatello, ID
PIK	Prestwick, UK
PIP	Pilot Point, AK
PIR	Pierre, SD
PIT	Pittsburgh, PA
PKA	Napaskiak, AK
PKB	Parkersburg, WV
PKC	Petropavlovsk-Kamchatsky, Russia
PLB	Plattsburgh, NY
PLN	Pellston, MI
PLS	Providenciales, Turks & Caicos Is
PMD	Palmdale/Lancaster, CA
PML	Port Moller, AK
PNC	Ponca City, OK
PNI	Pohnpei, Caroline Is
PNS	Pensacola, FL
POP	Puerto Plata, Dominican Rep
POS	Port of Spain, Trinidad & Tobago
POT	Port Antonio, Jamaica
POU	Poughkeepsie, NY
PPE	Puerto Penasco, México
PQI	Presque Isle, ME
PQM	Palenque, México
PRC	Prescott, AZ
PRG	Prague, Czech Republic
PSC	Pasco, WA
PSE	Ponce, PR
PSG	Petersburg, AK
PSM	Portsmouth, NH
PSP	Palm Springs, CA
PSR	Pescara, Italy
PTH	Port Heiden, AK
PTP	Pointe-à-Pitre, Guadeloupe
PTU	Platinum, AK
PTY	Panama City, Panamá
PUB	Pueblo, CO
PUW	Pullman, WA
PVD	Providence, RI
PVR	Puerto Vallarta, México
PWM	Portland, ME
PXM	Puerto Escondido, México

Q

QCC	Bella Coola, BC
QRO	Queretaro, México

R

RAP	Rapid City, SD
RDB	Red Dog, AK
RDD	Redding, CA
RDG	Reading, PA
RDM	Redmond, OR
RDU	Raleigh/Durham, NC
REK	Reykjavík, Iceland
REX	Reynosa, México
RFD	Rockford, IL
RHI	Rhinelander, WI
RIC	Richmond/Wmbg, VA
RIW	Riverton, WY
RKD	Rockland, ME
RKS	Rock Springs, WY
RNO	Reno, NV
ROA	Roanoke, VA
ROC	Rochester, NY
ROR	Koror, Palau Is
ROW	Roswell, NM
RSD	Rock Sound, Bahamas
RSH	Russian Mission, AK
RST	Rochester, MN
RSW	Southwest Florida Regional
RUH	Riyadh, Saudi Arabia
RUI	Ruidoso, NM
RUT	Rutland, VT
RWI	Rocky Mount/Wilson, NC

S

SAB	Saba, Netherlands Antilles
SAF	Santa Fe, NM
SAL	San Salvador, El Salvador
SAN	San Diego, CA
SAP	San Pedro Sula, Honduras
SAQ	San Andros, Bahamas
SAT	San Antonio, TX
SAV	Savannah, GA
SBA	Santa Barbara, CA
SBH	St Barthélémy, French Antilles
SBN	South Bend, IN
SBP	San Luis Obispo, CA
SBS	Steamboat Springs, CO
SBY	Salisbury, MD
SCC	Prudhoe Bay/Deadhorse, AK
SCE	State College, PA
SCL	Santiago, Chile
SCM	Scammon Bay, AK
SCQ	Santiago de Compostela, Spain
SCU	Santiago, Cuba
SCX	Salina Cruz, México
SDF	Louisville, KY
SDJ	Sendai, Japan
SDP	Sand Point, AK
SDQ	Santo Domingo, Dominican Rep
SDY	Sidney, MT
SEA	Seattle/Tacoma, WA
SEL	Seoul, Republic of Korea
SFB	Sanford, FL
SFG	St Martin, French Antilles
SFJ	Kangerlussuaq, Greenland
SFO	San Francisco, CA
SGF	Springfield, MO
SGU	Saint George, UT
SHA	Shanghai, China
SHD	Shenandoah Valley, VA
SHV	Shreveport, LA
SIN	Singapore
SIT	Sitka, AK
SJC	San Jose, CA
SJD	San José del Cabo/Los Cabos, México
SJO	San José, Costa Rica
SJT	San Angelo, TX
SJU	San Juan, PR
SKB	St Kitts, Leeward Islands
SLC	Salt Lake City, UT
SLK	Saranac Lake, NY
SLN	Salina, KS
SLP	San Luis Potosí, México
SLU	St Lucia, West Indies

SLW	Saltillo, México
SMF	Sacramento Metropolitan, CA
SML	Stella Maris, Long Islands, Bahamas
SMX	Santa Maria, CA
SNA	Orange County, CA
SNN	Shannon, Ireland
SNP	St Paul Island, AK
SOP	Pinehurst, NC
SOW	Show Low, AZ
SPI	Springfield, IL
SPK	Sapporo, Japan
SPN	Saipan, Mariana Is
SPS	Wichita Falls, TX
SPW	Spencer, IA
SQI	Sterling/Rock Falls, IL
SRQ	Sarasota/Bradenton, FL
SRZ	Santa Cruz, Bolivia
STC	St Cloud, MN
STG	St George Island, AK
STI	Santiago, Dominican Rep
STL	St Louis, MO
STN	London-Stansted, UK
STR	Stuttgart, Germany
STS	Santa Rosa, CA
STT	St Thomas, VI
STX	St Croix, VI
SUF	Lamezia Terme, Italy
SUN	Sun Valley, ID
SUR	Summer Beaver, ON
SUX	Sioux City, IA
SVC	Silver City, NM
SVD	Saint Vincent
SVO	Moscow-Sheremetyevo
SWF	Newburgh, NY
SXB	Strasbourg, France
SXF	Berlin-Schönefeld, Germany
SXM	St Maarten, Netherlands Antilles
SYB	Seal Bay, AK
SYD	Sydney, Australia
SYR	Syracuse, NY

T

TAB	Tobago, Trinidad & Tobago
TAM	Tampico, México
TAP	Tapachula, México
TBI	The Bight, Bahamas
TBN	Fort Leonard Wood, MO
TCB	Treasure Cay, Bahamas
TCL	Tuscaloosa, AL
TEX	Telluride, CO
TGU	Tegucigalpa, Honduras
TGZ	Tuxtla Gutierrez, México
THU	Pituffik (Thule), Greenland
TIJ	Tijuana, México
TKK	Truk (Chuuk), Caroline Is
TLC	Toluca, México
TLH	Tallahassee, FL
TLS	Toulouse, France
TLT	Tuluksak, AK
TLV	Tel Aviv, Israel
TNK	Tununak, AK
TOG	Togiak, AK
TOL	Toledo, OH
TPA	Tampa/St Petersburg, FL
TPE	Taipei, Taiwan
TPQ	Tepic, México
TRC	Torreón, México
TRI	Tri-City Airport, TN
TTN	Trenton, NJ
TUL	Tulsa, OK
TUP	Tupelo, MS
TUS	Tucson, AZ
TVC	Traverse City, MI
TVF	Thief River Falls, MN
TWA	Twin Hills, AK
TWF	Twin Falls, ID
TXK	Texarkana, AR
TXL	Berlin-Tegel, Germany
TYR	Tyler, TX
TYS	Knoxville, TN

U

UAK	Narsarsuaq, Greenland
UCA	Utica, NY
UGB	Ugashik Bay, AK
UGI	Uganik, AK
UIN	Quincy, IL
UIO	Quito, Ecuador
UMD	Uummannaq, Greenland
UNI	Union Island, Windward Islands
UNK	Unalakleet, AK
UPN	Urapan, México
UTO	Utopia Creek, AK
UUS	Yuzhno-Sakhalinsk, Russia
UVF	Hewanorra, West Indies

V

VAK	Chevak, AK
VCE	Venice, Italy
VCP	São Paulo-Viracopas, Brazil
VCT	Victoria, TX
VDZ	Valdez, AK
VEL	Vernal, UT
VER	Veracruz, México
VIE	Vienna, Austria
VIS	Visalia, CA
VIT	Vitoria, Spain
VLD	Valdosta, GA
VPS	Ft Walton Beach, FL
VRA	Varadero, Cuba
VSA	Villahermosa, México
VTU	Las Tunas, Cuba
VVI	Santa Cruz-Viru Viru, Bolivia
VVO	Vladivostok, Russia

W

WAW	Warsaw, Poland
WDG	Enid, AK
WMH	Mountain Home, AR
WNA	Napakiak, AK
WNN	Wunnummin Lake, ON
WRG	Wrangell, AK
WRL	Worland, WY
WTL	Tuntutuliak, AK
WWT	Newtok, AK
WYS	West Yellowstone, MT

X

XBE	Bearskin Lake, ON
XGR	Kangiqsualujjuaq, QC
XKS	Kasabonika, ON
XLB	Lac Brochet, MB
XPK	Pukatawagan, MB
XSC	South Caicos, Turks & Caicos Is
XSI	South Indian Lake, MB
XTL	Tadoule Lake, MB

Y

YAA	Anahim Lake, BC
YAC	Cat Lake, ON
YAG	Fort Frances, ON
YAJ	Lyall Harbour, BC
YAK	Yakutat, AK
YAM	Sault Sainte Marie, ON
YAP	Yap, Caroline Is
YAQ	Maple Bay, BC
YAT	Attawapiskat, ON
YAV	Miner's Bay, BC
YAX	Angling Lake, ON
YAY	St Anthony, NF
YBB	Townsite, NWT
YBC	Baie Comeau, QC
YBE	Uranium City, SK
YBG	Bagotville, QC
YBI	Black Tickle, NF
YBK	Baker Lake, NWT
YBL	Campbell River, BC
YBQ	Telegraph Harbour, BC
YBR	Brandon, MB
YBS	Opapamiska Lake/Musselwhite, ON
YBT	Brochet, MB
YBV	Berens River, MB

YBW	Bedwell Harbor, BC
YBX	Blanc Sablon, QC
YCB	Cambridge Bay, NWT
YCD	Nanaimo, BC
YCG	Castlegar, BC
YCH	Chatham, NB
YCK	Colville Lake, NWT
YCL	Charlo, NB
YCN	Cochrane, ON
YCO	Coppermine, NWT
YCQ	Chetwynd, BC
YCR	Cross Lake, MB
YCS	Chesterfield Inlet, NWT
YCY	Clyde River, NWT
YDA	Dawson City, YT
YDF	Deer Lake, NF
YDI	Davis Inlet, NF
YDL	Dease Lake, BC
YDN	Dauphin, MB
YDP	Nain, NF
YDQ	Dawson Creek, BC
YEG	Edmonton Intl, AB
YEK	Arviat, NWT
YER	Fort Severn, ON
YEV	Inuvik, NWT
YFA	Fort Albany, ON
YFB	Iqaluit, NWT
YFC	Fredericton, NB
YFH	Fort Hope, ON
YFO	Flin Flon, MB
YFR	Fort Resolution, NWT
YFS	Fort Simpson, NWT
YFX	Fox Harbour, NF
YGG	Ganges Harbor, BC
YGH	Fort Good Hope, NWT
YGK	Kingston, ON
YGL	La Grande, QC
YGO	Gods Narrows, MB
YGP	Gaspe, QC
YGQ	Geraldton, ON
YGR	Iles de la Madeleine, QC
YGT	Igloolik, NWT
YGV	Havre Saint Pierre, QC
YGW	Kuujjuarapik, QC
YGX	Gillam, MB
YGZ	Grise Fiord, NWT
YHA	Port Hope Simpson, NF
YHD	Dryden, ON
YHF	Hearst, ON
YHG	Charlottetown, NF
YHI	Holman Island, NWT
YHK	Gjoa Haven, NWT
YHM	Hamilton, ON
YHO	Hopedale, NF
YHR	Chevery, QC
YHY	Hay River, NWT
YHZ	Halifax, NS
YIB	Atikokan, ON
YIK	Ivujivik, QC
YIO	Pond Inlet, NWT
YIV	Island Lake/Garden Hill, MB
YJT	Stephenville, NF
YKA	Kamloops, BC
YKG	Kangirsuk, QC
YKK	Kikatla, BC
YKM	Yakima, WA
YKN	Yankton, SD
YKQ	Waskaganish, QC
YKU	Chisasibi, QC
YLC	Lake Harbour, NWT
YLE	Lac la Martre, NWT
YLH	Lansdowne House, ON
YLL	Lloydminster, AB
YLR	Leaf Rapids, MB
YLS	Lebel sur Quévillon, QC
YLW	Kelowna, BC
YMG	Manitouwadge, ON
YMH	Mary's Harbour, NF
YMM	Fort McMurray, AB
YMN	Makkovik, NF
YMO	Moosonee, ON
YMT	Chibougamau, QC
YMX	Mirabel, QC
YNA	Natashquan, QC
YNC	Wemindji, QC
YNE	Norway House, MB
YNG	Youngstown, OH
YNL	Points North Landing, SK
YNO	North Spirit Lake, ON
YNS	Nemiscau, QC
YOC	Old Crow, YT
YOG	Ogoki Post, ON
YOH	Oxford House, MB
YOJ	High Level, AB
YOP	Rainbow Lake, AB
YOW	Ottawa, ON
YPA	Prince Albert, SK
YPC	Paulatuk, NWT
YPE	Peace River, AB
YPH	Inukjuak, QC
YPI	Port Simpson, BC
YPJ	Aupaluk, QC
YPL	Pickle Lake, ON
YPM	Pikangikum, ON
YPO	Peawanuck, ON
YPR	Prince Rupert, BC
YPW	Powell River, BC
YPX	Povungnituk, QC
YQC	Québec City, QC
YQQ	Quaqtaq, QC
YQD	The Pas, MB
YQG	Windsor, ON
YQI	Yarmouth, NS
YQK	Kenora, ON
YQL	Lethbridge, AB
YQM	Moncton, NB
YQN	Nakina, ON
YQQ	Comox, BC
YQR	Regina, SK
YQT	Thunder Bay, ON
YQU	Grande Prairie, AB
YQX	Gander, NF
YQY	Sydney, NS
YQZ	Quesnel, BC
YRA	Rae Lakes, NWT
YRB	Resolute, NWT
YRD	Dean River, BC
YRF	Cartwright, NF
YRG	Rigolet, NF
YRJ	Roberval, QC
YRL	Red Lake, ON
YRN	Rivers Inlet, BC
YRS	Red Sucker Lake, MB
YRT	Rankin Inlet, NWT
YSB	Sudbury, ON
YSF	Stony Rapids, SK
YSG	Snowdrift, NWT
YSJ	St John, NB
YSK	Sanikiluaq, NWT
YSL	St Leonard, NB
YSM	Fort Smith, NWT
YSO	Postville, NF
YSP	Marathon, ON
YSR	Nanisivik, NWT
YST	Ste Therese Point, MB
YSY	Sachs Harbour, NWT
YTB	Hartley Bay, BC
YTE	Cape Dorset, NWT
YTF	Alma, QC
YTH	Thompson, MB
YTL	Big Trout Lake, ON
YTQ	Tasiujuaq, QC
YTS	Timmins, ON
YTZ	Toronto Island, ON
YUB	Tuktoyaktuk, NWT
YUD	Umiujaq, QC
YUL	Dorval, QC
YUM	Yuma, AZ
YUT	Repulse Bay, NWT
YUX	Hall Beach, NWT
YUY	Rouyn-Noranda, QC
YVC	La Ronge, SK
YVM	Broughton Island, NWT
YVO	Val d'Or, QC
YVP	Kuujjuaq, QC
YVQ	Norman Wells, NWT
YVR	Vancouver, BC
YVZ	Deer Lake, ON

YWB	Kangiqsujuaq, QC
YWG	Winnipeg, MB
YWH	Victoria Inner Harbour, BC
YWJ	Deline, NWT
YWK	Wabush, NF
YWL	Williams Lake, BC
YWP	Webequie, ON
YXC	Cranbrook, BC
YXD	Edmonton Municipal, AB
YXE	Saskatoon, SK
YXH	Medicine Hat, AB
YXJ	Fort St John, BC
YXL	Sioux Lookout, ON
YXN	Whale Cove, NWT
YXP	Pangnirtung, NWT
YXS	Prince George, BC
YXT	Terrace, BC
YXU	London, ON
YXY	Whitehorse, YT
YXZ	Wawa, ON
YYB	North Bay, ON
YYC	Calgary, AB
YYD	Smithers, BC
YYE	Fort Nelson, BC
YYF	Penticton, BC
YYG	Charlottetown, PEI
YYJ	Victoria, BC
YYL	Lynn Lake, MB
YYQ	Churchill, MB
YYR	Goose Bay, NF
YYT	St John's, NF
YYU	Kapuskasing, ON
YYY	Mont Joli, QC
YYZ	Toronto-Pearson International, ON
YZF	Yellowknife, NWT
YZG	Salluit, QC
YZP	Sandspit, BC
YZR	Sarnia, ON
YZS	Coral Harbour, NWT
YZT	Port Hardy, BC
YZV	Sept Îles, QC
YZY	Mackenzie, BC

Z

ZAC	York Landing, MB
ZBF	Bathurst, NB
ZCL	Zacatecas, México
ZEL	Bella Bella, BC
ZEM	East Main, QC
ZFD	Fond du Lac, SK
ZFN	Fort Norman, NWT
ZGI	Gods River, MB
ZIH	Ixtapa/Zihuatanejo, México
ZJN	Swan River, MB
ZKE	Kaschechewan, ON
ZLO	Manzanillo, México
ZMT	Masset, BC
ZPB	Sachigo Lake, ON
ZQS	Queen Charlotte Is, BC
ZRH	Zürich, Switzerland
ZRJ	Round Lake, ON
ZSA	San Salvador, Bahamas
ZSJ	Sandy Lake, ON
ZSW	Seal Cove, BC
ZTM	Shamattawa, MB
ZUM	Churchill Falls, NF
ZWL	Wollaston Lake, SK

AIRLINE INDEX

A

Abaco Air CAR-21
ABX Air US-1
Action Airlines US-137
Aero California MEX-1
Aero Postal de México MEX-10
Aerocaribbean CAR-1
Aerocaribe MEX-2
Aerochago CAR-21
Aeroejecutivo MEX-3
Aeroexo MEX-3
Aerogaviota CAR-2
Aerolíneas Internacionales MEX-4
Aerolitoral MEX-5
Aeromar MEX-6
AEROMEXICO MEX-7
Aeromexpress MEX-9
Aerotaxi CAR-21
Aerovías de México MEX-7
Air 500 . . . . CAN-51
Air Alliance CAN-1
Air Alma CAN-51
Air Anguilla CAR-21
Air Aruba CAR-3
Air Atlantic CAN-2
Air BC CAN-3
Air Canada CAN-4
Air Canada Connector . . . CAN-1
Air Canada Connector . . . CAN-3
Air Canada Connector . . CAN-11
Air Canada Connector . . CAN-12
Air Canada Connector . . CAN-27
Air Canada Connector . . CAN-39
Air Caraibes CAR-4
Air Cargo Carriers US-137
Air Cargo Express US-2
Air Caribbean CAR-5
Air Charter Express US-137
Air Charter/ Air Montréal CAN-51
Air Club International CAN-6
Air Creebec CAN-7
Air Georgian CAN-51
Air Guadeloupe CAR-6
Air Haiti CAR-21
Air Inuit CAN-8
Air Jamaica CAR-7
Air Jamaica Express CAR-8
Air Labrador CAN-9

Air Martinique CAR-9
Air Midwest US-3
Air Molokai US-137
Air Nevada US-137
Air North CAN-10
Air North Charter & Training CAN-10
Air Nova CAN-11
Air Nova CAN-42
Air Nunavut CAN-51
Air Ontario CAN-12
Air Sask Aviation CAN-33
Air Satellite CAN-51
Air South US-4
Air St Barthélémey CAR-21
Air St Martin CAR-21
Air St Thomas US-137
Air St-Pierre STP-1
Air Sunshine US-137
Air Taxi CAR-21
Air Tindi CAN-13
Air Transat CAN-14
Air Transport International US-5
Air Vegas US-137
Air Wisconsin US-6
Airborne Express US-1
Airlines of Carriacou CAR-21
Airpac Airlines US-137
Airspeed Aviation CAN-51
AirTran Airways US-7
Airwave Transport CAN-51
Aklak Air CAN-15
Alaska Airlines US-8
Alaska Airlines Commuter US-91
Alaska Central Express US-137
Alberta Citylink CAN-16
All Canada Express CAN-17
Allegheny Airlines US-9
Allegro MEX-11
ALM Antillean Airlines . . . CAR-10
Aloha Airlines US-10
Aloha Island Air US-66
Alpine Air US-137
America West Airlines . . . US-11
America West Express . . . US-73
American Airlines US-12
American Eagle US-51
American Eagle US-57
American Eagle US-103

American Eagle US-135
American International Airways US-14
American Trans Air US-15
Ameriflight US-137
Amerijet International US-16
APA International Air CAR-21
Arctic Circle Air Service US-137
Arriva Air International . . . US-137
Arrow Air US-17
Aspen Mountain Air US-18
Athabaska Airways CAN-18
Atlantic Coast Airlines US-19
Atlantic Southeast Airlines US-20
Atlas Air US-21
AvAtlantic US-22
Avia Air CAR-21
Aviación de Chiapas MEX-12
AVIACSA MEX-12
Aviation Québec Labrador CAN-51

B

Bahamasair CAR-11
Baker Aviation US-137
Baltimore Air Transport US-137
Bankair US-137
Baron Aviation Services US-137
Basler Airlines US-138
Baxter Aviation CAN-51
Bearskin Airlines CAN-19
Bellair US-138
Bemidji Airlines US-138
Bering Air US-138
Berry Aviation US-138
Big Sky Airlines US-23
Blackhawk Airways US-138
Borinquen Air US-138
Bradley Air Services CAN-20
Buffalo Airways CAN-21
Business Air US-138
Business Express Airlines US-24
BWIA International CAR-12

C

Calm Air International . . . CAN-22
Camai Air US-138
Canada 3000 Airlines . . . CAN-23

Canadian Airlines International CAN-24
Canadian Partner CAN-2
Canadian Partner CAN-22
Canadian Partner CAN-25
Canadian Partner CAN-30
Canadian Regional Airlines CAN-25
CanAir Cargo CAN-26
Cape Air US-138
Cape Smythe Air Service US-138
Capital Cargo International Airlines US-25
Cardinal Airlines CAR-21
Carib Aviation CAR-21
CaribAir............... US-138
Caribair (Dominican Republic) ... CAR-21
Caribair (Puerto Rico) ... CAR-21
Carnival Air Lines US-26
Casino Express.......... US-27
Cayman Airways........ CAR-13
CCAir US-28
Central Air Southwest ... US-138
Central Mountain Air.... CAN-27
Century Airlines......... US-138
Challenge Air Cargo US-29
Champion Air US-30
Chautauqua Airlines US-31
Cherry Air US-138
Chicago Express Airlines US-32
Circle Rainbow Air....... US-138
Coast Western Airlines............... CAN-51
Coastal Air Transport.... US-138
Colgan Air............. US-33
Columbia Pacific Airlines US-138
Comair US-34
Commercial Aviation.... CAN-51
Commutair US-35
Confortair............. CAN-51
Conquest Airlines US-36
Contact Air CAN-51
Continental Airlines US-37
Continental Express US-39
Continental Express US-63
Continental Micronesia ... US-40
Contract Air Cargo US-138
Corporate Air US-138
Corporate Express CAN-51
Corporate Express US-138
Corporate Express Airlines US-139

Coval Air............. CAN-51
CSA Air US-139
Cubana CAR-14
Custom Air Transport..... US-41

D

Delta Air Lines US-42
Delta Connection....... US-106
DHL Airways US-44
Downeast Express US-139

E

Eagle Air Services CAR-21
Eagle Canyon Airlines.... US-45
Eagle Jet Charter US-45
Eastwind Airlines........ US-46
Emery Worldwide Airlines US-100
Emery Worldwide Airlines US-47
Empire Airlines US-139
Enterprise Air CAN-51
ERA Aviation........... US-48
Evergreen International Airlines US-49
Executive Airlines US-50
Executive Airlines (Long Island) US-139
Executive Express II US-18
Express Airlines I US-51
Express One International US-52

F

F S Air Service US-139
Falcon Air Express US-53
FedEx................. US-54
Fine Air............... US-56
First Air.............. CAN-20
Flagship Airlines US-57
Flamenco Airlines US-139
Florida West International Airways..... US-58
Fly BVI.............. CAR-21
40-Mile Air............ US-139
Four Star Aviation US-139
Frontier Airlines......... US-59
Frontier Flying Service US-139

G

Gemini Air Cargo US-60
Grand Aire Express..... US-139
Grand Canyon.......... US-139
Grant Aviation US-139

Great American Airways............... US-61
Great Lakes Airlines US-62
Greenlandair GRE-1
Greyhound Air CAN-31
Gulfstream International Airlines US-63

H

Hageland Aviation Services........ US-139
Haines Airways US-139
Haiti Air Freight......... CAR-21
Haitian Aviation Line SA CAR-15
Halisa Air CAR-15
Hanna's Air Saltspring CAN-52
Harbor Airlines US-139
Harbour Air............ CAN-28
Hawaiian Airlines........ US-64
Hawkair Aviation Services CAN-52
Helenair CAR-21
Helijet Airways CAN-29
Horizon Air US-65

I

Iliamna Air Taxi US-139
Inter-Canadien CAN-30
InterIsland Airways CAR-21
Interprovincial.......... CAN-42
Island Air............. US-66
Island Air CAR-16
Island Airlines US-139
Island Express US-139

J

Jackson Air Service CAN-52

K

K D Air............... CAN-52
Kalitta Flying Service.... US-140
Kelowna Flightcraft Air Charter CAN-31
Kenmore Air US-140
Kenn Borek Air CAN-32
Ketchikan Air Service ... US-140
Keystone Air Services... CAN-52
Kistigan CAN-34
Kitty Hawk Air Cargo..... US-67
Kiwi International Air Lines US-68
Knighthawk Air Express............ CAN-52

L

La Ronge Aviation CAN-33
LAB Flying Service US-140
Labrador Airways CAN-9
Laker Airways US-69
Laker Airways
(Bahamas) CAR-17
Larry's Flying Service ... US-140
Las Vegas Airlines...... US-140
LIAT CAR-18
Líneas Aéreas Allegro .. MEX-11
Little Red Air Service ... CAN-52
Lone Star Airlines US-18
Lyndon Air Cargo US-70
Lynx Air............... US-140

M

Mahalo Air............. US-71
Martinaire US-140
Mas Air............... MEX-13
Maverick Airways US-72
Merlin Express US-140
Mesa Airlines US-73
Mesaba Airlines US-75
Methow Aviation US-140
Mexicana de Aviación... MEX-14
Mexicargo............. MEX-15
Miami Air International ... US-76
Miami Valley Aviation.... US-140
Mid-Atlantic Freight US-140
Midway Airlines......... US-77
Midway Connection...... US-62
Midwest Express........ US-78
Midwest Express
Connection US-105
Ministic Air CAN-34
Morningstar
Air Express........... CAN-52
Mountain Air Cargo..... US-140
Mountain Air Express US-79
Murray Aviation US-140
Mustique Airways CAR-22

N

Nakina Outpost Camps
& Air Service CAN-35
National Fisheries US-100
Nations Air Express...... US-80
Navair Charter CAN-52
Nevis Express CAR-22
New England Airlines ... US-140
North American
Airlines.............. CAN-52
North American
Airlines US-81
North Star Air Cargo ... US-140
North Vancouver
Airlines CAN-52
North-Wright Air CAN-38
Northern Air Cargo US-82
Northern
Dene Airways CAN-52
Northern
Thunderbird Air........ CAN-36
Northwest Airlines....... US-83
Northwest Airlink........ US-51
Northwest Airlink........ US-75
Northwest
Territorial Airways CAN-39
Northwestern
Air Lease CAN-37
NT Air................ CAN-36
NWT Air CAN-39

O

Olson Air Service US-140
Omni Air Express US-85

P

Pace Airlines US-86
Pacific Coastal
Airlines CAN-40
Pan Am Air Bridge US-87
Pan American
World Airways.......... US-88
Panagra Airways........ US-89
Paradise Island Airlines... US-90
Pem-air............... CAN-52
PenAir................ US-91
Peninsula Airways....... US-91
Perimeter Airlines CAN-41
Piedmont Air Cargo..... US-140
Piedmont Air
Transport............ US-140
Piedmont Airlines US-92
Pine State Airlines...... US-140
Planemaster Services ... US-140
Points North Air CAN-52
Polar Air Cargo US-93
Prestige Airways US-94
Pro Air................ US-95
Pro Mech Air.......... US-141
Prompt Air............ US-141
Propair CAN-52
Provincial Airlines CAN-42
PSA Airlines US-96

R

Ramp 66.............. US-141
Redwing Airways....... US-141
Reeve Aleutian Airways... US-97
Region Air CAR-22
Regional Express US-141
Reliant Airlines US-141
Reno Air US-98
Renown Aviation US-141
Rhoades International... US-141
Rich International
Airways.............. US-99
Royal Air Freight US-141
Royal Aviation......... CAN-43
Ryan Air US-141
Ryan International
Airlines US-100

S

Saber Cargo Airlines.... US-141
Samaritan Air Service... CAN-52
SAPSA............... CAR-22
Scenic Airlines US-101
Seair................ CAN-52
Servicios Aéreos
Litoral................ MEX-5
Servicios Aéreos
Profesionales CAR-22
Shuswap Air.......... CAN-52
Shuttle Inc. US-129
Sierra Pacific Airlines ... US-102
Sierra West Airlines...... US-141
Simmons Airlines US-103
Simo Air CAN-51
Skagway Air Service US-141
Sky Freighters CAN-53
Sky Trek
International Airlines US-104
Skyservice CAN-44
Skyward Aviation CAN-45
Skyway Airlines........ US-105
SkyWest Airlines....... US-106
SouthCentral Air US-141
Southern Air
Transport............ US-107
Southwest Airlines...... US-108
Spirit Airlines.......... US-109
Suburban Air Freight.... US-141
Suluit Air GRE-2
Summit Air Charters ... CAN-53
Sun Country Airlines ... US-110
Sun Jet International US-111
Sun Pacific
International US-112

Sunwest International
Aviation Services CAN-53

Sunworld International
Airlines US-113

Superior Aviation....... US-141

SVG Air CAR-22

T

TAESA MEX-16

Taino Air............. CAR-22

Taquan Air Service US-141

Tar Heel Aviation Inc US-141

Tatonduk
Flying Service US-141

TCI Skyking CAR-22

Telford Aviation US-142

Thunder Airlines CAN-53

Timberline Air CAN-53

TolAir Services US-142

Tower Air.............. US-114

Tradewinds Airlines US-115

TRADO CAR-22

Trans Air US-142

Trans Continental
Airlines US-117

Trans Florida Airlines ... US-142

Trans Island Air........ CAR-22

Trans North Aviation US-142

Trans States Airlines US-118

Trans World Airlines US-119

Trans-Air-Link US-116

Trans-Capital Air....... CAN-53

Trans-Côte CAN-53

Transfair CAN-53

TransMeridian Airlines... US-121

Transportes Aéreos
Aeromar.............. MEX-6

Transportes Aéreos
Ejecutivos............ MEX-16

Transportes Mas
de Carga MEX-13

Tropic Aire............. US-41

Turks & Caicos
Airways.............. CAR-19

TW Express US-118

U

Union Flights US-142

United Airlines......... US-122

United Express US-62

United Express US-73

United Express US-124

United Express US-133

United Feeder Service... US-124

United Parcel Service ... US-125

UPS CAN-17

UPS US-125

US Airways US-127

US Airways Express US-73

US Airways Express US-92

US Airways Express US-96

US Airways Express ... US-118

US Airways Shuttle ... US-129

US Jet................ US-130

V

V Kelner Airways CAN-53

ValuJet Airlines US-131

Vancouver
Helicopters CAN-29

Vancouver Island Air.... CAN-53

Vanguard Airlines US-132

Vieques Air Link US-142

Viking Express US-142

Voyageur Airways...... CAN-46

W

Walker's International ... US-142

Warbelow's
Airventures US-142

Wasaya Airways CAN-47

West Coast Air CAN-48

West Isle Air US-142

West Wind Aviation..... CAN-53

Westair US-142

WestAir
Commuter Airlines...... US-133

Western Express CAN-53

Western Pacific
Airlines............... US-134

Westjet.............. CAN-49

Wiggins Airways US-142

Wilderness Airline...... CAN-50

Williston Lake
Air Services CAN-53

Winair CAR-20

Windward Islands
Airways International ... CAR-20

Wings of Alaska US-142

Wings West Airlines US-135

World Airways......... US-136

Wright Air Service...... US-142

Y

Yute Air Alaska US-142

PHOTO CREDITS

Air Saint-Pierre: SPM 1; **Andrew Abshier:** USA 27; **Paul Bannwarth:** USA 136; **Boeing:** USA 122; **Michael Bolden:** USA 83; **Scott Brandenburg:** USA 42; **British Aerospace:** Canada 11; **Phil Brooks:** USA 15; **Dave Campbell:** USA 7, 87; **Mike Chew:** USA 98; **Ray Cormack:** Canada 1, 2, 19, 20, 30; **Bill Crimmins:** USA 35; **Maurice Cutler:** USA 73; **Jeffrey S DeVore:** USA 95; **Dornier:** Caribbean 8; **Mark Durban:** USA 41, **Elliot Epstein:** USA 45; **Glen Etchells:** Canada 42; **Lawrence Feir:** USA 47, 100, 115; **Rob Finlayson:** COVER, USA 12, 57; **Fokker:** USA 77; **Winfried Giese:** USA 14; **Phil Glatt:** USA 49; **Len Gold:** USA 130; **Augusto Gómez Rojas:** México 5, 6, 14; **Denis Goodwin:** USA 92; **Derek Gould:** Canada 26; **Robert S Grant:** Canada 9, 22, 35; **Stephen L Griffin:** USA 26, 40, 54, 61, 64, 78, 81, 88, 99, 101; **Brian K Gustafson:** USA 4, 20, 121; **Eddy Gual/Aviation Photography of Miami:** USA 56; **Steve Haltvick:** USA 90; **George W Hamlin:** USA 19, 30, 60, 76, 102, 109, 129, 131, México 16; **Brett Hammerstrom:** USA 110; **Bill Hough:** USA 24; **Andrew Hunt:** USA 21, 43, 93; **Gary Jennings:** USA 2, 37, 48, 69, 82, 97, 107, Canada 43; **William Jesse:** Canada 29; **Erik Johannesson:** Canada 50; **Mike Keenan:** USA 31, 34, Canada 7, 10, 13, 16, 23, Caribbean 13; **John Kimberley:** Canada 27, 36, 46; **Steve Kinder:** México 13; **KIWI International:** USA 68; **Espeth Kurthi:** Caribbean 5; **Christian Laugier:** USA 114; **Rainer Leisewitz:** Caribbean 7; **Frank Litaudon:** Caribbean 4, 9, 20; **Jean-Marie Magendie:** Canada 6; **Hernán Matos:** USA 50; **Nick Mills:** USA 94, 127, México 7, Caribbean 15; **Vicki Mills:** USA 58; **Stéphane Mutzenberg:** México 3; **Malcolm Nason:** México 10; **Pace Airlines:** USA 86; **Steven J Pinnow:** USA 6, 16, 17, 22, 29, 33, 52, 62, 67, 75, 103, 105, 117, 118, 124, Caribbean 12; **Norbert Raith:** USA 28, 36, 39, 51, México 11; **Raytheon:** USA 3, 74; **Rob Rennert:** USA 9, Canada 31; **Mike Reyno:** Canada 28; **Jeremy Rice:** Caribbean 16; **S Runge:** Caribbean 1, 2; **SAAB/Norman Pealing via Defford Taylor:** USA 91; **Zenon G Sanchez Zamudio:** Canada 44, México 4, 9; **Bob Shane:** USA 10, 11, 25, 53, 59, 66, 71, 72, 79, 80, 104, 108, 112, 113, 119, 134, México 15; **Robbie Shaw:** Greenland 1, 2; **Tom Sheridan:** USA 63, 89, 111, 116, Canada 14, Caribbean 6, 11, 17, 18, 19; **SkyWest:** USA 106; **A J Smith:** USA 46, 85; **SPA Photography:** Canada 24; **Ed Stephens:** USA 18; **Gary Tahir:** Canada 4; **Henry Tenby:** USA 70, Canada 3, 8, 12, 15, 18, 21, 25, 32, 33, 34, 37, 38, 39, 40, 41, 45, 47, 48, 49, Caribbean 3; **Jim Thompson:** USA 96; **John van den Berg/Caribbean Aviation Curaçao:** Caribbean 10; **Joe G Walker:** USA 1, 23, 125, México 12; **John Wegg:** USA 8, 32, 65, 84, 132, 133, 135, Canada 17, Caribbean 14; **Tony Works:** USA 44; **Peter Zastrow:** USA 5

With acknowlegement also to Canadian section editorial assistant Anna Arcari

NOTES:

NOTES:

NOTES: